OHIO
SCIENCE
FUSiON

fusion [FYOO • zhuhn] a combination of two
or more things that releases energy

This Write-In Student Edition belongs to

Abby mccloskey

Teacher/Room

Tipp

Consulting Authors

Michael A. DiSpezio
Global Educator
North Falmouth, Massachusetts

Marjorie Frank
Science Writer and Content-Area Reading Specialist
Brooklyn, New York

Michael Heithaus
Executive Director, School of Environment, Arts, and Society
Associate Professor, Department of Biological Sciences
Florida International University
North Miami, Florida

Donna Ogle
Professor of Reading and Language
National-Louis University
Chicago, Illinois

Front Cover: *stingray* ©Jeffrey L. Rotman/Corbis; *moth* ©Millard H. Sharp/Photo Researchers, Inc.; *astronaut* ©NASA; *thermometer* ©StockImages/Alamy; *gear* ©Garry Gay/The Image Bank/Getty Images.

Back Cover: *geyser* ©Frans Lanting/Corbis; *frog* ©DLILLC/Corbis; *flask* ©Gregor Schuster/Getty Images; *rowers* ©Stockbyte/Getty Images.

Printed in the U.S.A.

ISBN 978-0-544-31781-9

13 14 15 0928 20 19

4500745958   ABCDEFG

Program Advisors

Paul D. Asimow
Professor of Geology and Geochemistry
California Institute of Technology
Pasadena, California

Bobby Jeanpierre
Associate Professor of Science
Education
University of Central Florida
Orlando, Florida

Gerald H. Krockover
Professor Emeritus of Earth,
Atmospheric, and Planetary Science
Education
Purdue University
West Lafayette, Indiana

Rose Pringle
Associate Professor
School of Teaching and Learning
College of Education
University of Florida
Gainesville, Florida

Carolyn Staudt
Curriculum Designer for Technology
KidSolve, Inc.
The Concord Consortium
Concord, Massachusetts

Larry Stookey
Science Department
Antigo High School
Antigo, Wisconsin

Carol J. Valenta
Associate Director of the Museum and
Senior Vice President
Saint Louis Science Center
St. Louis, Missouri

Barry A. Van Deman
President and CEO
Museum of Life and Science
Durham, North Carolina

Ohio Reviewers

Brian Geniusz, MEd.
Science Curriculum Leader
Worthington Schools
Worthington, Ohio

Richard J. Johnson, Jr., MEd.
Science Department Chair
Eastlake Middle School
Eastlake, Ohio

Robert Mendenhall
Curriculum Director
Toledo Public Schools
Toledo, Ohio

Power up with Ohio Science Fusion!

Grade 4

Your program fuses . . .

e-Learning & Virtual Labs

Labs & Explorations

Write-In Student Edition

. . . to generate new energy for today's science learner— you.

Write-In Student Edition

S.T.E.M.
Engineering & Technology
STEM activities throughout the program!

Be an active reader and make this book your own!

Write your ideas, answer questions, make notes, and record activity results right on these pages.

Learn science concepts and skills by interacting with every page.

Is Energy

...in your house need energy.
...frigerator and washing machine.
...three other things in your
...or school that use energy?

...ading As you...d these two pages, find and underline
...of energy. Then...two sources of energy.

...do you and...have
...energy. Gasoli...the
...won't go any...e it

...object move
...ty to cause
...g that moves ha
...nsformed from one for
...e transferred from one le
...here does energy come fr
...some sources of energy on t

This man r
do you thir
healthful fe
they will ha

A

e-Learning & Virtual Labs

Digital lessons and virtual labs provide e-learning options for every lesson of *ScienceFusion*.

Do it!

90.00 ºC

Copper
Steel
Iron
Wood

Choose a material to be used in the simulation.

Choose a material to be used in the simulation.

8 of 13

What Are Mixtures and Solutions?

combine to make mixtures?

solids with solids

liquids with gases

solids with liquids

liquids with liquids

click all the images that fit with your idea of what a mixture is.

5 of 15

On your own or with a group, explore science concepts in a digital world.

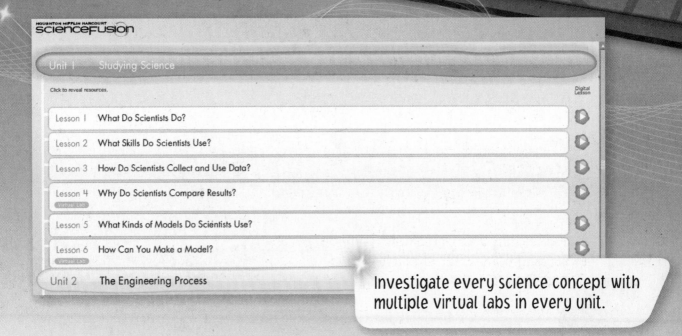

Investigate every science concept with multiple virtual labs in every unit.

Continue your science explorations with these online tools:

→ ScienceSaurus   → People in Science

→ NSTA SciLinks   → Media Gallery

→ Video-based Projects   → Vocabulary Cards

→ Science Readers for Ohio with complete AUDIO!

What Is Matter?

What Is Matter?

Sculpting with Physical Properties

Labs & Explorations

Science is all about doing.

Exciting investigations for every lesson.

Ask questions and test your ideas.

Draw conclusions and share what you learn.

How Can You Model a School?

There are many types of models: mental models, two-dimensional, three-dimensional, and computer models. In this activity, you'll model a part of your school in two ways.

...wing or modeling program

1 With a team, choose a part of your school to model. It may be a single room, a floor, or a whole building.

2 Next, choose two types of models to make. Get permission from your teacher to carry out your plans.

3 With your team, choose the materials you will use. Make any measurements you need, and record them carefully.

4 Make the two models, and compare them to those of other teams.

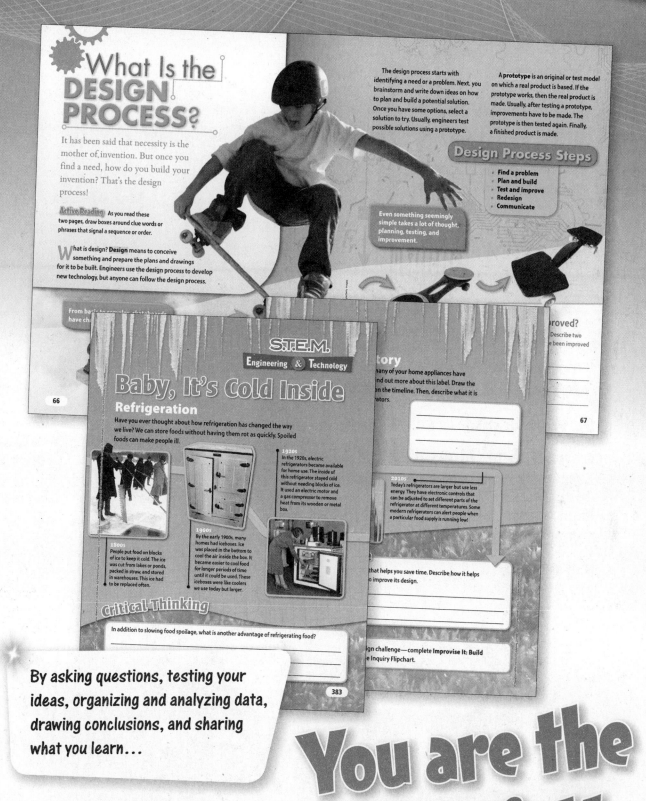

What Is the DESIGN PROCESS?

It has been said that necessity is the mother of invention. But once you find a need, how do you build your invention? That's the design process!

Active Reading As you read these two pages, draw boxes around clue words or phrases that signal a sequence or order.

What is design? **Design** means to conceive something and prepare the plans and drawings for it to be built. Engineers use the design process to develop new technology, but anyone can follow the design process.

The design process starts with identifying a need or a problem. Next, you brainstorm and write down ideas on how to plan and build a potential solution. Once you have some options, select a solution to try. Usually, engineers test possible solutions using a prototype.

A **prototype** is an original or test model on which a real product is based. If the prototype works, then the real product is made. Usually, after testing a prototype, improvements have to be made. The prototype is then tested again. Finally, a finished product is made.

Design Process Steps

- Find a problem
- Plan and build
- Test and improve
- Redesign
- Communicate

Even something seemingly simple takes a lot of thought, planning, testing, and improvement.

66

67

S.T.E.M.
Engineering & Technology

Baby, It's Cold Inside
Refrigeration

Have you ever thought about how refrigeration has changed the way we live? We can store foods without having them rot as quickly. Spoiled foods can make people ill.

1800s
People put food on blocks of ice to keep it cold. The ice was cut from lakes or ponds, packed in straw, and stored in warehouses. This ice had to be replaced often.

1900s
By the early 1900s, many homes had iceboxes. Ice was placed in the bottom to cool the air inside the box. It became easier to cool food for longer periods of time until it could be used. These iceboxes were like coolers we use today but larger.

1920s
In the 1920s, electric refrigerators became available for home use. The inside of this refrigerator stayed cold without needing blocks of ice. It used an electric motor and a gas compressor to remove heat from its wooden or metal box.

2010s
Today's refrigerators are larger but use less energy. They have electronic controls that can be adjusted to set different parts of the refrigerator at different temperatures. Some modern refrigerators can alert people when a particular food supply is running low!

Critical Thinking

In addition to slowing food spoilage, what is another advantage of refrigerating food?

383

By asking questions, testing your ideas, organizing and analyzing data, drawing conclusions, and sharing what you learn...

You are the scientist!

Contents

PHYSICAL SCIENCE

© Houghton Mifflin Harcourt Publishing Company

Safety in Science

Indoors Doing science is a lot of fun. But, a science lab can be a dangerous place. Falls, cuts, and burns can happen easily. When you are doing a science investigation, you need to be safe. Know the safety rules and listen to your teacher.

Adult scientists have to follow lab safety rules, too.

Pay attention to these safety rules.

1. **Think ahead.** Study the investigation steps so you know what to expect. If you have any questions, ask your teacher. Be sure you understand all caution statements and safety reminders.

2. **Be neat and clean.** Keep your work area clean. If you have long hair, pull it back so it doesn't get in the way. Roll or push up long sleeves to keep them away from your activity.

3. **Oops!** If you spill or break something, or get cut, tell your teacher right away.

4. **Watch your eyes.** Wear safety goggles anytime you are directed to do so. If you get anything in your eyes, tell your teacher right away.

5. **Yuck!** Never eat or drink anything during a science activity.

6. **Don't get shocked.** Be careful if an electric appliance is used. Be sure that electric cords are in a safe place where you can't trip over them. Never use the cord to pull a plug from an outlet.

7. **Keep it clean.** Always clean up when you have finished. Put everything away and wipe your work area. Wash your hands.

8. **Play it safe.** Always know where to find safety equipment, such as fire extinguishers. Know how to use the safety equipment around you.

Outdoors

Lots of science research happens outdoors. It's fun to explore the wild! But, you need to be careful. The weather, the land, and the living things can surprise you.

This scientist has to protect his eyes.

Follow these safety rules when you're doing science outdoors.

1 **Think ahead.** Study the investigation steps so you know what to expect. If you have any questions, ask your teacher. Be sure you understand all caution statements and safety reminders.

2 **Dress right.** Wear appropriate clothes and shoes for the outdoors. Cover up and wear sunscreen and sunglasses for sun safety.

3 **Clean up the area.** Follow your teacher's instructions for when and how to throw away waste.

4 **Oops!** Tell your teacher right away if you break something or get hurt.

5 **Watch your eyes.** Wear safety goggles when directed to do so. If you get anything in your eyes, tell your teacher right away.

6 **Yuck!** Never taste anything outdoors.

7 **Stay with your group.** Work in the area as directed by your teacher. Stay on marked trails.

8 **"Wilderness" doesn't mean go wild.** Never engage in horseplay, games, or pranks.

9 **Always walk.** No running!

10 **Play it safe.** Know where safety equipment can be found and how to use it. Know how to get help.

11 **Clean up.** Wash your hands with soap and water when you come back indoors.

Studying Science

Big Idea

Scientists use scientific inquiry methods and critical thinking during investigations to answer questions about the world around us.

OHIO 4.SIA.1, 4.SIA.2, 4.SIA.3, 4.SIA.4, 4.SIA.5, 4.SIA.6

I Wonder Why

Why is the work of a scientist doing field research similar to the work of a scientist doing research in a laboratory? *Turn the page to find out.*

Here's Why All scientists ask questions, answer them with investigations, and communicate their results to other scientists.

In this unit, you will explore the Big Idea, the Essential Questions, and the Investigations on the Inquiry Flipchart.

Levels of Inquiry Key ■ DIRECTED ■ **GUIDED** ■ INDEPENDENT

Track Your Progress

Big Idea Scientists use scientific inquiry methods and critical thinking during investigations to answer questions about the world around us.

Essential Questions

Now I Get the Big Idea!

Science Notebook
Before you begin each lesson, be sure to write your thoughts about the Essential Question.

© Houghton Mifflin Harcourt Publishing Company (tr) ©Jeff Rotman/Getty Images; (bkg) ©Alexis Rosenfeld/Photo Researchers, Inc.; (border) ©NDisc/Age Fotostock

OHIO **4.SIA.1** Observe and ask questions about the natural environment; **4.SIA.2** Plan and conduct simple investigations; **4.SIA.5** Communicate about observations, investigations and explanations; and

Lesson **1**

Essential Question

What Do Scientists Do?

Engage Your Brain!

Find the answer to the following question in this lesson and record it here.

Biologists make observations about living things. What are some observations you can make about lizards?

_____

_____

_____

_____

Active Reading

Lesson Vocabulary

List the terms. As you learn about each one, make notes in the Interactive Glossary.

_____ _____

_____ _____

_____ _____

Main Ideas

In this lesson, you'll read about how scientists do their work. Active readers look for main ideas before they read to give their reading a purpose. Often, the headings in a lesson state its main ideas. Preview the headings in this lesson to give your reading a purpose.

The Role of Scientists

It's career day for Mr. Green's fourth-grade class! Mr. Green invited a scientist named Dr. Sims to talk to the class. The students are ready, and they have many questions to ask.

Active Reading As you read these two pages, turn the heading into a question in your mind. Then underline the sentence that answers the question.

What do scientists do?

▶ Write a question you would ask a scientist.

_____

_____

_____

_____

"Thank you for inviting me to your school! My name is Dr. Sims, and I am a scientist. A **scientist** asks questions about the natural world. There are many kinds of scientists and many questions to ask!

Science is the study of the natural world. Earth scientists study things such as rocks, weather, and the planets. Physical scientists study matter and energy. Life scientists, like me, study living things. I am a wildlife biologist, which means I study animals in the wild.

Scientists work alone and in teams. Sometimes, I travel alone on long hikes to watch animals. At other times, I ask other biologists to go with me. I share ideas with other scientists every day.

Science is hard work but fun, too. I like being outdoors. Discovering something new is exciting. The best part, for me, is helping animals. The best way to explain what a scientist does is to show you."

▶ For each area of science, write one question a scientist might ask.

Earth Science

_____

_____

_____

Life Science

_____

_____

_____

Physical Science

_____

_____

_____

Do you work all by yourself?

Is it fun to be a scientist?

Making Observations and Asking Questions

Dr. Sims looks around the classroom. She observes everything for a few moments. Then she asks questions about what she sees.

How does that plant produce offspring?

Does the lizard's skin ever change colors?

Does the goldfish spend more time near the top or at the bottom of the aquarium?

▶ Ask your own well-defined question about the classroom in the photo to the right.

_____

_____

_____

▶ Name five things you observe in this classroom.

_____

_____

Scientists make observations about the world around them. An **observation** is information collected using the five senses.

Scientists ask well-defined questions about their observations. Notice that Dr. Sims asks questions about the living things in the classroom. That's because she is a wildlife biologist. You might ask different questions if you observed different things.

Dr. Sims asks, "How would you answer my question about the goldfish?" One student suggests recording observations in a Science Notebook. Another student suggests using a stopwatch to collect information about the goldfish.

Dr. Sims says, "I can plan and implement a descriptive investigation." Scientists conduct an **investigation** to answer questions. The steps of planning and implementing an investigation may include asking questions, making inferences, selecting appropriate equipment or technology, collecting and analyzing data, and communicating results supported by data.

Experiments

Dr. Sims seems very excited to talk about investigations. She says, "Describing what you see is one kind of investigation. Other investigations include doing an experiment."

Active Reading As you read these two pages, circle the vocabulary term each time it is used.

A Fair Test

An *experiment* is a fair test. It can show that one thing causes another thing to happen. In each test, you change only one factor, or *variable*. To be fair and accurate, you conduct the experiment multiple times.

To test something else, you must start a new experiment. Being creative and working in teams can help scientists conduct experiments.

Carlos is conducting an experiment. He gives the lizard fruit and crickets to see which will be eaten. The food is the only variable that is changed. Each day, the lizard gets two different types of food at the same time and in the same amounts.

Scientific Methods

Scientific investigations use scientific methods. Scientific methods may include the following activities:

- make observations

- ask a well-defined question

- form a hypothesis

- plan and conduct an experiment

- collect, record, and analyze data

- draw conclusions

- communicate results

Sometimes, these steps are done in this order. At other times, they're not.

A **hypothesis** is an idea or explanation that can be tested with an investigation. Dr. Sims gives the students an example from their classroom. She says, "I hypothesize that this lizard eats more insects than fruit."

▶ Talk with other students in your class. Then write a hypothesis to explain what makes the lizard in the photo change color.

_____

_____

_____

_____

_____

_____

Other Kinds of Investigations

Dr. Sims smiles. She says, "I hope this doesn't confuse anyone, but doing an experiment is not always possible."

Many science questions cannot be answered by doing an experiment. Here's one question: What kind of lizard have I found? This question can be answered by using an identification guide. Here's another question: What causes the sun to seem to rise and set? This question can be answered by making and using a model of Earth and the sun. Here's another: At what time of year does a state get the most rain? This question can be answered by looking for patterns through many years of rainfall records. Here's another: How did people who lived 100 years ago describe Mars? This question can be answered with research. Research includes reading what others have written and asking experts.

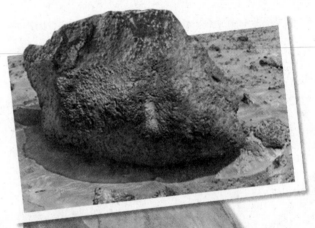

What is the surface of Mars like? This question is hard to answer with an experiment. NASA scientists sent robot spacecraft to Mars. Cameras on these spacecraft take pictures of the planet for scientists to observe.

Use an Identification Guide

Draw lines to match the lizard with its description.

Texas Horned Lizard

- Colors: brownish
- Body: wider and flatter than other lizards
- Tail: straight and shorter than the body
- Spines: several short horns on head, spiny scales on sides of body

Common Chameleon

- Colors: green, yellow, gray, or brown
- Eyes: big and bulge out from side of head
- Body: tall and flat, a ridge of scales along the backbone
- Tail: curls for grasping branches

Common Iguana

- Colors: green, gray, brown, blue, lavender, or black
- Spines: along center of back and tail
- Body: Large flap of skin under the chin

Scientists Share Their
Results as Evidence

Dr. Sims says, "Tell me something you know. Then tell me *how* do you know."

Active Reading As you read these two pages, draw two lines under the main idea.

When scientists explain how things work, they must give evidence. **Evidence** is data gathered during an investigation. Scientists should examine all sides of scientific evidence as they develop scientific explanations. Evidence might support a hypothesis, or it might not. For example, think about the class with their lizard. The students state this hypothesis: Lizards eat more insects than fruit. They carry out an experiment, putting crickets and fruit in the lizard's tank. After two hours, they observe how much food is left, and repeat the steps each day for a week.

The students report that their lizard ate more crickets than fruit. She says, "What is your evidence?" The students share their recorded results. They report that the lizard ate 13 crickets and no fruit.

Once evidence is gathered, a scientist can analyze the data and interpret patterns. Scientists use data that can be observed and measured to construct reasonable explanations for things that happen in the natural world.

Science Notebook

A *conclusion* is an explanation based on evidence. Communicate written results by stating conclusions supported by the data below.

Evidence

We used thermometers and found that when the air temperature changed by 5 degrees, a chameleon's skin color changed.

Conclusion

_____
_____
_____
_____

Evidence

We measured the temperature at the same time each morning and each afternoon for one month. Each day, the air temperature was higher in the afternoon than in the morning.

Conclusion

_____
_____
_____
_____
_____

Evidence

Paper Airplane Wingspan (cm)	Time in the Air (sec)
5	7
10	12
15	21
20	28

Conclusion

_____
_____
_____

When you're done, use the answer key to check and revise your work.

Fill in the missing words to tell what scientists do.

Summarize

Mr. Brown's fourth-grade class wants a pet in their classroom. Their teacher says they have to think like a (1) _____ to care for animals. The students know that means (2) _____ about the natural world. The class wonders what kinds of animals make good classroom pets. They decide to do an (3) _____ to find out. They go to the library and use books and websites to (4) _____ pets.

The class concludes that guinea pigs are the best pets for their classroom. Mr. Brown asks them what (5) _____ they have to support their conclusion. The students explain that guinea pigs are quiet and gentle. They are also active in the daytime and sleep at night.

Once the guinea pigs are in the classroom, the students watch and listen. They keep a Science Notebook and list all their (6) _____. Then, students ask (7) _____ based on what they observe. One is: What does it mean when the guinea pigs make squeaking sounds? Two students have a (8) _____ : guinea pigs make that noise when they want to be fed.

Mr. Brown suggests that the students record the time when they hear the sound and write down what they are doing at the same time. After a few days, the students see that their guinea pigs make that noise just as the zippered bag that holds the fresh vegetables is opened. So, what do you think the sound means? (9) _____

_____

Answer Key: 1. scientist, 2. asking questions, 3. investigation, 4. research, 5. evidence, 6. observations, 7. questions, 8. hypothesis, 9. It means they want to eat the vegetables right away.

Name _____

Word Play

1 Use the words in the box to complete the puzzle.

Across

5. An explanation based on evidence

7. Scientists do one of these to answer questions

Down

1. An idea or explanation that can be tested with an investigation

2. To share the results of investigations

3. A person who asks questions about the natural world

4. You ask this

6. A kind of investigation that is a fair test

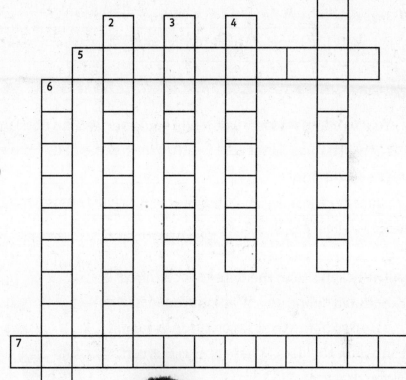

| communicate | conclusion | experiment* | hypothesis* |
| investigation* | question | scientist* | |

*Key Lesson Vocabulary

Apply Concepts

2 Choose an object to observe. List some observations. Then ask some well-defined questions related to your observations.

Name of Object: _____   Questions: _____

Observations: _____   _____

_____   _____

_____   _____

_____   _____

3 Your family uses steel wool soap pads for cleaning pots and pans. Often they get rusty after use. What could you do to stop the pads from rusting? Write a hypothesis you could test. _____

_____

4 The graph shows the data collected from a national online poll in which students were asked to name their favorite lunch food. Analyze the data. What conclusions can you draw? _____

_____

_____

_____

_____

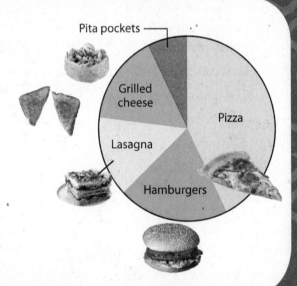

Take It Home!

You can think like a scientist at home, too. Which window cleaner leaves fewer streaks? What kind of bird did I see outside my window? Make a list of questions with your family. Investigate them together.

Essential Question

What Skills Do Scientists Use?

Engage Your Brain!

Find the answer to the following question in the lesson and record it here.

Splash it. Pour it. Freeze it. Make bubbles in it. What skills might a scientist use to test how water behaves?

_____

_____

_____

_____

Active Reading

Lesson Vocabulary

List the terms. As you learn about each one, make notes in the interactive Glossary.

_____

_____

_____

_____

Visual Aids

In this lesson, you'll see large graphics with labels. The labels call attention to important details. Active readers preview a lesson's graphics and decide how the information in them provides details about the main idea.

Inquiry Flipchart p. 4—Pendulum Swing/Pantry Investigation

Everyday Science Skills

Do you ask questions about the world around you? If so, you use these science skills all day, every day—just like a scientist!

Active Reading As you read the next four pages, circle the names of nine science skills.

As you read about scientists, think
→ **"Hey, I can do this, too!"**

Infer

Scientists *infer* how things work by thinking about their observations. A biologist may infer that the color patterns of fish enable them to blend in and avoid predators.

Observe

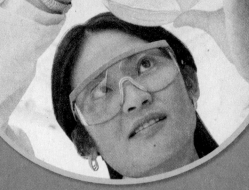

Scientists may *observe* many things, such as changes in color, temperature, and bubbling.

Scientists use inquiry skills every day—and so do you. When you observe, you use your five senses to get information. Let's say you smell cheese, bread, and spicy odors. You *infer* "I think we are having pizza for lunch today!" An **inference** is a statement that explains an observation.

When you think about how things are the same and different, you *compare* them. For example, your family wants to adopt a new kitten. You compare different kittens, looking for one that is playful and friendly. When you decide which kitten is the best, you *communicate* that decision to your family. You can communicate by speaking, writing, and by using pictures or models.

Compare

Scientists *compare* objects and things that happen.

▶ Practice the skill of *comparing*. List ways these two fish are similar and different.

Powder–Blue Tang   Porcupinefish

Similarities	Differences

Communicate

▶ Scientists *communicate,* or share, their results and inferences with other scientists. What did you communicate today?

_____

_____

_____

Think Like a Scientist

Scientists use these skills every day in their investigations. Find out what they are and when you might use them.

Predict

Scientists use their observations and existing research to make predictions about what will happen in the future. For example, a meteorologist uses weather patterns to determine whether it will rain over the weekend.

Use Variables

When scientists plan experiments, they think, "What is the one thing I will change?" That one thing is a variable. Let's say you want to find out how cold a freezer has to be to make fruit pops. The variable that you will change is the temperature inside the freezer.

Some science skills are part of doing science investigations, including experiments. They may sound unfamiliar to you. But when you read about these skills, you might realize that you already use them.

Plan and Conduct Investigations

Scientists plan and conduct investigations that will answer science questions. Say you want to know how salty water must be to make an egg float. First, you think about the steps you'll take to find the answer. Next, you gather the materials you'll use. Then, you test the amount of salt.

▶ You are a marine biologist. You study living things in the ocean. What is one investigation you might plan?

_____

_____

_____

Predict what a marine biologist might look for on a dive.

_____

_____

_____

_____

Hypothesize

Scientists hypothesize when they think of a testable statement that tries to explain an observation. Suppose you notice that water seems to evaporate at different rates from containers with different shapes. What would you hypothesize is a cause?

Draw Conclusions

Scientists draw conclusions when they use evidence to evaluate a hypothesis. If you investigate how the size of a sail affects how quickly a toy boat moves, you might conclude that boats with larger sails move faster because larger sails collect more wind.

Math and Science Skills

Using rulers and balances. Putting things in order. Measuring the speed of a car. Making tables and graphs. Sounds like math, but it's science, too!

Active Reading As you read this page, turn the heading into a question in your mind. Then underline the parts of the text that answer the question.

Every scientist uses math. Let's say you are a marine biologist who studies whales. You *classify* whales by how much they weigh or how long they are from head to tail. You put them in *order* when you arrange them by length from smallest to largest. You *use numbers* to tell how many are alive today. You *use time and space relationships* to investigate when and where they migrate each year. You *measure* how long they are and how much food they eat. You *record and display* the results of your investigations in writing and in tables, graphs, and maps.

Beyond the Book

Do research to collect data about whale migration. Construct maps using tools to organize, examine, and evaluate your data. Construct reasonable explanations about patterns of whale migration based on the data collected as well as your map.

Classify and Order

You classify things when you put them into groups. To put things in order, you may make a list in which position matters, such as ordering bird species by how fast they fly or move.

Measure

In science and math, you measure by using tools to find length, width, height, mass, weight, volume, and elapsed time.

Use Numbers

You use numbers when you observe by counting or measuring. You also use numbers to compare and order. And, you use numbers to describe speed and force.

Do the Math!

Compare Numbers

Some of the world's biggest mammals live under the oceans' waves. The table gives the names of several kinds of whales and the number that scientists estimate are alive today.

Kind of Whale	Population
Beluga whale	200,000
Blue whale	14,000
Fin whale	55,000
Humpback whale	40,000
Minke whale	1,000,000
Pilot whale	1,200,000
Sei whale	54,000
Sperm whale	

1. Which two kinds of whales have the closest number alive?

_____

2. How many more Pilot whales are there than Minke whales?

_____

3. Scientists estimate there are about three hundred and sixty thousand sperm whales alive today. Write that number, using numerals, in the table.

Use Time and Space Relationships

You use timing devices, including clocks and stopwatches, to collect, record, and analyze information about time. You can predict when it will be high tide or low tide. You can also determine how the planets move in space.

Record and Display Data

You record and analyze information using tools, including notebooks and computers. You display, or show, data so that it's easy to understand by making tables, graphs, or diagrams.

Critical Thinking Skills

Have you ever asked yourself if the results of a scientific investigation are correct or make sense? If so, you've used critical thinking skills.

Scientists in all fields use critical thinking skills to propose and examine scientific explanations and evidence related to those explanations. For example, scientists determine if an explanation is reasonable or is supported by valid data. Data collected through direct observation is called **empirical evidence**. Scientists use empirical evidence to analyze, evaluate, and critique the results of scientific investigations. To *analyze* is to think about all the pieces and parts that contribute to something. To *evaluate* is to examine something and decide if it has worth or value. To *critique* is to carefully judge something based on your knowledge, findings, and beliefs.

Logical Reasoning

When you use critical thinking, you also use logic. Logic requires you to use reason and order to figure out if something makes sense. When you use logical reasoning, you do not include your emotions or opinions. Scientists in all fields use logical reasoning to draw conclusions based on evidence.

Use Empirical Evidence

Careful observations and measurements are empirical evidence; observations that include opinions are not. For example, recording the temperature of a mixture is empirical evidence. However, saying the mixture feels warm is an opinion. When you analyze, evaluate, and critique an explanation, you see if it is based on empirical evidence.

Experimental Testing

Scientists perform an experiment to test a hypothesis. These experiments can be conducted in a laboratory or outdoors. Some scientific explanations are based on evidence from experiments. For example, suppose a scientist wants to find out how quickly Arctic ice freezes and thaws. He would design an experiment to test a specific hypothesis related to this question. He would then analyze the data he collected in order to help answer his question.

Observational Testing

It is not always possible to answer a question by conducting an experiment. For example, astronomers study objects in space such as planets and stars. Since these objects are very far away, the only way to study them is to observe their patterns. Scientists use observational testing to compare their patterns and draw conclusions.

Alternative Explanations

When you analyze, evaluate, and critique a scientific investigation, an important question to ask is, "Might there be another possible explanation for this data?" This would be an alternative explanation. For example, you might conclude from an investigation that bees that pollinate red flowers produce more honey than bees that pollinate yellow flowers. Other factors may also account for the difference in honey production. Always consider alternatives when you analyze, evaluate, and critique a scientific explanation.

Alternative Explanations

Milo concluded that the number of chirps crickets make each minute is based on when the sun sets at night. Suggest an alternative explanation for the number of times crickets chirp.

_____

_____

_____

_____

_____

When you're done, use the answer key to check and revise your work.

Fill in the missing skills in the column where they belong.

Summarize

Skills Scientists Use

Everyday Science Skills	1. _____
	2. _____
	3. _____
	4. _____
Science Investigation Skills	5. _____
	6. _____
	7. _____
	8. _____
	9. _____
Math and Science Skills	10. _____
	11. _____
	12. _____
	13. _____
	14. _____
Critical Thinking Skills	15. _____
	16. _____
	17. _____
	18. _____
	19. _____

Answer Key: 1–4, infer, communicate, compare, observe; **5–9,** predict, use variables, plan and conduct investigations, draw conclusions, hypothesize; **10–14,** measure, classify and order, record and display data, use time and space relationships, use numbers; **15–19,** logical reasoning, use empirical evidence, observational testing, experimental testing, alternative explanations

Name _____

Word Play

1 It's easy to get tongue-tied describing what scientists do. Look at the statements below. Switch the red words around until each statement about inquiry skills makes sense.

In order to sort his beakers and other tools, Dr. Mallory hypothesizes each object by size and shape. _____

Gabriella measures that her dog will want his favorite food for dinner, because she has observed him eat it quickly many times before. _____

Kim predicts when planning an experiment with her older brother. She keeps everything the same during their procedure, except for the one factor being tested. _____

After completing an experiment and summarizing her findings, Dr. Garcia classifies what she has learned with other scientists. _____

Dr. Jefferson studies the age of rocks and fossils. She uses variables to tell how old each specimen is. _____

Before conducting his experiment for the science fair, Derrick uses time and space relationships about which sample of fertilizer will make his tomato plant grow the fastest.

_____

To find out how long it takes Deshawn to ride his bike 100 m, Jessica communicates the time with a stopwatch. _____

Apply Concepts

2 Write how you would use numbers to investigate each object.

_____   _____   _____

_____   _____   _____

_____   _____   _____

_____   _____   _____

_____   _____   _____

3 For each picture, what kinds of observations could you record on a calendar?

_____   _____   _____

_____   _____   _____

_____   _____   _____

_____   _____   _____

_____   _____   _____

4 Shauna records the following information while conducting an investigation about plants. Circle the statements that are examples of empirical evidence. Then write to explain your choices.

- Soil temperature: 26°C
- Weight of plants: light
- Favorite plant: tulips

- Hours of sunlight: 12 hr
- Size of plants: big
- Average weekly growth: 3 cm

_____

_____

_____

5 Identify the type of testing used in each example below.

| Kate counts the number of birds that visit a feeder. | Lushen draws the different phases of the moon. | Dean records the volume of several mixtures. |

_____   _____   _____

_____   _____   _____

6

Trial Number	Time to Get to Cheese
2	59 seconds
4	48 seconds
6	32 seconds
8	29 seconds

The data table records the number of times a mouse ran through a maze to get to a piece of cheese.

Use logical reasoning to analyze and evaluate the data to draw a conclusion.

_____

_____

_____

_____

_____

Enrico concludes from the data that all mice really like cheese. Is his conclusion logical? Explain.

_____

_____

_____

_____

_____

Take It Home!

There are many books in the library about scientists and how they think about the world around them. Pick a book with a family member. Find examples of the skills you've learned about and make a list.

OHIO **4.SIA.1** Observe and ask questions about the natural environment; **4.SIA.3** Employ simple equipment and tools to gather data and extend the senses; **4.SIA.4** Use appropriate mathematics with data to construct reasonable explanations; **4.SIA.5** Communicate about observations, investigations and explanations; and **4.SIA.6** Review and ask questions — about the observations and explanations of others.

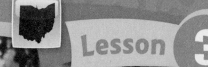

Lesson 3

Essential Question

How Do Scientists Collect and Use Data?

Engage Your Brain!

Find the answer to the following question in this lesson and record it here.

Are the ladybugs on this tree identical to each other? How would you investigate this question?

_____

_____

_____

_____

Active Reading

Lesson Vocabulary

List the terms. As you learn about each one, make notes in the Interactive Glossary.

_____ _____

_____ _____

_____ _____

Main Idea and Details

Details give information about a topic. The information may be examples, features, or characteristics. Active readers stay focused on the topic when they ask, What facts or information do these details add to the topic?

Inquiry Flipchart p. 5 — Rain, Rain, Come Again/Who's Wet? Who's Dry?

pp. 6–9 — Science Tools Activities

Research Is the Key

Tiny insects fly and flash on a summer night. Are you curious about them? Do you wonder how to find out what they are and how they light up? Do some research!

Active Reading As you read the next page, check the research sources you have used.

Natural history museums have insect collections as well as scientists who can answer questions about them.

Often scientists ask themselves, "What do other scientists know about this?" To find out, they do *research*. When you research, you use reference materials and talk to experts to learn what is known. So, if you want to learn what scientists know about fireflies, you can do these things:

- Use an encyclopedia.

- Read a book.

- Read science articles.

- Visit a museum.

- E-mail a scientist.

- Visit science websites.

These kinds of resources may have plenty of information about fireflies. But you will still have questions they do not answer. That's when you conduct your own investigations.

Do the Research!

You just saw bees flying in and out of a hole in an old tree. You know it's not a good idea to get too close. So, how can you find out what bees do inside a tree? What research resource would you go to first? Explain why.

_____

_____

_____

_____

Science Tools

What comes to mind when you hear the word *tools*? Hammers, saws, and screwdrivers? What about computers and calculators? These are both science tools.

Active Reading As you read these two pages, circle the lesson vocabulary each time it is used.

Scientists use all kinds of tools to collect, record and analyze information. Many turn the five senses into "super-senses." Tools enable scientists to see things that are far away, to smell faint odors, to hear quiet sounds, and to feel vibrations their bodies can't.

Let's say you want to observe craters on the moon. A telescope, which makes faraway objects look closer, will turn your sense of sight into "super-vision."

Hand Lens
An ant looks larger in a magnifying box or with a hand lens.

What if you're interested in studying tiny critters, such as leaf cutter ants? Use a hand lens to collect information about and to better analyze these ants. Hand lenses make small objects look bigger. Is the ant crawling away too fast to see it with the hand lens? Try gently placing the ant in a magnifying box. The top of the box has a lens in it, too.

Wondering what the ant's bite marks look like? Place a tiny piece of a cut leaf under a microscope. A **microscope** is a tool for looking at objects that cannot be seen with the eye alone.

▶ Predict how you could use a microscope to collect and analyze information about an ant. Make a drawing and add labels.

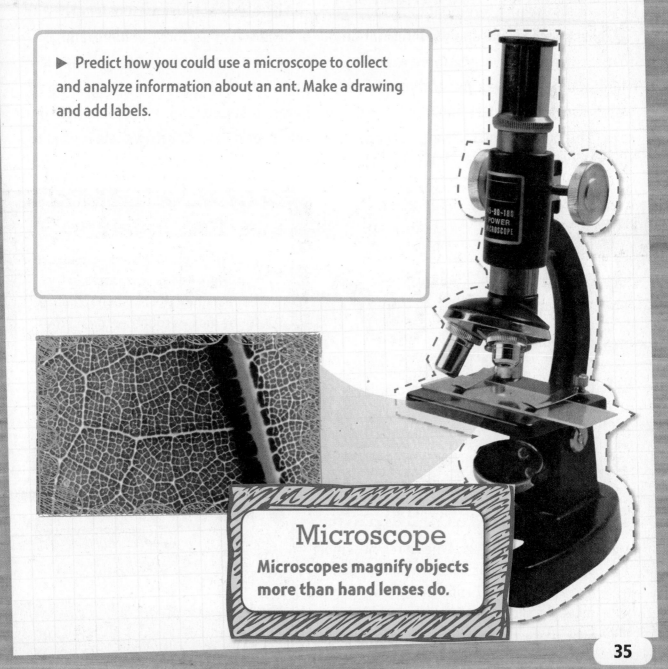

Microscope

Microscopes magnify objects more than hand lenses do.

Measurement Tools

What's the biggest bug in the world? How far can a grasshopper hop? How long can a butterfly fly? How do scientists find exact answers?

Scientists use measurement tools to collect, record, and analyze information to make their observations more exact. Think about it this way. You and your friend watch two grasshoppers hop. Your friend says, "This one jumped farther." But you think the other one jumped farther. To find out for sure, you need to measure.

There are tools to measure length or distance, mass, force, volume, and temperature. Most scientists use metric units with these tools. For example, a **pan balance** is used to measure mass with units called grams (g). A **spring scale** is used to measure force in units called newtons (N).

Pan Balance

Place the object you want to measure on one pan. Add gram masses to the other pan until the two pans balance. Add the masses together to find the total in grams (g).

Triple Beam Balance

A **triple beam balance** measures mass more exactly than a pan balance. It has one pan and three beams. To find the mass in grams, move the sliders until the beam balances.

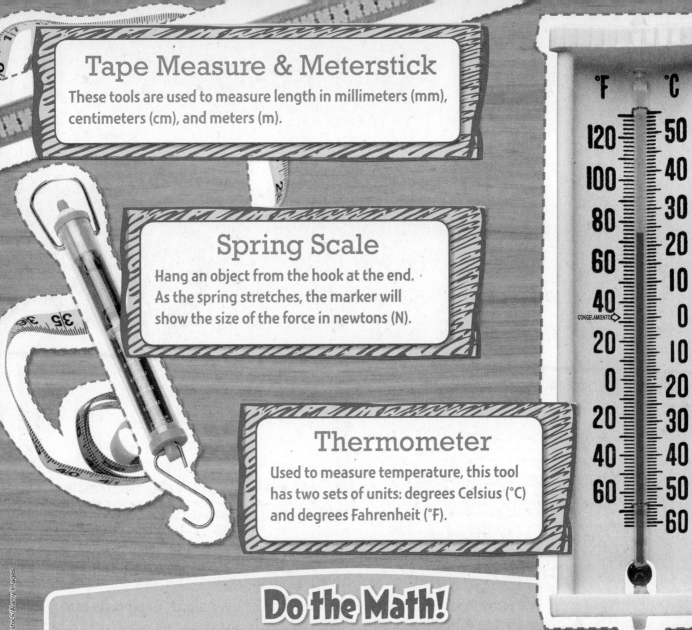

Tape Measure & Meterstick

These tools are used to measure length in millimeters (mm), centimeters (cm), and meters (m).

Spring Scale

Hang an object from the hook at the end. As the spring stretches, the marker will show the size of the force in newtons (N).

Thermometer

Used to measure temperature, this tool has two sets of units: degrees Celsius (°C) and degrees Fahrenheit (°F).

Do the Math!
Make Measurements

Use the metric ruler below to collect and record information about the length of the stick insect's body. Use the correct unit.

Find an object in your classroom to measure with a spring scale. Write the name of the object and number of units.

Look at the thermometer on this page. Record the temperature in degrees Celsius (°C) and degrees Fahrenheit (°F).

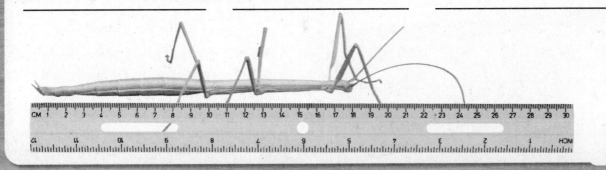

More Science Tools

The wings of a hummingbird beat rapidly. A river surges through a canyon. Light reflects off a mirror. Science tools help scientists observe nature in action.

As you read these two pages, circle the names of four science tools that are described.

Many science tools help scientists make detailed observations in order to collect and record information. A camera is a tool that provides scientists with a permanent record. Scientists can use cameras to record the progress of a science experiment to analyze later. Still images help scientists study details. For example, pictures of shadows can show how they change over a day. Scientists may use video images to study animal behavior or other moving objects. For instance, they might use slow-motion video to observe the rapidly moving wings of a hummingbird.

Camera

A camera is any device that records an image. Scientists can use digital cameras, smartphones, and tablets to take pictures as a way to collect and record information.

Other tools help scientists observe events or living things that are difficult to see with the eyes alone. Geologists may use a stream table to model the movement of sediment in water. A collecting net can be used for up-close observation of living organisms. Physicists use mirrors to study and analyze how light behaves. In addition to the tools shown on these pages, scientists use many other tools to collect, record, and analyze information.

Stream Table

A stream table is a type of model scientists use to observe and collect information about how water moves in sources too large to study in person.

Mirror

A mirror has a smooth, shiny surface. It can be used to collect information about how light is reflected or about optical illusions. A concave or a convex mirror can help scientists observe how light reflects. Scientists use mirrors and lasers to form 3-D pictures called holograms and to make precise measurements of distant objects.

Collecting Net

A collecting net is made up of a hoop, a handle, and netting. Scientists can use collecting nets to gather living specimens, such as insects, for close observation without causing any harm.

Lights, Camera, Action

Think of some nonliving things or events in nature. List three objects you could collect, record, and analyze information about using a still camera. List three events you could collect, record, and analyze information about using a video camera.

_____

_____

_____

_____

Recording and Displaying Data

You're crawling through a tropical jungle.
A butterfly flutters by. Then another appears.
How will you keep track of how many you see?

As you read these two pages, turn each heading
into a question that will point you to the main idea. Underline the
answers to your questions in the text.

A poster is one way
to display data.

© Houghton Mifflin Harcourt Publishing Company (bkgd) ©Clearviewstock/Alamy

Recording Data

The bits of information you observe are called **data**. Some data are in the form of numbers. For example, the number of butterflies you see in an hour is a piece of data. Other data are in the form of descriptions. Examples include written notes, diagrams, audio recordings, and photographs.

Only observations are data. So when you think, "There are more butterflies here than in Canada," that's a guess, not data.

Displaying Data

The data you record as you investigate may be correct, but not easy to understand. Later, you can decide how to display the data. For example, you might use your scribbled notes from the jungle to draw a map showing where you saw each butterfly. You might compare the number of each kind of butterfly you found in a circle graph. You might use a bar graph to show the number of butterflies you saw each hour.

Data Two Ways

The table on the left lists six butterflies and the number of wing flaps each one made as it passed by an observer. The bar graph on the right can display the same data. Use the data in the table to complete the graph.

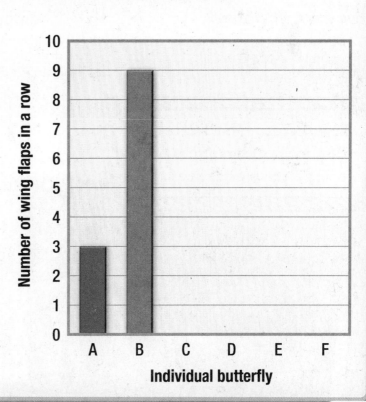

Individual Butterfly	Number of Wing Flaps in a Row
A	3
B	9
C	4
D	3
E	3
F	10

Using Data

You see on the news that the number of honeybees in the United States is decreasing. What is happening to them? How do scientists use data to solve problems and share information?

Drawing Conclusions

You've recorded your data. You've displayed it in a way that is easy to understand. Your next step is to analyze, or look for patterns in, the data. You might identify a trend, or a direction in the data over time. For example, you might conclude that the number of honeybees in your hometown has decreased by 30% in the last five years. What's next?

Communicating

Scientists communicate in many ways. They may work together to collect data. They compare their data with other scientists doing similar investigations. They report their results and conclusions by giving talks and writing reports. Conclusions often lead to new questions to investigate. Scientists are still studying why the number of honeybees is decreasing.

Scientists can share data as they make observations by using electronic devices.

4:25 PM

SEND▶

Dr. Ruiz,

Just checked the hives on Elm Street. There are many dead bees, and fewer honeycombs than last month.

Dr. Preston

Scientists may work alone or in teams to analyze data and draw conclusions.

▶ A database is a collection of information or objects. Databases are organized so they are easy to search—like a search website. How would you search a database of insect facts to see what others have learned about the decrease in the number of honeybees?

_____

_____

_____

_____

Museums often have large collections of specimens, so scientists can compare what they have found to what's in a museum.

When you're done, use the answer key to check and revise your work.

The outline below is a summary of the lesson. Complete the outline.

Summarize

I. Research Is the Key

    A. Scientists do research to find out what others know.

    B. Reference sources you can use:

        1. encyclopedias

        2. _____

        3. _____

        4. _____

        5. _____

        6. _____

II. Science Tools

    A. Scientists use tools to make the senses more powerful.

    B. Tools that aid the sense of sight:

        1. telescope

        2. _____

        3. _____

        4. _____

III. _____

    A. pan balance

    B. triple beam balance

    C. spring scale

    D. tape measure/meterstick

    E. _____

IV. More Science Tools

    A. camera

    B. _____

    C. _____

    D. _____

V. Recording and Displaying Data

    A. Data are the bits of information you observe.

    B. Ways to display data:

        1. tables

        2. _____

        3. _____

Answer Key: I.B.2–6 (in any order) books, science articles, museums, contact a scientist, science websites
II.B.2–4 (in any order) hand lens, magnifying box, microscope III. Measurement Tools III.E. thermometer
IV.B–D (in any order) stream table, mirror, collecting net V.B.2–3 (in any order) maps, graphs

Name _____

Word Play

1 Put the mixed-up letters in order to spell a science term from the box.

tada

eama supteer

crasheer

priclg harce

croopsmice

gripes clans

montumceica

axingbynim fog

metermother

lap cannaeb

circle graph	communicate	data*	magnifying box	microscope*
pan balance*	research	spring scale*	tape measure	thermometer

* Key Lesson Vocabulary

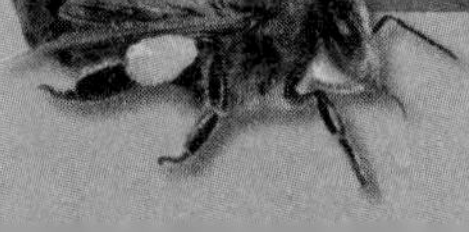

Apply Concepts

2 Someone gives you an object. You think it's a rock, but you aren't sure. Write how you could use each resource below to do research about the object.

encyclopedia   websites   books

_____   _____   _____

_____   _____   _____

_____   _____

contact a scientist   museum

_____   _____

_____   _____

_____   _____

3 Draw lines to match the tool to its use.

pan balance   to measure force

spring scale   to look closely at insects outdoors

thermometer   to measure mass

microscope   to find temperature

hand lens   to view objects too small to be
                     seen with the eye alone

Take It Home! Tell your family about the measurement tools scientists use. Discuss ways your family measures at home. Find and learn to use these tools. Hint: Does your kitchen have tools for measuring foods?

Inquiry Flipchart page 10

Lesson **4**

INQUIRY

OHIO **4.SIA.3** Employ simple equipment and tools to gather data and extend the senses; **4.SIA.5** Communicate about observations, investigations and explanations; and **4.SIA.6** Review and ask questions about the observations and explanations of others.

Name _____

Essential Question

Why Do Scientists Compare Results?

Set a Purpose
What will you learn from this investigation?

_____

_____

_____

Think About the Procedure
Which tool will you use to measure mass?

_____

_____

_____

Which units of length will your group use? Explain your choice.

_____

_____

_____

_____

Record Your Data
In the space below, construct a simple table to collect, record, and organize your measurements.

Draw Conclusions

Of the three measurement tools you used, which was the easiest to use? The hardest? Explain.

_____

_____

_____

_____

Analyze and Extend

1. Why is it helpful to communicate your written results with others?

_____

_____

_____

_____

2. What should you do if you find out that your measurements are very different from those of other teams?

_____

_____

_____

3. Which other characteristics of the object can you measure?

_____

_____

_____

_____

4. These pictures show two more measurement tools. Describe how you could use each tool to measure and collect information about an object.

Graduated cylinder

_____

_____

_____

_____

5. Which other questions would you like to ask about science tools?

_____

_____

_____

_____

_____

_____

_____

John Diebold

Dr. John Diebold spent much of his life studying Earth's oceans. He worked in the lab and in the field. He studied volcanoes, ancient ice sheets, and faults that cause earthquakes under water. Dr. Diebold improved the design of the *air gun*, a tool used to make underwater sound waves. Then he used these sound waves to make 3-D pictures of the ocean floor.

Much of Earth's oceans are too deep to study directly. John Diebold used many tools like this air gun to help people study the ocean floor from the surface.

Meet the Inventors

These gears are many times smaller than a millimeter! Dr. Culpepper's tools can be used to assemble objects this small.

Martin Culpepper

Dr. Martin Culpepper is a mechanical engineer. He invents tools that work with machines so small you cannot see them with a regular light microscope. These machines are many times smaller than the thickness of a human hair! One day these tiny machines could be used to find cancer cells. Unlike Dr. Diebold, Dr. Culpepper does most of his research in a lab. His lab has to be dust-free—a tiny bit of dust could ruin the results of his investigations.

Field Versus Lab

In the Field Scientists often work in the field, or the world outside of labs. What did Dr. Diebold learn from his studies in the field?

Research done by Dr. Diebold and others in the field led to the development of maps like this one. The map shows rock and sediment layers beneath the ocean floor.

This tool is a tiny lifter! It moves and sets into position the incredibly small parts of tiny machines.

In the Lab Why do you think Dr. Culpepper builds machines in a lab? Why would he not build them in the field?

Think About It!

How might a scientist's work be both in the field and in a lab? Think of an example.

OHIO **4.SIA.2** Plan and conduct simple investigations; **4.SIA.3** Employ simple equipment and tools to gather data and extend the senses; **4.SIA.5** Communicate about observations, investigations and explanations; and

Essential Question

What Kinds of Models Do Scientists Use?

Engage Your Brain!

Find the answer to the following question in this lesson and record it here.

This is a scale model of the moon. What can scientists learn by studying it?

_____

_____

_____

_____

Active Reading

Lesson Vocabulary

List the terms. As you learn about each one, make notes in the Interactive Glossary.

_____

_____

_____

Signal Words: Comparisons

Signal phrases show connections between ideas. Words that signal comparisons, or similarities, include *like, better than, also, alike, as close as,* and *stands for.* Active readers remember what they read because they are alert to signal phrases that identify comparisons.

Models and Science

Native Americans had mental models for the sun, moon, and planets. Several tribes in North America tell stories of the beginning of time, when Earth did not exist. All of the animals applied mud to the shell of a turtle. Earth was born when the mud became thick and large on the turtle's back.

Make a Two-dimensional Model!

Good models are as close to the real thing as possible. Draw a floor plan of a room in your home. Show the doorways and windows. Show the objects that sit on the floor. Add labels. Be as accurate as you can!

A toy car. A doll's house. A person who shows off clothes on a runway. These are all models. But what is a model in science?

Active Reading As you read these two pages, draw a star next to what you think is the most important sentence. Be ready to explain why.

Scientists make models to represent the natural world. In science, a **model** represents something real that is too big, too small, too far away, or has too many parts to investigate directly. For example, our solar system is too big to see all its parts at once. So, scientists use models to investigate the motion of planets, moons, and other solar system objects. They can use the models to predict when an asteroid will pass close to Earth.

Models can take many forms. A *mental model* is a picture you make in your mind. A good thing about this kind of model is that you always have it with you! A **two-dimensional model** has length and width. It can be a drawing, a diagram, or a map.

Models do have limitations, including accuracy and size. Our solar system is so large, an accurate model would also need to be large so that it includes enough detail.

Other Models Scientists Use

Do the Math!

Use Fractions

You plan to make a model of the solar system. You make the tiniest ball of clay you can for Mercury. The ball is 4 mm across. If Mercury were that size, the chart shows how big all the other objects in your model would be.

Object	Diameter (mm)
Sun	1,100
Mercury	4
Venus	9
Earth	10
Mars	5
Jupiter	110
Saturn	92
Uranus	37
Neptune	36

1. Which fraction tells how the size of Mars compares to Earth?

_____

2. Which object is about 1/4 the diameter of Neptune?

_____

3. Which object is about 1/9 the diameter of Saturn?

_____

You see thousands of stars in the night sky. You point to a very bright star. Suddenly, you are zooming through space. As you get closer, the star gets bigger and brighter. Your trip isn't real, but it feels like it is. It's another kind of model!

Three-Dimensional Models

The more a model is like the real thing, the better it is. If the object you want to model has length, width, and height, a **three-dimensional model** is useful. Such a model can show the positions of planets, moons, and the sun better than a two-dimensional model can.

If you want to compare sizes and distances in a model, then you make a *scale model*. The scale tells how much smaller or bigger the model is than the real thing. For example, a model railroad may have a scale of 1 to 48. This means each one inch on the model stands for 48 inches on the real train.

Computer Models

What if you want to understand how asteroids move through the solar system? You'd use a computer model. A **computer model** is a computer program that models an event or an object. Some computer models make you feel like you are moving through the solar system!

Weather Models Save Lives

Dangerous weather can happen suddenly. Hurricanes, tornadoes, floods, and winter storms can harm people, pets, and homes. How can models save lives?

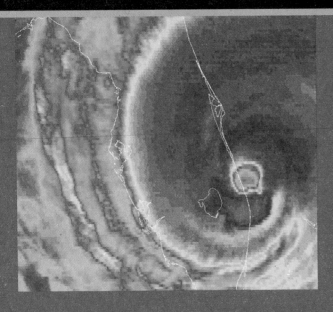

Data from Space

Satellites circle Earth 24 hours each day. Images and other weather data are beamed back to Earth. It's called *real-time* data because scientists see the pictures almost as soon as they are taken. This image shows the path of a hurricane. The colors are not real. Scientists choose them to show differences in wind speeds, heights of clouds, and other factors.

Using Models

Meteorologists use satellite data to make computer models of weather. They model hurricanes, tornadoes, and thunderstorms. The models are used to predict how and where storms will get started.

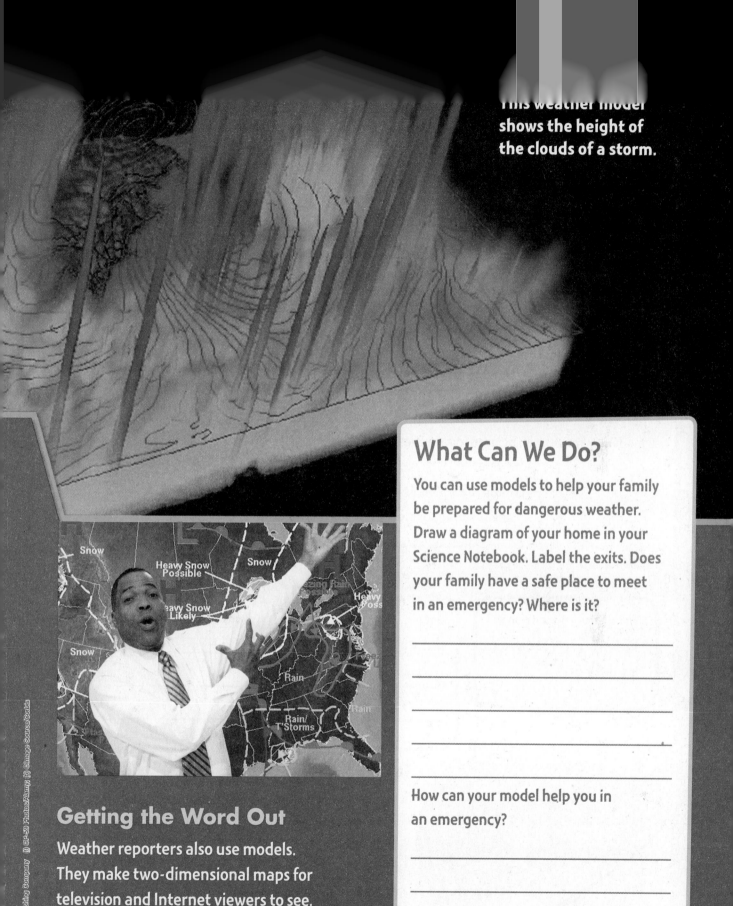

This weather model shows the height of the clouds of a storm.

What Can We Do?

You can use models to help your family be prepared for dangerous weather. Draw a diagram of your home in your Science Notebook. Label the exits. Does your family have a safe place to meet in an emergency? Where is it?

_____

_____

_____

_____

_____

How can your model help you in an emergency?

_____

_____

_____

_____

Getting the Word Out

Weather reporters also use models. They make two-dimensional maps for television and Internet viewers to see. These maps can change to show how soon and where bad weather will be.

Sum It Up!

When you're done, use the answer key to check and revise your work.

Use information from the summary to complete the graphic organizer in your own words.

Summarize

For scientists, a model represents the natural world—something real that is too big, too small, too far away, or has too many parts to investigate directly. Scientists use models to investigate and understand real places and objects. Models do have limitations, including accuracy and size. Several kinds of models are used in science. Two-dimensional models, such as drawings, diagrams, and maps, have length and width. Three-dimensional models have length, width, and height. Computer models are computer programs that behave like the real thing. Some models, such as models of storms, can be used to save lives.

Main Idea: Models in science are like real things and are used to understand real things.

Detail: Two-dimensional models are flat, like a map or a diagram.

Detail:
_____
_____
_____

Detail:
_____
_____
_____
_____

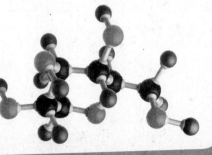

© Houghton Mifflin Harcourt Publishing Company   (l) ©Dorling Kindersley/Getty Images, (r) ©Dorling Kindersley/Getty Images

Answer Key: 1. Three-dimensional models have length, width, and height. 2. Computer models are computer programs that act like the real thing.

Name _____

Word Play

1 Use the words in the box to complete the puzzle.

computer model*   real-time
mental model   model*
scale model   satellite
two-dimensional model*   weather
three-dimensional model*
*Key Lesson Vocabulary

Across

2. A type of model that is in your head
4. Something that represents the real thing
6. These kinds of models can save lives
7. A type of model that has length and width
9. A device that sends weather images back to Earth

Down

1. A type of model made with a computer program
3. A type of model that has length, width, and height
5. In this type of model, a measurement on the model stands for a measurement on the real thing
8. Data that scientists can see as soon as it is collected

Apply Concepts

Tell how making or using each model listed below could help people.

2 A model to show where lightning is likely to strike

_____

_____

_____

3 A model to show where water flows during a storm

_____

_____

_____

4 A model to show how traffic moves in a city

_____

_____

5 Give an example of a model that is limited by accuracy and size. Identify the model's specific limitations.

_____

_____

_____

Many kids' toys are models of real things. Challenge your family to find such toys at home, in ads, or where you shop. Ask yourself: How is this toy like the real thing? How is it different?

Inquiry Flipchart page 12

OHIO **4.SIA.2** Plan and conduct simple investigations; **4.SIA.3** Employ simple equipment and tools to gather data and extend the senses; **4.SIA.5** Communicate about observations, investigations and explanations; and

Name _____

Essential Question

How Can You Model a School?

Set a Purpose
Which inquiry skills will you practice in this investigation?

_____

_____

_____

Think About the Procedure
How will you decide which part of your school you will represent using a model?

_____

_____

_____

_____

How will you choose the two types of models you will use?

_____

_____

_____

_____

Record Your Observations
Identify and describe the part of your school you represented using models.

_____

_____

_____

_____

Identify the two types of models you used and describe your models.

_____

_____

_____

_____

_____

_____

Draw Conclusions

What was something you learned about your school from making the models?

_____

_____

_____

Analyze and Extend

1. Why is it helpful to compare results with others?

_____

_____

_____

_____

2. Identify your models' limitations, including its accuracy.

_____

_____

_____

_____

_____

3. Why is it important to be accurate when making your measurements?

_____

_____

_____

_____

4. What was the hardest part of making the models? Was size a limitation during the planning and development of your model? Explain.

_____

_____

_____

_____

_____

_____

_____

5. Why is it important for engineers to make and try out models before making a real building or bridge?

_____

_____

_____

_____

6. What other things or places would you like to learn about by making a model? Explain why.

_____

_____

_____

7. What other questions would you like to ask about making models?

_____

_____

_____

Unit 1 Review

Vocabulary Review

Use the terms in the box to complete the sentences.

> inference
> investigation
> observation
> pan balance
> spring scale

1. When people collect data by using their five senses,

   they make a(n) _____.

2. A tool used to collect and analyze information about

   the mass of an object is a(n) _____.

3. When people ask questions, make observations, and use other methods to gather data about an event

   or object, they are doing a(n) _____.

4. Someone who makes a statement that explains an

   observation is making a(n) _____.

5. If you want to collect and analyze information about the pull of a force, such as the force of gravity, you would use

   a tool called a(n) _____.

Science Concepts

Fill in the letter of the choice that best answers the question.

6. Amira wants to compare close-up views of different bird feathers. Which tool should she use to collect and analyze this information?

   (A) magnet

   (B) meterstick

   (C) microscope

   (D) pan balance

7. Camilla is studying minerals in different rocks. Which would not help Camilla collect and record data about a rock?

   (A) measuring the volume of the rock

   (B) inferring the rock is millions of years old

   (C) testing the effect of dripping vinegar onto the rock

   (D) observing the minerals that make up the rock

8. Junichi used a computer to look at this three-dimensional model of his classroom.

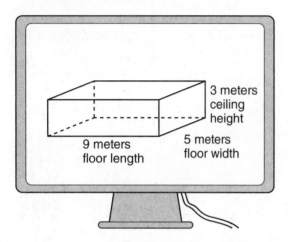

3 meters
ceiling
height

9 meters
floor length

5 meters
floor width

How can he use this model to find out if his classroom is longer than it is tall?

(A) He can look at the length of the floor.

(B) He can look at the height of the ceiling.

(C) He can compare the length and the width.

(D) He can compare the length and the ceiling height.

9. Julia concludes that a certain type of plant grows best in sandy soil. Rico suggests that this plant type grows best because it has the right amount of water. Which critical thinking skill is he using?

(A) alternative explanation

(B) experimental testing

(C) logical reasoning

(D) observational testing

10. Diego has been observing how well one plant type grows in different locations. He concludes a location with bright sunlight is the best. Which of the following is an example of empirical evidence he could use in support of his conclusion?

(A) His friend told him that all plants need bright sunlight to grow.

(B) Plants he kept in shade grew better than plants he kept in sunlight.

(C) Plants he kept in shade did not grow as well as plants he kept in sunlight.

(D) He thinks the plants he kept in sunlight would have grown better with more water.

11. A scientist uses steps of the scientific method to conduct an investigation. She analyzes the data she has collected and recorded through observation. What should she do next?

(A) draw a conclusion

(B) make a hypothesis

(C) conduct an experiment

(D) study the data one more time

12. Seiji records the number of birds he sees each day at a bird feeder. Which is the best method for Seiji to record his data?

(A) bar graph

(B) camera

(C) diagram

(D) model

13. A scientist has spent one year conducting an experiment. He concludes that the evidence from his experiment does not support his hypothesis. What should the scientist do next?

(A) Forget this experiment and choose a new problem.

(B) Try to make up evidence that supports his hypothesis.

(C) Look at the evidence and see if he can make a new hypothesis.

(D) Look at the information and find a different way to organize his results.

14. Gia hypothesizes that hot water will cause a sugar cube to dissolve faster than cold water will. She investigates by filling three cups: one with hot water, one with cold water, and one with ice water. She drops a sugar cube in each cup. Which observation will help Gia decide whether her hypothesis is correct?

(A) which cup the sugar cube dissolves in first

(B) the time it takes for two sugar cubes to dissolve

(C) changes in water temperature from start to finish

(D) changes in the size of the sugar cube in cold water

15. The local news station asks viewers to measure the amount of rain that falls in their neighborhoods. Four measurements are shown below.

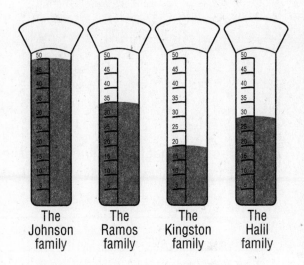

The Johnson family   The Ramos family   The Kingston family   The Halil family

Which family measures the most rain?

(A) Halil family

(B) Johnson family

(C) Kingston family

(D) Ramos family

16. Scientists state a hypothesis before conducting an experiment. Which step should a scientist also do before conducting an experiment?

(A) ask questions

(B) draw conclusions

(C) communicate results

(D) record and analyze results

Apply Inquiry and Review the Big Idea

Write the answers to these questions.

17. Luis fed his cat in the kitchen. These pictures show what Luis saw as he left the kitchen and then what he saw when he returned.

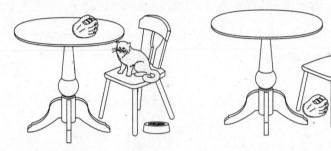

Luis figured out that the cat jumped on the table and knocked the mitt onto the floor. What inquiry skill did Luis use? Give a reason for your answer.

_____

_____

18. Write three observations about this leaf.

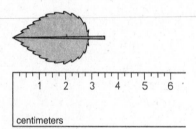

My Observations

a. _____

b. _____

c. _____

19. Marie collects data during an experiment. She records the mass of several soil samples, as shown in this data table.

Sample A	Sample B	Sample C
45 g	25 g	38 g

What is the average mass of these soil samples? _____.

The Engineering Process

Big Idea

Engineers use a process to design products and processes that solve human problems.

OHIO 4.SIA.2, 4.SIA.3, 4.SIA.4, 4.SIA.5

I Wonder Why

Ancient people used stone tools. Today, scientists study these tools to learn how ancient people lived. I wonder how scientists know why ancient people made these tools? *Turn the page to find out.*

Here's Why Throughout history, people have designed and built tools to help meet their needs. Whether a tool is a simple stone or a high-tech electronic device, it can help solve a problem. By figuring out how an ancient tool was used, scientists can draw conclusions about the needs of the person who made it.

In this unit, you will explore the Big Idea, the Essential Questions, and the Investigations on the Inquiry Flipchart.

Levels of Inquiry Key ■ DIRECTED ■ GUIDED ■ INDEPENDENT

Big Idea Engineers use a process to design products and processes that solve human problems.

Track Your Progress

Essential Questions

Now I Get the Big Idea!

Science Notebook
Before you begin each lesson, be sure
your thoughts about the Essential Que

OHIO **4.SIA.2** Plan and conduct simple investigations; **4.SIA.5** Communicate about observations, investigations, and explanations; and

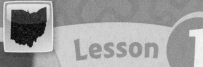

Lesson **1**

Essential Question

What Is an Engineering Design Process?

🧠 Engage Your Brain!

Find the answer to the following question in this lesson and record it here.

Why would a car company want a wooden car?

_____

_____

_____

_____

Active Reading

Lesson Vocabulary

List the terms. As you learn about each one, make notes in the Interactive Glossary.

_____

_____

_____

Signal Words: Sequence

Signal words show connections between ideas. Words that signal sequence include *now, before, after, first,* and *next.* Active readers remember what they read because they are alert to signal words that identify sequence.

What Is ENGINEERING?

From the food we eat and the clothes we wear, to the cars we drive and the phones we talk on, science is at work in our lives every day.

Active Reading As you read the next page, circle the main idea of the text, and put brackets [ ] around each detail sentence.

Electrical engineers use their knowledge of physics to build things like this robot.

Knowledge of math and geology allows surveyors to make maps of Earth.

This biomedical engineer uses his knowledge of biology to make glass eyes.

Look around. Many of the things you see are products of engineering. **Engineering** is the use of scientific and mathematical principles to develop something practical. Some engineers use biology. Others use geology, chemistry, or physics.

Engineers use this knowledge to create something new. It might be a product, a system, or a process for doing things. Whatever it is, it's practical. People use it. Engineers develop things that people use.

▶ In the space below, draw a picture of something you can see around you that was probably designed by an engineer.

What Is the DESIGN PROCESS?

It has been said that necessity is the mother of invention. But once you find a need, how do you build your invention? That's the design process!

Active Reading As you read these two pages, draw boxes around clue words or phrases that signal a sequence or order.

What is design? **Design** means to conceive something and prepare the plans and drawings for it to be built. Engineers use the design process to develop new technology, but anyone can follow the design process.

From basic to complex, skateboards have changed over time.

The design process starts with identifying a need or a problem. Next, you brainstorm and write down ideas on how to plan and build a potential solution. Once you have some options, select a solution to try. Usually, engineers test possible solutions using a prototype.

A **prototype** is an original or test model on which a real product is based. If the prototype works, then the real product is made. Usually, after testing a prototype, improvements have to be made. The prototype is then tested again. Finally, a finished product is made.

Design Process Steps

- Find a problem
- Plan and build
- Test and improve
- Redesign
- Communicate

Even something seemingly simple takes a lot of thought, planning, testing, and improvement.

How was it improved?

Look at the skateboards. Describe two design features that have been improved over time.

_____

_____

_____

_____

Design
YOU CAN USE

Look around you at all the things you use every day. Do you have ideas about improving them?

As you read these two pages, find and underline the meaning of the word *prototype*.

Who Needs It?

The first step in any design process is identifying a need or problem. Is there a chore that could be easier, a tool that could work much better, a car that could go faster or be safer? Often, the design process begins with the phrase "What if?"

Prototype!

A prototype is a test version of a design. To build a prototype, a person has to have plans. Early sketches give a rough idea. More detailed drawings provide exact measurements for every piece. Keeping good records and drawings helps to make sure that the prototype can be replicated.

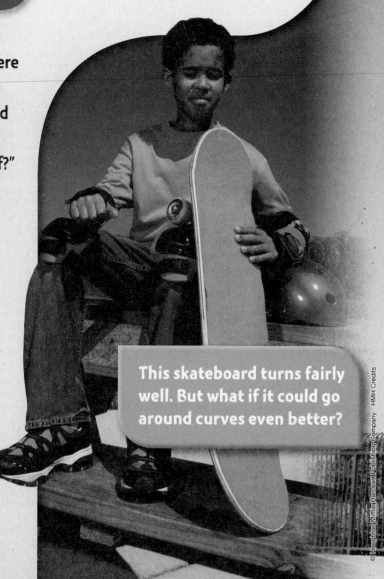

This skateboard turns fairly well. But what if it could go around curves even better?

Details

Draw a blueprint of a school supply, favorite toy, or tool. Label its parts and include exact measurements.

Sketches and detailed drawings are an important step in planning a product.

Every part of a product can become an opportunity for a design change.

wheel

trucks

deck

Are We DONE YET?

Now that the prototype has been built, can the final product be far behind? Yes, it can. But it might not be. It all depends.

Active Reading As you read these two pages, draw a box around the clue word or phrase that signals one thing is being contrasted with another.

Test It and Improve It!

Prototypes are carefully tested. This testing helps answer questions such as, *Does it work the way it should? Is it easy to use? How does it hold up under normal working conditions?*

The first prototype you build may pass all its tests. If so, the prototype can go into production. However, it is more likely that testing shows that the design needs to change. Once the test results are analyzed, it's back to the drawing board. The product may need only a few minor improvements, or it may need to be completely redesigned.

If a prototype works as expected, it will become a finished product.

Redesign and Share

When a prototype fails to meet a design goal, it may be redesigned. Redesign takes advantage of all work done before. Good design features are kept, and those that fail are discarded.

When the final working prototype is done, team members communicate the design. Sketches, blueprints, and test data and analysis are shared. Often, the product details are recorded in a legal document called a *patent*.

Sometimes, one prototype leads to ideas for others.

Spin Off!

Imagine a normal bicycle. Now think of three ways it could be modified to work better in different environments.

_____

_____

_____

_____

_____

New ideas keep the engineering design process constantly moving forward.

Sum It Up!

When you're done, use the answer key to check and revise your work.

Use information in the summary to complete the graphic organizer.

Summarize

The first step in the design process is to identify a need or a problem to be solved. The next step is to plan and build a prototype. Brainstorming ideas and drawing detailed sketches of potential solutions are important parts of this step. The third step is to test and improve a prototype. After testing, a prototype might need to be redesigned and tested again. A prototype that meets all its design goals is ready for production. The final step in the design process is to communicate to others the details of a working prototype.

1 The design process starts with identifying a need or _____ _____.

3 _____ _____ _____

5 The final step in the design process is to _____ _____.

2 _____ _____ _____ _____

4 _____ _____ _____ _____

Answer Key: 1. problem to be solved 2. The second step in the design process is to plan and build a prototype. 3. The third step is to test and improve the prototype. 4. After testing, a prototype might need to be redesigned and tested again. 5. communicate

Name _____

Word Play

1 Use the clues to help you write the correct word in each row. Some boxes have been filled in for you.

A. To conceive something and prepare plans to build it

B. The use of scientific and mathematical principles to develop something practical

C. A prototype may undergo many rounds of this.

D. Engineers have to be familiar with these principles.

E. The answer to a problem

F. A test version of something

G. Is identified during the first step in the design process

H. What comes after sketches, plans, and the prototype?

I. Something that people will use is described as this.

J. Engineers have to be familiar with these principles.

Apply Concepts

2 Write numbers in the circles to put the pictures in the correct order.

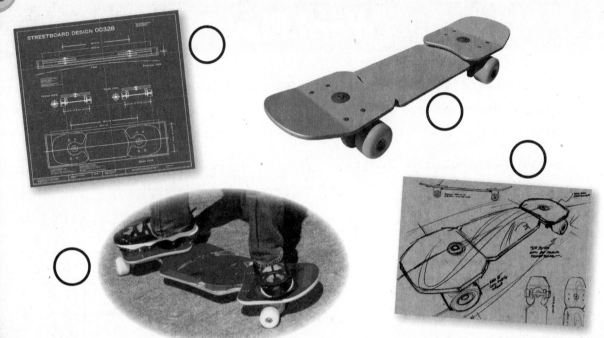

3 How is a prototype different from the finished product?

_____

_____

_____

_____

_____

4 Why is it better to build and test a prototype of a product than to produce tens of thousands of the product and then test it?

_____

_____

_____

5 The owner of a safety apparel company asks an engineer to "design a better helmet for skateboarders." How would you improve this instruction?

_____

_____

_____

_____

_____

_____

_____

_____

6 Which job is more likely to be done by an engineer? Why?

Developing a new material that will be used to make the outer covering of vitamin capsules	Determining how vitamins are absorbed into the bloodstream

_____

_____

_____

_____

_____

7 The engineers at an appliance company have developed a new dishwasher. It looks very different from previous models. The controls look different and work differently. The part of the machine that heats the water has been completely redesigned. Now that the plans are completed, should the company start producing thousands of these dishwashers? Why or why not?

_____

_____

_____

_____

_____

_____

_____

_____

_____

_____

_____

_____

Take It Home!

With your family, find a product in your home that needs improving. Suppose you work for the company that makes this product and brainstorm a new prototype to test.

OHIO **4.SIA.5** Communicate about observations, investigations and explanations; and

Name _____

Essential Question

How Can You Design a Solution to a Problem?

Set a Purpose
What do you think you will learn from this experiment?

_____

_____

_____

_____

Think About the Procedure
How will the equipment you design be similar to safety belts and airbags in a car?

_____

_____

_____

_____

_____

_____

Why is it a good idea to make sure the plastic bag is tightly sealed before you test your prototype?

_____

_____

_____

Record Your Data
In the space below, draw a table to record the materials you used in your prototype and your observations from each test.

Draw Conclusions

What conclusions can you draw as a result of your test observations?

_____

_____

_____

_____

Analyze and Extend

1. Was your design successful? Why or why not?

_____

_____

_____

_____

2. Based on your results, how could you improve your design? Describe and draw the changes you would make to your prototype.

_____

_____

_____

_____

3. Were there any aspects of someone else's design you might incorporate into your design?

_____

_____

_____

4. What is the difference between a successful design and a successful prototype?

_____

_____

_____

_____

_____

5. Think of other questions you would like to ask about forces and transportation.

_____

_____

_____

_____

OHIO **4.SIA.2** Plan and conduct simple investigations; **4.SIA.3** Employ simple equipment and tools to gather data and extend the senses; **4.SIA.4** Use appropriate mathematics with data to construct reasonable explanations; **4.SIA.5** Communicate about observations, investigations and explanations; and

Lesson 3

Essential Question

What Is Technology?

Engage Your Brain!

Find the answer to the following question in the lesson and record it here.

This robot is riding a bicycle, just like a human, and not falling over. How is this possible?

_____

_____

_____

_____

Active Reading

Lesson Vocabulary

List the terms. As you learn about each one, make notes in the Interactive Glossary.

_____

_____

_____

Main Ideas

The main idea of a paragraph is the most important idea. The main idea may be stated in the first sentence, or it may be stated elsewhere. Active readers look for main ideas by asking themselves, What is this paragraph mostly about?

Inquiry Flipchart p. 15 — Goals, Inputs, and Outputs/All Systems Go!

85

Grappler

TOOLS RULE!

A bulldozer and a shovel serve the same purpose. However, because of a bulldozer's size, it can move huge amounts of material much more quickly than a shovel can.

Look in your desk. Do you see pens and pencils? Scissors? A ruler? All of these things are tools.

Active Reading As you read these two pages, put brackets [ ] around the sentences that describe a problem. Underline the sentences that describe the solution.

Planting a vegetable garden? You'll need a shovel, a rake, and a spade. All these items are tools. A **tool** is anything that helps people shape, build, or produce things to meet their needs.

Your family's toolbox probably contains a hammer and screwdrivers. Construction workers have similar tools that do the same jobs, only on a larger scale. Instead of hammering nails by hand, construction workers use tools that quickly drive nails into wood with the push of a button. Their tools are sized and powered differently to meet different needs.

Some tools are designed to do one task. You use a pen to write a note to a friend. You keep your science notes organized in a notebook. You talk to your grandmother on the phone. What if you had one tool that could do all these tasks? A smartphone is a tool that can help you send a message, organize information, *and* talk to people.

A smartphone, like all tools, is an example of technology. **Technology** is any designed system, product, or process that people use to solve problems. Technology doesn't have to be complex. The pencil you write with and the cell phone you text with are both technology. Technology changes as the needs of people change.

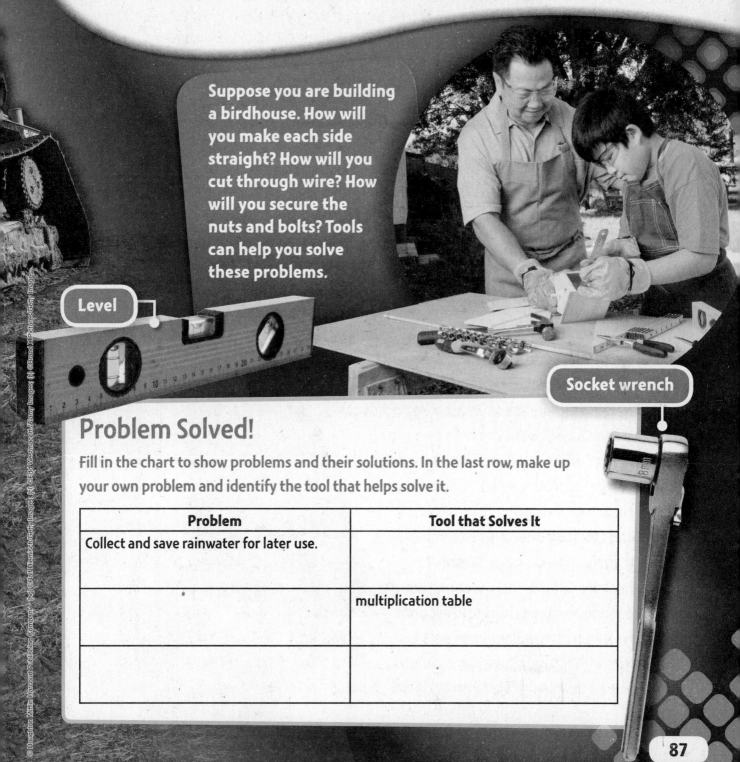

Suppose you are building a birdhouse. How will you make each side straight? How will you cut through wire? How will you secure the nuts and bolts? Tools can help you solve these problems.

Level

Socket wrench

Problem Solved!

Fill in the chart to show problems and their solutions. In the last row, make up your own problem and identify the tool that helps solve it.

Problem	Tool that Solves It
Collect and save rainwater for later use.	
	multiplication table

WHAT IS TECHNOLOGY?

Vending machines, televisions, and video games are examples of technology products you know—but there are more. Technology is all around you.

Active Reading As you read this page, underline technology products. On the next page, circle the paragraph that describes examples of a technology process.

A video game is the end product of a technology process. Programming a video game involves technology you can't hold in the palm of your hand.

You've learned that technology is any designed system, product, or process. A *technology product* is anything designed to meet a need or desire. Some people think that electronics are the only type of technology product. However, most technology products do not use electricity!

This book, the desk it is on, and the backpack you use to take it home are all technology products. Your bike and the sidewalk you ride it on are technology products, too. Technology products can be very large or very small. They can be a single thing like a stone brick or made of many things put together. Some technology products, such as medicine, are made to keep us healthy. Others, such as construction tools, are made to shape the world around us. We also invent technology products just to have fun.

▶ Circle three examples of technology in this photo.

The way a product is made is also a form of technology. A *technology process* is a series of steps used to achieve a goal or make a product. The steps in a technology process are like the steps in a scientific investigation. They are carefully designed for doing something a certain way.

Many things you do are a technology process. You follow a series of steps to make gelatin dessert, tie your shoelaces, and add music to your MP3 player. If you have ever played baseball, you are familiar with its rules. The rules of a game are a technology process.

Safety gear and clothing are types of technology that help baseball players perform. The bleachers and the backstop are types of technology that let spectators watch safely.

Play Ball

The ballpark, scoreboard, rules, and baseball equipment are all examples of technology. How can technology help deliver the game's events to people who aren't at the ballpark?

_____

_____

_____

TECHNOLOGICAL SYSTEMS

The next time you ride in a car, look at how many parts it has. It took many tools and hundreds of steps to produce this technology.

Active Reading As you read this page, underline the sentence that describes what makes a designed system.

Groups of things that work together to achieve a goal make up a *system*. Tools, parts, and processes that work together form a *designed system*. Designed systems help us travel and ship goods. They help us communicate and grow our foods.

You are a part of many designed systems. Whether you ride the bus or walk to school, you are a part of a transportation system. This system is made up of the sidewalks, roads, and traffic signs. It also includes the cars, buses, planes, and trains that move people and materials from place to place.

Designed systems help us shape the world around us. When you ride around your town, you might see cars, roadways, buildings, or farm fields. All these things make up the *designed world*. The designed world is the part of your community that is designed and built by people.

Many designed systems work together in the designed world. For example, the agricultural system produces the food that we need. Ships, trains, and trucks in the transportation system carry food where it is needed.

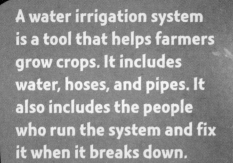

A water irrigation system is a tool that helps farmers grow crops. It includes water, hoses, and pipes. It also includes the people who run the system and fix it when it breaks down.

PARTS OF A DESIGNED SYSTEM

Part	Example: Rail Transportation System
Goal—what the system aims to do	Goal—to move cargo and passengers safely from place to place
Input—what is put into the system to meet the goal	Inputs—fuel for the train, cargo, and people to ride the train
Processes—describe how the goal is to be achieved	Processes—train tracks and departure and arrival schedules
Output—the end product	Output—safe and timely delivery of people and cargo
Feedback—information that tells whether or not the output is successful	Feedback—records of whether trains left and arrived on time

A railroad system includes trains, rails, and safety signals at road crossings. The system also has parts you can't see. Radio signals keep track of where trains are. The signals raise and lower crossing arms, too.

Tech Systems

What do you think would be the goal of a farming system?

_____

_____

_____

THE GOOD AND THE BAD OF IT

A light bulb that can save you $100 a year? What's the catch?

Active Reading As you read this page, draw a box around the main idea.

Compact fluorescent lights (CFLs) and light emitting diodes (LEDs) use less energy than incandescent bulbs. However, CFLs contain mercury, which can be hazardous if the bulbs break open, and LEDs are more expensive than regular light bulbs.

Technology is constantly changing. Anyone can invent or improve a technology product or process. It takes new ideas and knowledge for technology to change. The goal of any new technology is to better meet people's needs. However, new technology can also bring new risks.

Changes in technology often involve making things safer, quicker, easier, or cheaper. For example, people once used candles and lanterns to light their homes. These things helped people see at night, but they could also cause fires. Electricity and incandescent light bulbs helped solve this problem, but this technology also has its risks.

We burn coal to generate electricity. When coal burns, harmful ash and gases are produced. The potential harm these substances can cause leads to negative feedback. Such feedback helps people think of ways to improve technology.

Sometimes the problems with a technology are caused by the way people use technology. For instance, pesticides are helpful technology products. They are used to protect people, crops, and farm animals from harmful organisms. However, when used incorrectly, they can contaminate the soil, the water, and the air. Living things exposed to pesticides by accident can get sick and die.

Do the Math!
Interpret a Table

Use the data in the table to answer the questions below.

Light Bulb Cost Comparisons		
	25-Watt CFL	100-Watt incandescent
Cost of bulb	$3.40	$0.60
Bulb life	1,667 days (4.5 years)	167 days (about half a year)
Energy cost per year	$6.00	$25.00
Total cost over 4.5 years	$27.00	$118.50

1. How much more is the total cost of an incandescent bulb than a CFL?

_____

2. How much would your yearly energy cost be if you had 20 CFL bulbs in your home?

_____

3. Which bulb lasts longer?

_____

Airplanes can transport a lot of people at one time. However, they burn a lot of fuel and release pollution into the atmosphere. Engineers redesign airplanes to improve their performance.

OUT WITH THE OLD

Computers, cell phones, and flat-screen TVs are fun and useful. But like all technology, electronic gadgets have drawbacks.

Electronic technology seems to change at the blink of an eye. New electronic devices rapidly replace old ones. People benefit from new or improved electronic devices, but they also bring new problems.

Not long ago, most televisions and computer monitors were large, bulky things. New technology has made these large devices a thing of the past. They have been replaced by thin, lightweight flat screens.

But what do we do with old electronics? Some are taken apart and recycled; however, like the devices shown on this page, most end up in landfills. At landfills, electronics may release harmful chemicals into the environment.

Many electronic devices contain lead. Lead can be harmful to people and other organisms in the environment.

Electronics are helpful communication, work, and entertainment tools. They can also be a distraction. Some people spend a lot of time playing video games or on the Internet. They send text messages or listen to MP3 players while they are with other people. Some might even operate electronics while driving and cause a safety hazard for themselves and others.

People can solve these problems. They can set limits on computer and game time. They can put the phone away and pay attention to people and driving. These are ways to be responsible with technology.

▶ On the chart below, fill in the pros and cons of each electronic technology. Some examples have been provided for you.

	Pros	Cons
Television	can be educational; can provide breaking news quickly	
Smartphones		can take time away from doing other activities or being social; can cause drivers to be a hazard
Video games	fun; can be social when played with others	

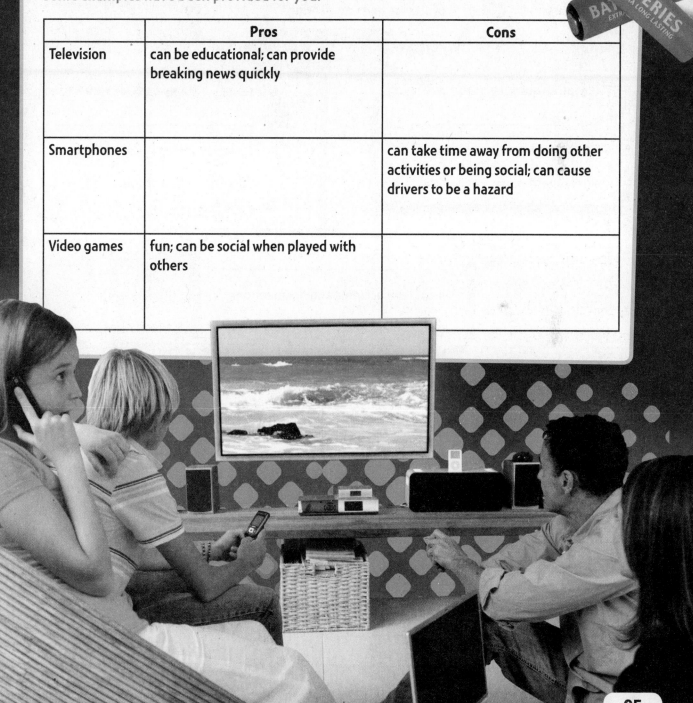

When you're done, use the answer key to check and revise your work.

Complete the graphic organizer below.

1 _____ changes with new ideas and knowledge of science and engineering.

is made up of any

2 _____ is tools, parts, and processes that work together.

4 _____ is a series of steps used to achieve a goal or make a product.

3 _____ includes electronic and nonelectronic devices that meet a need or a desire.

Summarize

Fill in the missing words that help summarize ideas about technology.

A shovel is a tool that can help move dirt. A [5] _____ can do the same job in a bigger way. Tools are technology that help people shape, build, or produce things. [6]_____ changes to meet the growing needs and desires of people.

A computer is an electronic product of technology. A [7]_____ is a nonelectronic product of technology. [8]_____ and [9]_____ often work in teams to develop new technology.

With technology, there is often risk to people and to the [10]_____.

Name _____

Word Play

1 Use the clues below to fill in the words of the puzzle.

1. Any designed system, product, or process

2. Anything that helps people shape, build, or produce things to meet their needs

3. Tools, parts, and processes that work together

4. Things that are made to meet a need

5. The end product or service of a system

6. Anything that is put into a system to meet a goal

7. Information that tells whether or not the output is successful

8. This is made up of all products of technology

9. A series of steps that result in a product

designed world

feedback   input

process   products

output   system

technology*   tool*

*Key Lesson Vocabulary

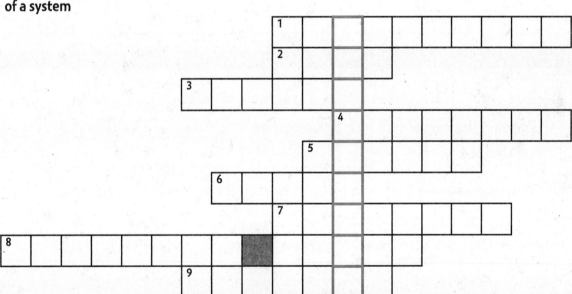

Read down the squares with red borders. The word will answer the question below.

Murata Boy is a bicycling robot. He can ride forward, backward, and stop without falling over. Where does he get the ability to do it?

__ __ __ __ __ __ __ __ __

Apply Concepts

Passenger jets can transport people quickly from one place to another. Modern computer electronics help pilots fly these planes.

2 Describe two technological systems that are related to airplanes.

_____

_____

_____

3 What are some of the risks of global airline travel? What are some of the benefits?

_____

_____

_____

4 Write a problem associated with each example of electronic technology.

1. Compact fluorescent light bulbs

_____

_____

_____

2. Video games

_____

_____

_____

3. Cell phones

_____

_____

_____

Take It Home!

Work with a family member to make a list of tools found in your kitchen. Sort the items in your list into simple and complex tools. Share your work with your class. Explain how you categorized the items in your list.

OHIO 4.SIA.4 Use appropriate mathematics with data to construct reasonable explanations; **4.SIA.5** Communicate about observations, investigations and explanations; and

Name _____

Essential Question

How Do We Use Technology?

Set a Purpose

What do you think you will learn from this activity?

_____

_____

Think About the Procedure

What does the spring scale measure?

_____

Why is it a good idea to repeat each trial in Steps 1 and 2 three times?

_____

_____

_____

What is being modeled when some of the marbles are replaced with cubes?

_____

_____

Record Your Data

Record your observations for Trials 1–3 in the space below.

	Measured Force (N)		
Trial	Bare table	Marbles	Marbles and cubes
1			
2			
3			
Average			

Draw Conclusions

Calculate the average force needed to move the book stack in each setup. Show your work and record your answers in the table above.

Draw Conclusions (continued)

Which problem did the tool you built help solve?

_____

_____

Which setup required the greatest amount of force to move the book stack? Why?

_____

_____

_____

_____

_____

Analyze and Extend

1. Which products of technology did you use to build your tool?

_____

_____

_____

2. What other objects could you have used in place of marbles?

_____

_____

_____

3. In the space below, draw a bar graph to show the average force needed to move the book stack in each setup.

4. What could cause the marbles to become more like cubes?

_____

_____

_____

_____

5. How could you redesign this tool to move larger things?

_____

_____

_____

_____

8 Things YOU SHOULD KNOW ABOUT Ayanna Howard

1 Dr. Ayanna Howard is a roboticist. She designs and builds robots.

2 Dr. Howard is making robots that will make decisions without the help of people.

3 To get a robot to make decisions on its own, Dr. Howard must teach the robot how to think.

4 Dr. Howard uses computer programs to teach robots. She observes the robots. Then she changes her computer programs to get better results.

5 Dr. Howard studies how robots can help explore outer space and unsafe places on Earth.

6 Dr. Howard taught a robot called SmartNav to move around things in its path. This robot could explore the surface of Mars.

7 Scientists want to understand why the ice in Antarctica is melting. Dr. Howard's SnoMote robots can safely gather data on the cracking ice sheets.

8 In 2003, Dr. Howard was named a top young inventor.

Now You Be a Roboticist!

1 What is Dr. Howard investigating?

2 Why does Dr. Howard test the robots?

3 What scientific question does Dr. Howard's SnoMote help answer?

4 If you were a roboticist, what kind of robot would you make?

5 What steps would you take in making your robot?

6 Draw a picture of your robot.

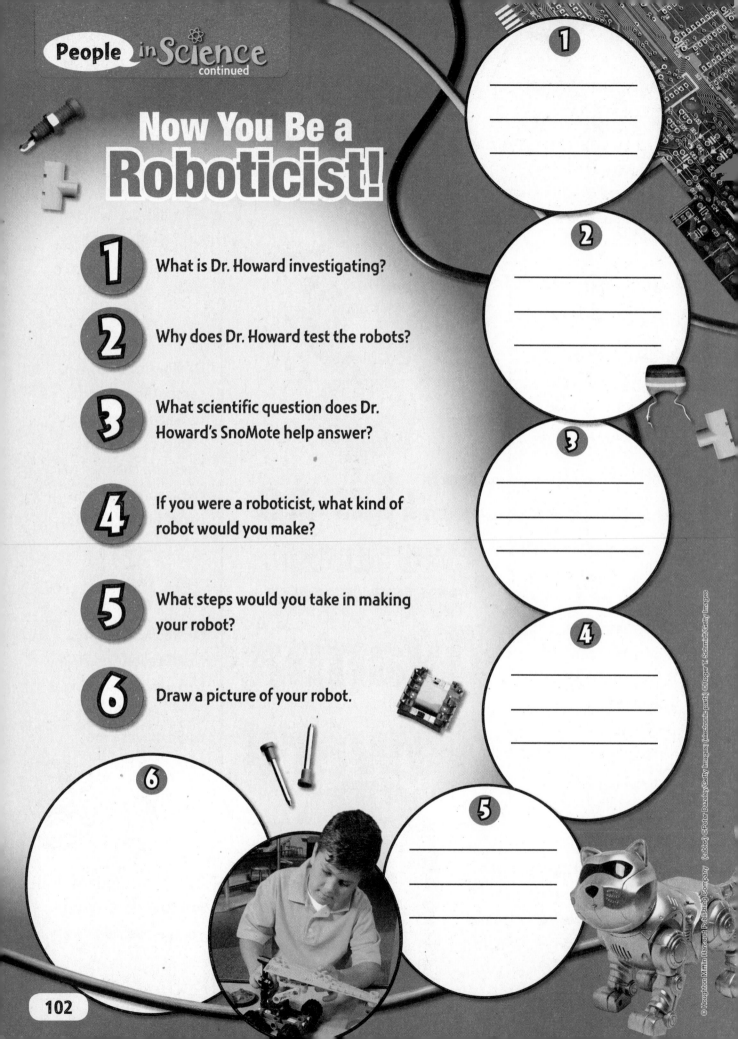

Unit 2 Review

Name _____

Vocabulary Review

Use the terms in the box to complete the sentences.

> design
> designed system
> engineering
> process
> prototype
> technology
> technology product
> tool

1. Anything that is made to meet a need or desire is

   a(n) _____.

2. To conceive of something and prepare the plans and drawings

   for it to be built is _____.

3. A designed system, product, or process that people use to solve

   problems is called _____.

4. A series of steps used to achieve a goal or make a product is

   called a(n) _____.

5. The use of scientific and mathematical principles to develop

   something practical is called _____.

6. An original or test model on which a real product is based is

   called a _____.

7. Tools, parts, and processes that work together form

   a(n) _____.

8. Anything that helps people shape, build, or produce things

   to meet their needs is called a _____.

© Houghton Mifflin Harcourt Publishing Company (border) ©NDisc/Age Fotostock

Unit 2   103

Science Concepts

Fill in the letter of the choice that best answers the question.

9. A group of researchers is working on a way to make winter coats warmer. The first coat the researchers design is not very warm. What should they do?

  (A) They should try again without using tools.

  (B) They should find a different designed system.

  (C) They should continue their work without using technology.

  (D) They should examine their test data for ways to improve the coat's design.

10. Sylvia works for a car company. She uses her knowledge of math and science to design dashboards that make it easier to operate cars. What is Sylvia's profession?

  (A) analyst

  (B) biologist

  (C) engineer

  (D) geologist

11. Marco is using this object to help him find information for a report.

Which statement best describes this object?

  (A) It is a technology process.

  (B) It is an engineer.

  (C) It is a prototype.

  (D) It is a tool.

12. Researchers want to build a new type of spaceship for transporting astronauts to the moon. What should they do **first**?

  (A) They should test the prototype.

  (B) They should plan a prototype.

  (C) They should build a model.

  (D) They should evaluate how the prototype worked.

13. Bulldozers, measuring cups, pencils, and hammers are all examples of tools. What else can be said about all of them?

  (A) They are all technology products.

  (B) They are all in the prototype stage.

  (C) They all release harmful gases into the atmosphere.

  (D) They all require power sources other than their users.

14. New solutions to problems often begin with a "What if?" question. Which "What if?" question might an engineer ask after seeing the electrical energy station shown below?

  (A) What if we burned trees instead of coal?

  (B) What if we could find even more coal to burn?

  (C) What if we all threw away all of our electrical appliances?

  (D) What if we could burn coal to make electricity without polluting the air?

15. Angie tested a reflector that she hopes will make bicycles safer. Although her first test went well, she repeated the test three more times. Which of these statements is **true**?

(A) She skipped the step of asking "What if?"

(B) She wasted her time by repeating the same test.

(C) She obtained unreliable data, because there were more chances for mistakes.

(D) She obtained more accurate data than if she had only tested the reflector once.

16. You probably use the tools shown below every day.

Which statement about these tools is **true**?

(A) They cost about the same to produce.

(B) They are both examples of technology.

(C) They are examples of identical technology.

(D) They are each designed for many different tasks.

17. Sometimes, a prototype tests poorly or fails completely. What should be done when that happens?

(A) The prototype should be abandoned.

(B) A second prototype should be built.

(C) The prototype should be modified, with the good parts of it kept.

(D) The prototype should be examined to see if it has other uses.

18. A fuel-efficient automobile is an example of a designed system. What is an example of feedback for such an automobile?

(A) safe arrival at the destination

(B) fuel for the car and the roads on which it will travel

(C) data on how much fuel the car used to travel 100 km

(D) to move a family of four 100 km using only 2 liters of gasoline

19. Long ago, there were few roads. Now there are many roads. How has a system of roads changed most communities?

(A) People can easily get from one place to another.

(B) People live closer to where they work and drive less.

(C) People travel less and rarely see family members that live far away.

(D) Use of fossil fuels has decreased with the increase in roads and highways.

Apply Inquiry and Review the Big Idea

Write the answers to these questions.

20. This picture shows solar cells on the roof of a house. These cells take solar energy and convert it into electricity that appliances in the house need to function.

a. How is this an example of a designed system?

_____

_____

_____

b. Identify the goal, input, output, and feedback of this system.

_____

_____

_____

21. An engineer follows the design process to improve soccer shoes. First, he studies shoes on the market and reads about what people have to say about them. Then, he starts to design his prototype.

a. Why is it important for the engineer to keep good notes during the design process?

_____

_____

b. Why should the engineer build a prototype of the shoes?

_____

_____

c. Describe a part of the design process the engineer should do **after** testing the prototype.

_____

_____

_____

_____

_____

_____

Earth's Surface

Big Idea

The shape of Earth's land changes over time. 70% of Earth's surface is covered in water, which travels through the water cycle.

OHIO 4.ESS.1, 4.ESS.2, 4.ESS.3, 4.SIA.1, 4.SIA.5

I Wonder How

Hocking Hills in Ohio has many different types of landforms, including cliffs and caves. How does water shape the landforms? *Turn the page to find out.*

Here's how Water weathers rock changing the shape and size of the land. Water also erodes rock moving it from place to place. A melting glacier also dramatically changed the landforms in Hocking Hills over 10,000 years ago.

In this unit, you will explore the Big Idea, the Essential Questions, and the Investigations on the Inquiry Flipchart.

Levels of Inquiry Key ■ DIRECTED ■ GUIDED ■ INDEPENDENT

Track Your Progress

Big Idea The shape of Earth's land changes over time. 70% of Earth's surface is covered in water, which travels through the water cycle.

Essential Questions

Now I Get the Big Idea!

Science Notebook

Before you begin each lesson, be sure to write your thoughts about the Essential Question.

OHIO **4.ESS.1** Earth's surface has specific characteristics and landforms that can be identified.

Lesson **1**

Essential Question

What Is the Water Cycle?

Engage Your Brain!

Find the answer to the following question in this lesson and record it here.

Where is all this water going?

_____

_____

_____

_____

Active Reading

Lesson Vocabulary

List the terms. As you learn about each one, make notes in the Interactive Glossary.

_____   _____

_____   _____

_____   _____

_____

Sequence

In this lesson, you'll read about a process of change called the *water cycle*. As you read about the water cycle, focus on the sequence, or order, of events in the process. Active readers stay focused on a sequence when they mark the transition from one step in a process to another.

Water
on the Move

The water that you drink may have once been under ground or high in the sky. How does water get from Earth's surface to the air and back again?

Active Reading As you read the next page, underline sentences that explain the sun's role in the water cycle.

▶ On the diagram, draw an *X* on three places that illustrate where water evaporates from Earth's surface. Circle places that illustrate condensation of water above Earth's surface.

Earth's water is always being recycled. It evaporates from bodies of water, the soil, and even from your skin. Water exits plants' leaves through a process called transpiration. In the air, winds and clouds can help move water from one place to another.

Condensation   **Transpiration**

Evaporation

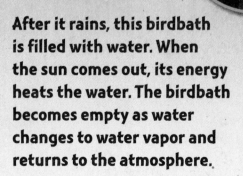

After it rains, this birdbath is filled with water. When the sun comes out, its energy heats the water. The birdbath becomes empty as water changes to water vapor and returns to the atmosphere.

About 70 percent of Earth's surface is covered by water. Most of the water is stored in oceans. Water moves between Earth's surface and the atmosphere through a process called the **water cycle**.

The sun provides the major source of energy for water to move through the water cycle. Sunlight heats up water near the ocean's surface. It causes water to evaporate. **Evaporation** is the change from a liquid to a gas. When water evaporates, it forms a gas called *water vapor*.

Water vapor rises into the atmosphere. The **atmosphere** is the mixture of gases that surrounds Earth. In the atmosphere, water vapor cools to form clouds. At any time, about three-fifths of Earth's surface is covered by clouds.

Precipitation

Glacier

Precipitation

Lake

Surface Runoff

River

Groundwater

What Goes **Up** Comes **Down**

What happens to water vapor after it rises into the air above Earth's surface? How does it become puffy white clouds or raindrops that fall on your head?

Active Reading As you read these pages, write numbers next to sentences and phrases to sequence and describe how water moves above Earth's surface through the water cycle.

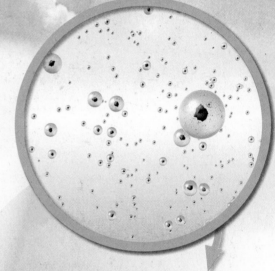

Water vapor condenses around salt and dust particles in the air to form these water droplets.

Condensation

Think again of the ocean. Water from the ocean's surface evaporates. As water vapor rises into the atmosphere, it cools. When water vapor loses enough energy, it condenses to form liquid water. **Condensation** is the change of a gas into a liquid.

There are tiny solid particles in the atmosphere. Water vapor condenses around these particles to form water droplets. A few water droplets are almost too small to see. However, when billions of droplets are close together, they form clouds.

Clouds can be made of water droplets, ice crystals, or both. They can form high in the sky or just above the ground. *Fog* is a cloud that forms near the ground.

Water vapor may condense on cool surfaces, too. It's why the cool glass below seems to "sweat." *Dew* is water droplets that form on objects near the ground.

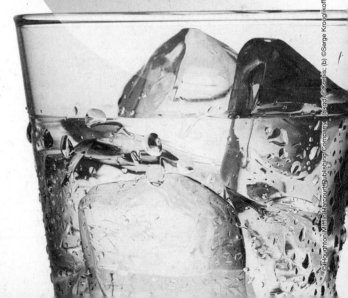

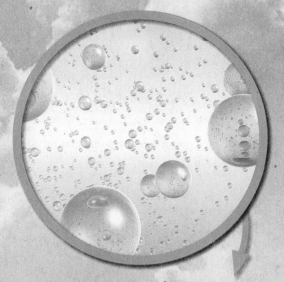

Water droplets in a cloud collide and join together. It takes many droplets to form a single raindrop.

Precipitation

Air currents keep water droplets in the air. But as droplets and snow crystals grow inside clouds, they become too heavy and fall to Earth as precipitation. **Precipitation** is water that falls from clouds to Earth's surface. Rain, snow, and hail are all forms of precipitation.

Precipitation that falls into the oceans may quickly evaporate back into the atmosphere. Precipitation that falls on land may be stored, it may flow across the land, or it may be used by living things. Depending on where it falls, water from precipitation may move quickly or slowly through the water cycle.

Do the Math!
Order Fractions

A raindrop is many times bigger than a water droplet and a dust particle. The table shows the size of droplets and dust particles in relation to the size of raindrops. Order the fractions from least to greatest.

Fractions	Ordered fractions
$\frac{1}{100}$	
$\frac{1}{1}$	
$\frac{1}{5,000}$	
$\frac{1}{20}$	

Use the ordered fractions to correctly label the items on the diagram.

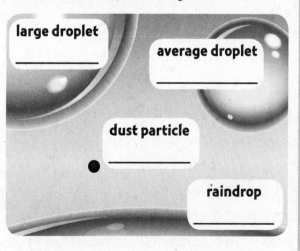

large droplet
_____

average droplet
_____

dust particle
_____

raindrop
_____

Where Does Water Go?

Most precipitation falls into oceans and evaporates back into the air. But some water takes a more roundabout path on its way through the water cycle.

Active Reading As you read these pages, identify and underline sentences and phrases that describe the movement of water on Earth's surface.

Imagine a rainstorm. Heavy rain falls on the ground. Some of this water will evaporate from shallow puddles quickly. It goes from Earth's surface directly back into the atmosphere.

Much of the rainfall will not reenter the atmosphere right away. Some will seep into the ground. Water that is stored underground is called **groundwater**. Groundwater can be found near the surface or very deep underground. Some groundwater may eventually return to the surface at places such as natural springs. Then it moves on through the water cycle.

As rainwater soaks into the ground, it fills up spaces between soil particles and cracks in rocks. Water that seeps deep underground becomes groundwater. Groundwater moves very slowly—if at all!

114

When glaciers melt, they quickly release stored water. Some of it may evaporate, some may seep into the ground, and some may move across the land as runoff.

Not all of the water that falls on land evaporates right away or seeps into the ground. **Runoff** is water that cannot soak into the ground and instead flows across Earth's surface. Too much precipitation may cause runoff. Runoff often flows into streams, rivers, and lakes. It may also flood low-lying areas.

Precipitation that falls in cold places may become part of a glacier. A *glacier* [GLAY•sher] is a large, slow-moving mass of ice. Water can be stored in glaciers for a very long time. Eventually, though, glaciers melt. Meltwater from glaciers can form lakes, flow into oceans, or become groundwater. Melting glaciers can increase the amount of runoff in a place.

Runaway Water

The picture shows runoff on a city street. Describe how this runoff could move through the water cycle on Earth's surface.

_____

_____

_____

_____

_____

_____

A Precious Resource

Can you name all the ways that you use water? Water is an important resource used by all living things. People often need to share and conserve their sources of fresh, clean water.

LEGEND

Ogallala Aquifer

Active Reading As you read these two pages, find and underline at least three facts about aquifers.

When you turn on a faucet, water flows out. Where does it come from? People can get fresh water from rivers or lakes. They can also get fresh water from aquifers. An *aquifer* [AH•kwuh•fuhr] is a body of rock that stores groundwater. People can drill into an aquifer and pump the water to the surface.

The water in aquifers can run low if people use more than can be replaced by precipitation. Human activities can also pollute aquifers. States that share aquifers work together to find solutions to these problems. They want to make sure there is enough fresh, clean water for everyone.

The Ogallala Aquifer covers about 450,000 square kilometers and is the largest aquifer in the United States. It supplies almost one-third of all groundwater used for irrigation within the U. S.

Why Worry About Water?

Why is it important to care for our aquifers?

_____

_____

_____

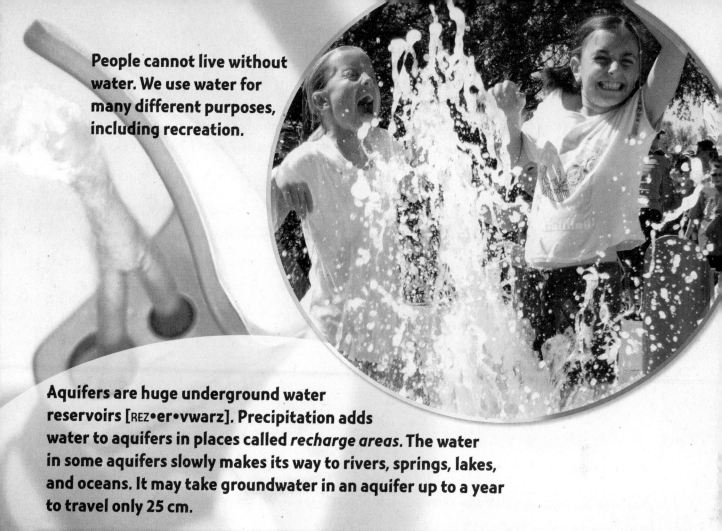

People cannot live without water. We use water for many different purposes, including recreation.

Aquifers are huge underground water reservoirs [REZ•er•vwarz]. Precipitation adds water to aquifers in places called *recharge areas*. The water in some aquifers slowly makes its way to rivers, springs, lakes, and oceans. It may take groundwater in an aquifer up to a year to travel only 25 cm.

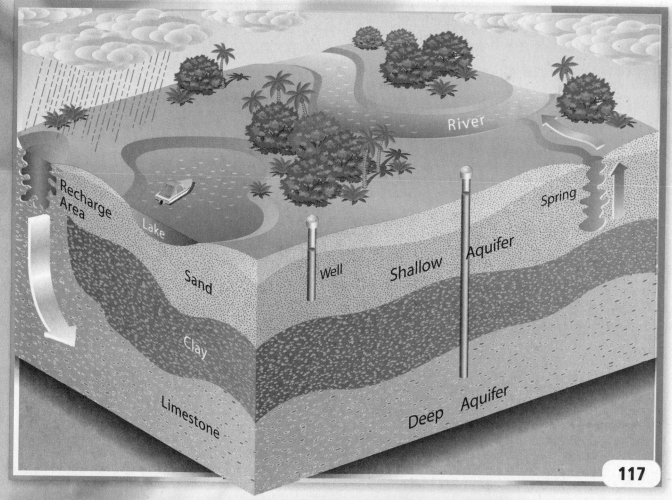

Recharge Area

Lake

Sand

Well

Shallow

Aquifer

Spring

River

Clay

Limestone

Deep Aquifer

Sum It Up!

When you're done, use the answer key to check and revise your work.

Write the term that matches each photo and caption.

1 Water can be stored for a long time in a large, slow-moving mass of ice.

_____

2 Water can also be stored underground between the spaces in soil particles or cracks in rocks.

_____

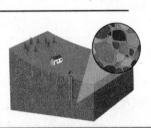

3 During heavy rains, some water might not soak into the ground. Instead, it flows down slopes and across Earth's surface.

_____

Summarize

Fill in the missing words to describe the water cycle.

The water cycle shows how water moves from Earth's surface to the 4. _____ and back again. The 5. _____ provides the energy for the water cycle. Water on the surface of the ocean heats up. During 6. _____ , it changes from a liquid to a gas. As 7. _____ rises into the atmosphere, it cools. During 8. _____ , it changes from a gas to a liquid. Billions of water droplets form a 9. _____ . When the droplets get too large for air currents to keep them up, they fall to Earth's surface as 10. _____ .

© Houghton Mifflin Harcourt Publishing Company

Answer Key: 1. glacier 2. groundwater 3. runoff 4. atmosphere 5. sun 6. evaporation 7. water vapor 8. condensation 9. cloud 10. precipitation

Brain Check

Name _____

Word Play

1 Use the clues to fill in the missing letters of the words.

1. g _ _ _ _ _ w _ _ ⃝_   Water stored underground
                    10

2. _ o _ d _ _ _ _ _ _ _ _ _   The changing of water from a gas to a liquid

3. _ a _ _ _ _ _ ⃝c _ _   The movement of water from Earth's surface to the
                  7   atmosphere and back again

4. _ t _ _ _ p _ _ _ ⃝ Mixture of gases that surrounds Earth
                    4

5. _ r _ ⃝i _ _ _ _ _ t _ _ _   Water that falls from clouds to Earth's surface
          8

6. ⃝u _ _ _ _ _   Water that flows across Earth's surface
   5

7. g⃝_ _ ⃝i _ _   A huge mass of frozen water that moves slowly
   9   6

8. _ r _ n _ _ i _ _ ⃝_ _ _   The process in which plants return water vapor
                    3   to the atmosphere

9. ⃝_ t _ _ _ _ a _ _ _   Water as a gas
   1

10. _ v _ _ o _ ⃝t _ o _   The changing of water from a liquid to a gas
                  2

Bonus: Solve the Riddle!

Use the circled letters in the clues above to solve the riddle.

What is water's favorite way to travel?

On a ___ ___ ___ ___ ___ ___ ___ ___ ___ ___
      1   2   3   4   5   6   7   8   9   10

Apply Concepts

2 Number the sentences to place the steps of cloud formation in order. Then describe what causes water vapor to condense as it rises into the atmosphere.

_____ Water vapor condenses around tiny particles.

_____ Water is heated by the sun.

_____ Water evaporates into the air.

_____ Billions of water droplets join together.

_____

_____

3 Use this picture to illustrate how water moves on and above Earth's surface through the water cycle. Use arrows to show how the water moves and use wavy lines to show evaporation.

4 Describe how the water cycle would be affected if water could not condense in the atmosphere.

_____

_____

_____

_____

5 In the spaces below, draw and label examples of water in the atmosphere as a solid, a liquid, and a gas. Hint: Wavy lines may be used to represent water vapor.

_____   _____   _____

_____   _____   _____

6 Each illustration shows a part of the water cycle. Label each as *evaporation*, *precipitation*, or *condensation*. Then describe what happens during each process.

_____   _____   _____

_____   _____   _____

_____   _____   _____

7 The picture shows stored water being used to irrigate crops. Circle and label the source of the water. How may this stored water be renewed?

_____

_____

_____

_____

8 During an ice age, water is stored in glaciers. The picture shows land area before and after an ice age. How are land area and the oceans affected during an ice age?

Land Area
■ Current Day
■ Last Ice Age

_____

_____

_____

_____

_____

9 About how much of Earth's surface is covered by water? Where can most of the water be found?

_____

_____

Take It Home!

Share what you have learned about water with your family. Tell them why it is important to conserve water. Set up a barrel outside to catch rainwater. Use the rainwater to wash your car or water your garden.

OHIO **4.ESS.1** Earth's surface has specific characteristics and landforms that can be identified.

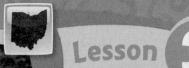

Lesson **3**

Essential Question

What Are Some Features Found on Earth's Surface?

Engage Your Brain!

Find the answer to the following question in this lesson and record it here.

What processes caused caves like these to form?

_____

_____

_____

_____

Active Reading

Lesson Vocabulary

List the terms. As you learn about each one, make notes in the Interactive Glossary.

_____

_____

_____

Compare and Contrast

Many ideas in this lesson are connected because they explain comparisons and contrasts—how things are alike and different. Active readers stay focused on comparisons and contrasts when they ask themselves, How are these things alike? How are they different?

Inquiry Flipchart p. 19 — Model the Flow of a River/Wandering Landforms?

139

That's a Landform!

Is there a Riverfront Avenue near you? What about a Mountain Drive or a Hill Street? Where do you think these names come from?

A delta forms at the mouth of a river, where sediment weathered and eroded by the river is deposited.

Mountains are the result of Earth's internal forces. They are often found near the edges of continents.

Erosion and deposition by wind shapes sand into dunes.

Active Reading As you read these two pages, draw two lines under each main idea.

Streets are often named after nearby landforms. A **landform** is any recognizable feature on Earth's surface shaped by natural causes. Mountains, plateaus, and plains are landforms. These are very large features, but landforms vary in size. A gentle rising hill and a small glacial lake are also landforms.

Surface and internal processes shape landforms. On the surface, weathering and erosion break down landforms. Deposition builds landforms from eroded sediments. Below Earth's surface, the movement of molten and solid rock also shapes landforms.

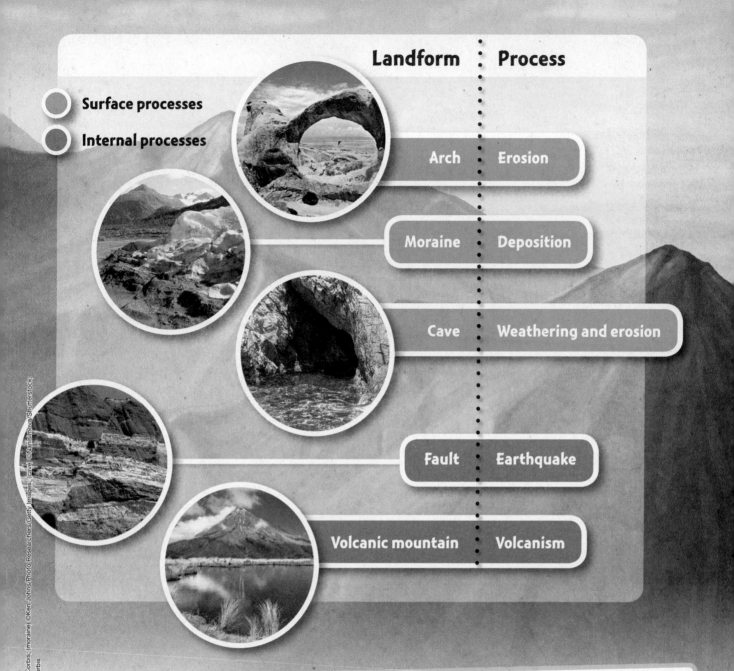

Surface processes

Internal processes

Landform	Process
Arch	Erosion
Moraine	Deposition
Cave	Weathering and erosion
Fault	Earthquake
Volcanic mountain	Volcanism

My Neighborhood Landforms

Study the chart at the top of this page. Then make an entry with information about a landform in Ohio. Make sure to draw or paste a picture. After you're finished, share the information with your teacher or classmates.

Landform	Process

Slow Work at the Surface

"Hello . . . *Hello*. . . *Helloo*. . . *Helloooo*." You hear the spooky echo inside a cave. You wonder, "How long did it take for this place to form?"

Little by little, water can dissolve rock near Earth's surface to form tunnels and even large caves!

Active Reading As you read these two pages, circle two clue words or phrases that signal a detail such as an example or an added fact.

The processes that shape landforms work at different rates. Most caves, for example, form slowly over thousands or even millions of years as groundwater dissolves rock near Earth's surface. Besides forming caves, water can also slowly carve wide valleys and deep canyons.

A *valley* is a depression between mountains. A narrow valley with high walls is called a canyon. The walls of the Grand Canyon, for instance, rise more than 1,500 meters above the canyon's floor!

Canyons don't have well-developed flood plains. A flood plain is the flat, wide area alongside a river. Frequent floods deposit nutrient-rich sediment on flood plains, which makes them good for agriculture.

drumlins

kames

kettles

eskers

erratics

Glacier Features

These glacial landforms are characterized by their composition. They are made of bits of rock ranging in size from dust-sized grains of sand and clay to car-sized boulders.

Glaciers shaped the landscape in much of North America. Gravity caused these ice sheets to flow downhill. They scraped and leveled the land like bulldozers. When the glaciers melted, they left behind mounds of sediments called kames, moraines, drumlins, and eskers. The melted glacier water formed the Great Lakes and thousands of smaller lakes called kettles.

Landform Trek

Rivers form V-shaped valleys. Glaciers form U-shaped valleys. Label these pictures, and describe the characteristics of each landform. What would it be like to hike to the top of each of these valleys?

_____

_____

_____

Fast Work on the Surface

Landslide! Some landforms can be shaped at incredible speeds.

After weathering weakens and breaks rocks, gravity causes the pieces on mountains, cliffs, and cave roofs to slide or fall quickly and without warning.

Active Reading As you read these two pages, write numbers next to the appropriate sentences or phrases to show the order of an event.

Sometimes surface processes can change landforms in a short time. In the Great Lakes region, for example, severe storms known as November gales produce storm waves. When these waves crash onshore, they erode bluffs, beaches, and dunes. They also can deposit sand just beyond the beach area to form landforms called outwash fans.

outwash fan

bluff

dunes

dunes

beach

Along riverbanks, lakeshores, and coastlines, water can quickly build or tear down landforms.

Away from coasts, rivers carry on the work of reshaping landforms. Some rivers, such as the Mississippi River, "snake" through their flood plains along large, curved paths called meanders. Strong currents can change these paths. They can erode riverbanks, widening channels. During floods, water can erode the narrow strip of land between closely spaced loops. This results in a new landform called an oxbow lake.

Oxbow lakes don't last forever. They shrink as water evaporates and seeps into the ground. In time, sediment fills in the old channel, and plants begin to grow.

n Mifflin Harcourt Publishing Company • Image Credits: (tc) ©Allan Baxter/Photodisc/Getty Images

Changing Beaches and Flood Plains

Beaches and flood plains are important natural resources. Use information from this lesson to make a list of processes that can build up and tear down these landforms.

_____

_____

Forged Slowly from Within

The Rocky and the Appalachian Mountains formed at different times. How can we tell which is older just by looking at them?

Rocky Mountains

Active Reading As you read this page, put brackets [ ] around each detail sentence. Underline the main idea the details help explain.

Earth is made of layers. We live on the solid, outer layer, or crust. The crust is broken into pieces called plates. Another layer of rock below the crust is hot and soft. The plates move on top of this soft rock. As the plates move, they may collide, pull apart, or slide past each other. Landforms such as mountains and rift valleys are the result of these slow motions.

In places where plates are pulling apart, a rift valley may form. The word *rift* means tear—so a rift valley is a tear in the crust. Basins are large, bowl-shaped dips in the land. They are the lowest point in a rift valley. Water that flows into a rift valley basin may form a lake or an inland sea.

A *plateau* is a large, flat block of land that is higher than its surroundings. Mountains and plateaus form where plates collide. These collisions can push rock from the ocean floor high into the sky a few centimeters at a time!

146

Plates

Motion at the edges of plates shapes landforms. Faults are fractures, or breaks on the crust, where large blocks of land move. Along the San Andreas Fault in California, the Pacific and North American plates slide past each other.

Most plateaus are formed by the same slow processes that build up mountains. Some form as erosion turns the surrounding land into plains.

San Andreas Fault

North American plate

Eurasian plate

Himalayan Mountains

African plate

Pacific plate

South American plate

African Rift Valley

Australian plate

Andes Mountains

Antarctic plate

The African Rift Valley runs nearly 1,600 kilometers from north to south. Lake Tanganyika, one of the largest in the world, formed as water flowed into its basin.

Locate the Landform

On the map, locate and circle the San Andreas Fault, the African Rift Valley, and the Andes Mountains. Then indicate whether plates colliding, pulling apart, or sliding past each other formed each of these features.

_____

_____

_____

Appalachian Mountains

The Appalachian Mountains were once as high and jagged as the Rocky Mountains. Over time, weathering and erosion smooth and lower the shape of mountains.

Fast Work from Within

A towering volcano built in a year?!! Yes, it grew on a cornfield. Read on to find out more!

In 1943, Mexican farmers watched a volcano grow out of their cornfield, nearly overnight. The Parícutin volcano grew to a height of over 300 meters in its first year!

Active Reading As you read these two pages, draw circles around two things that are being compared.

Volcanic eruptions can quickly shape landforms. A **volcano** is a place where hot gases, ash, and melted rock come out of the ground onto Earth's surface. Some volcanoes erupt explosively, sending ash and hot rock into the air. Lava, or molten rock, oozes out and gently flows down the slope of other volcanoes. In places such as Iceland and Hawai'i, volcanoes are building up new land in the middle of the ocean!

A steady flow of molten rock from Earth's interior builds the islands of Hawai'i. Lava flows from the Kīlauea Volcano on Hawai'i's main island have added nearly 220 hectares (540 acres) of land to the island since 1983.

Earthquakes also can change the land quickly. They occur when forces within Earth release energy. We sense earthquakes as a shaking of the ground. Earthquakes are common at the boundary between two plates, but they can happen anywhere. Large earthquakes can shape landforms such as landslides, cliffs, waterfalls, and lakes.

The Hebgen [HEB•gen] Lake Earthquake of 1959 caused a large landslide. The landslide blocked the Madison River, forming Earthquake Lake. The lake is six miles long and nearly 200 feet deep.

The same earthquake formed this cliff near Red Canton Creek, Montana. A cliff is an earth wall with a steep slope. This cliff is 19 feet tall!

Do the Math!
From Lava to Land

A hectare is a metric unit used to measure land area. It's equivalent to 10,000 m². Use information from this lesson and problem-solving skills to calculate the number of square meters that the Kīlauea Volcano has added to the island of Hawai'i to date.

_____

_____

It Pays to Know Your Land!

Suppose you're a chief engineer in charge of building a highway across a river valley. How would knowledge of landforms and the processes that shape them influence your decisions?

Every day, engineers have to answer questions like this one. They work together with Earth scientists such as geologists, hydrologists, and geotechnicians to find answers. They know that landforms provide clues about the characteristics of Earth materials and structures.

People need to use different techniques to build lasting structures on some landforms. On a flood plain, for example, bedrock, or solid rock, might be found beneath thick layers of soft sediment. To anchor structures, engineers may need to drive long concrete posts deep into the ground.

Schmalkalden, Germany

Finding bedrock is often not the most important thing for engineers. In places where bedrock is made of soft rock, it's important to avoid building on top of caves.

Many cities are located near rivers. To keep these cities safe from flooding, city planners and scientists work together. They build dams and levees to control water flow. They also set aside undeveloped land to divert floodwaters when the dams and levees aren't enough.

Working with soft sediment might not be a problem near the valley walls. The bedrock might be exposed on the surface. But building there isn't trouble-free. Engineers and city planners worry about future landslides trapping people in buildings and blocking important access roads.

Construction near the banks of a river can be an even greater challenge. There, the seasonal changes in the level and speed of the river must be planned for. When building a bridge, for example, engineers need to design foundations that can resist the forces of water erosion.

People need to know about the processes that shape landforms. They can use this knowledge to build safer and long-lasting structures.

Now You Be the Chief

Suppose you're a scientist or an engineer designing a construction project near a lakeshore, a fault, or a volcano. Identify some design problems and solutions associated with building on one of these areas.

_____

_____

_____

_____

_____

_____

_____

When you're done, use the answer key to check and revise your work.

Change the part of the summary statement in blue to make it correct.

1 Landforms are recognizable surface features shaped by human activity and catastrophic events.

_____
_____
_____

2 Landforms vary in size and are formed by the same slow processes.

_____
_____
_____

3 Surface processes such as volcanism and earthquakes shape landforms.

_____
_____
_____

4 Mountains and plateaus are landforms common in places where plates slide past each other.

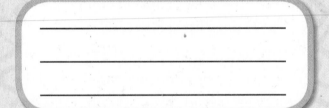

5 The nutrient-rich soils found in flood plains are the result of November gales around the Great Lakes.

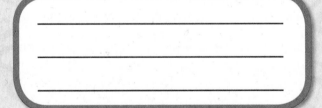

Answer Key: 1. natural processes 2. are formed at different rates by surface and internal processes 3. weathering, erosion, and deposition 4. collide 5. sediment deposited by frequent floods

Name _____

Word Play

1 Use the words from the lesson to complete each sentence.

1. Plateaus, mountains, and plains are examples of _____.

2. Landforms are shaped by _____ processes such as weathering and erosion.

3. Landforms produced by volcanic eruptions and earthquakes are the result of _____ processes.

4. Moraines, eskers, and drumlins are landforms produced by _____.

5. A canyon is a narrow valley with high walls and a poorly developed _____ _____.

6. A _____ _____ is a kind of storm that can quickly shape beach landforms.

7. In places where plates collide, _____ may form.

8. _____ build up the land as molten rock from inside Earth flows onto the surface.

Figure out how to place the answers in the boxes below so that the letters in the red boxes complete the answer to the riddle.

Riddle: What do Mr. Hill, Mrs. River, and Johnny Cliff have in common?

Answer: There is a _____ in their names.

Apply Concepts

2 Identify and label the landform images below. Then describe their characteristics.

_____

Sample answer:

_____

_____

3 In the first box, draw a landform produced by a slow change. In the second box, draw a landform produced by a rapid change.

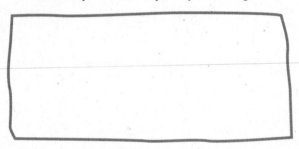 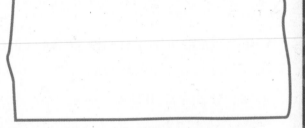

4 Look at the picture. Draw on the picture to show how the river channel would change during a flood. Identify any new landforms produced by the flood.

_____

_____

_____

Take It Home!

Discuss what you've learned about landforms with your family. Together, identify at least three landforms that are located near your community. Draw a map that includes these landforms to share with your classmates.

OHIO 4.SIA.1 Observe and ask questions about the natural environment;
4.SIA.5 Communicate about observations, investigations and explanations; and

S.T.E.M.
Engineering & Technology

Extreme Weather Gear

To survive in extreme cold, people need special clothing. Layers that serve different purposes provide the protection. But the layers can't be too bulky, or the wearer won't be able to move around easily.

Headwear

Down coat

Mittens/gloves

Down pants

Insulated boots

Boots need to be waterproof, warm, and lightweight. Your feet are far from your heart, so it is harder for warm blood to keep them warm. So gear for hands and feet must be very effective.

This fabric's outer layer keeps out water and wind. Inner layers provide insulation and help keep the body dry.

Think About It

Keeping warm is important, but so is keeping dry! Clothing that causes a person to sweat can be dangerous. Wet skin can chill quickly. How could extreme-weather clothing be designed to prevent that?

_____

_____

Dressing to deal with extreme weather conditions applies not only to the cold. The body needs protection in extreme heat as well.

What gear would you wear to protect yourself in the environment below? Draw the gear, and explain what protection it provides.

_____

_____

_____

_____

You are going on a hike. The weather forecast predicts rain. What would you wear? From what materials should your clothing be made?

_____

_____

Build On It!

Rise to the engineering design challenge—complete **Design It: Build a Seismograph** in the Inquiry Flipchart.

Inquiry Flipchart page 21

Lesson **4**

INQUIRY

OHIO **4.ESS.1** Earth's surface has specific characteristics and landforms that can be identified. **4.ESS.2** The surface of Earth changes due to weathering. **4.ESS.3** The surface of Earth changes due to erosion and deposition. **4.SIA.5** Communicate about observations, investigations and explanations; and

Name _____

Essential Question

How Does Water Change Earth's Surface?

Set a Purpose
What will you learn from this activity?

_____

_____

_____

Think About the Procedure
1. **What do the materials in the activity represent?**

_____

_____

_____

2. **Why do you position the tray to produce a slope?**

_____

_____

_____

Record Your Data
Use the table below to record your observations. Draw or describe your model's appearance before and after you pour the water.

	Top view	Front view	Side view
Before water			
After water			

Draw Conclusions

What happened to the sugar under the clay?

_____

_____

_____

Describe how your model demonstrates a process that shapes landforms.

_____

_____

_____

Analyze and Extend

1. What would you expect to happen in places with steeper slopes where water moves downhill faster?

_____

_____

_____

2. What would you expect to happen in places where it rains daily compared to places that receive very little rain?

_____

_____

_____

3. What is the role of the clay in this model? What does it represent?

_____

_____

_____

4. What additional factors could affect the rate of cave formation?

_____

_____

_____

5. Explain how you could test the effect of one of the factors you listed in question 4.

_____

_____

_____

6. What other questions do you have about how water weathers rock?

_____

_____

_____

_____

Ask a Seismologist

Q. What do seismologists do?

A. They use advanced tools to detect the tiniest movements in Earth's crust. They can learn a lot about earthquakes this way.

Q. Why is seismology important?

A. Seismologists warn people about where some earthquakes might happen in the future. They can also warn people when earthquakes happen under the ocean.

Q. How do seismologists know where natural disasters will happen?

A. Seismologists watch places where Earth's plates rub and move. They also watch hot spots around the world. These are places where magma from under Earth's crust comes to the surface. Hot spots are among the places where volcanoes form.

Be a Seismologist!

Look at the world map. Numbers are placed where earthquakes are most likely. Write each number below the description that correctly explains why earthquakes happen there.

Pacific Ring of Fire: A place where many volcanoes are found because of ocean trenches and plate movements

_____

hot spot: A place far from tectonic plate boundaries where a plate moves slowly over a hole below it that lets out magma

_____

plate boundaries: A place where tectonic plates push against each other and shift positions

_____

mountain-building area: A place where plates move under or over each other to raise the surrounding land

_____

Unit 3 Review

Vocabulary Review

Use the terms in the box to complete the sentences.

> deposition
> erosion
> flood plain
> landform
> precipitation
> runoff
> sediment
> weathering

1. Water that falls from clouds to Earth's surface

   is _____.

2. Any recognizable feature on Earth's surface shaped by

   natural causes is a _____.

3. The process of moving weathered rock from one place

   to another is called _____.

4. Water that cannot soak into the ground and instead flows

   across Earth's surface is _____.

5. Weathering by wind, water, and ice produces

   _____.

6. The flat, wide area alongside a river is a

   _____.

7. The process of rock breaking apart from water, wind, or ice

   is known as _____.

8. A river slowly erodes a steep hill, which causes sediment
   to travel downstream and to eventually drop through a

   process called _____.

Science Concepts

Fill in the letter of the choice that best answers the question.

9. Which of the following sequences shows how water may move from an ocean to land and back to an ocean?

(A) precipitation → runoff → cloud formation → groundwater

(B) evaporation → cloud formation → precipitation → runoff

(C) groundwater → cloud formation → precipitation → runoff

(D) cloud formation → precipitation → evaporation → runoff

10. Taro is studying the water cycle. He knows that energy is needed for matter to move and change state. What is a major source of energy for the water cycle process?

(A) clouds

(B) the oceans

(C) mountains

(D) the sun

11. Kyle knows that slow changes to Earth's surface are caused by many things. Which would most likely be caused by deposition from ice?

(A) delta

(B) glacier

(C) moraine

(D) sand dune

12. Alexa observed this landform on a trip to Alaska.

What is this landform and how did it form?

(A) It is a valley carved by a glacier.

(B) It is a dune that formed as wind eroded sand.

(C) It is an arch carved by a slow-moving river.

(D) It is a delta that formed when a river deposited sediment.

13. This picture illustrates how a puddle changes over the course of a day.

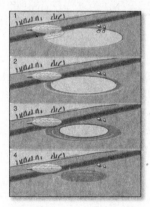

Which process is taking place?

(A) condensation

(B) evaporation

(C) precipitation

(D) runoff

14. An airplane pilot observed the following landform from his plane.

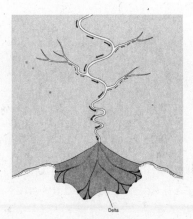

Delta

Which statement explains how slow changes to Earth's surface caused it to form?

(A) deposition and erosion from wind

(B) erosion and deposition from water

(C) erosion and weathering from ice

(D) weathering and deposition from wind

15. Natural processes change Earth's surface. Some of these processes affect humans and human-made structures.

Which Earth process most likely caused the damage in this picture?

(A) an earthquake

(B) a volcanic eruption

(C) erosion by strong winds

(D) water freezing in a crack in the road

16. Kaylee is doing a report on landforms caused by slow changes to Earth's surface. Which topic in her report is most likely caused by erosion and deposition from wind?

(A) glacial moraine

(B) river delta

(C) sand dune

(D) sea arch

17. Dewayne's family takes a trip through the desert. He observes an arch. Which statement best describes how the desert rock formed?

(A) deposition from water and ice

(B) deposition from water and wind

(C) weathering from water and ice

(D) weathering from water and wind

18. Oceans get fresh water from precipitation and rivers. However, ocean water levels do not change very much as a result. Why are these levels not greatly affected?

(A) Water is constantly seeping into the ocean floor.

(B) Water is constantly evaporating over the ocean's surface.

(C) Water is constantly flowing back into rivers from the oceans.

(D) Water is constantly deposited back on land by ocean wave action.

Apply Inquiry and Review the Big Idea

Write the answers to these questions.

19. Anish is doing a science investigation. Her setup is shown below.

Identify two Earth processes being modeled. Describe what will happen when Anish pours the water over the sand. Predict what would happen if Anish propped up one end of the pan before she poured the water over the sand.

_____

_____

_____

_____

20. Changes to Earth's surface by water over a long period of time form many of Earth's landforms. Describe the processes that shape each of the following landforms.

a. canyon _____

_____

b. river delta _____

_____

c. sea arch _____

_____

d. cave _____

_____

e. rift valley _____

_____

Living Things and Their Environments

Big Idea

Living organisms are adapted to live in specific environments. Changes to environments affect an organism's survival.

OHIO 4.LS.1, 4.SIA.1, 4.SIA.2, 4.SIA.3, 4.SIA.5

I Wonder Why

Why are conservation areas like this one in Ohio so important to the survival of endangered animals like gorillas and rhinos? *Turn the page to find out.*

Here's why Many animals are in danger of extinction due to changes in their environments such as severe droughts and habitat loss. Breeding programs such as the ones at The Wilds and the Columbus Zoo have been successful in stabilizing the populations of many species.

In this unit, you will explore the Big Idea, the Essential Questions, and the Investigations on the Inquiry Flipchart.

Levels of Inquiry Key ■ DIRECTED ■ GUIDED ■ INDEPENDENT

Track Your Progress

Big Idea Living organisms are adapted to live in specific environments. Changes to environments affect an organism's survival.

Essential Questions

Now I Get the Big Idea!

Science Notebook

Before you begin each lesson, be sure to write your thoughts about the Essential Question.

Essential Question

How Are Living Things Adapted to Their Environment?

🧠 Engage Your Brain!

Find the answer to the following question in this lesson and record it here.

How do the characteristics of this fox help it survive in its environment?

It's fur is really thick fur witch keeps them warm. They sleep in dens that are in the ground.

Active Reading

Lesson Vocabulary

List the terms. As you learn about each one, make notes in the Interactive Glossary.

_____ _____

_____ _____

_____ _____

_____

Signal Words: Details

This lesson gives details about the types of adaptations that help plants and animals survive in different environments. Signal words, such as *for example, for instance,* and *like,* link main topics to added details. Active readers look for signal words that link a main topic to its details.

Life on the Blue Planet

Because most of Earth is covered by water, it is often called the Blue Planet. Life is found in water, on land, and everywhere in between!

Active Reading As you read this page, circle signal words that indicate details about the environment.

The **environment** consists of all the living and nonliving things in an area. Look at the picture on these pages. The environment shown here includes the animals, plants, water, soil, air, and everything else in the picture. Animals and plants depend on their environment to meet their needs. For example, the zebras in the picture get food, water, and shelter from their environment.

Earth has many types of environments. For instance, Arctic environments are very cold; tropical rainforests are very hot. Some types of environments are deep in the ocean. Others are on dry land with very little rainfall. Because there are so many types of environments on Earth, there are also many types of living things. Each living thing, or organism, is able to survive in its own environment.

All living things need food, water, air, and shelter. Organisms in the same environment share resources.

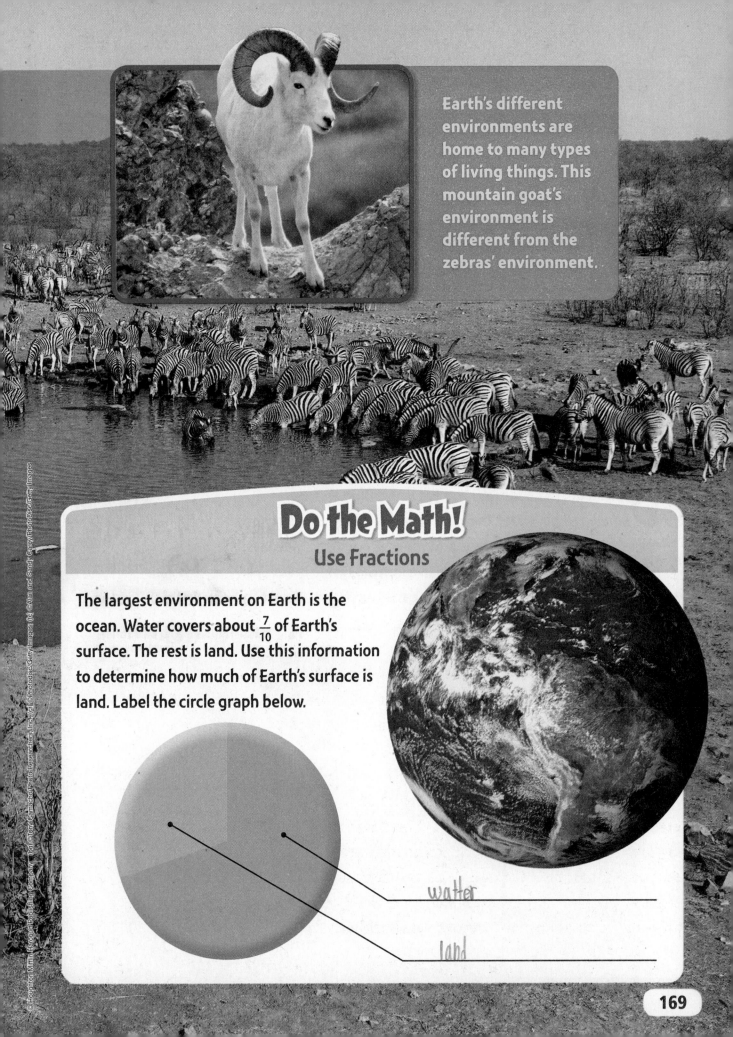

Earth's different environments are home to many types of living things. This mountain goat's environment is different from the zebras' environment.

Do the Math!

Use Fractions

The largest environment on Earth is the ocean. Water covers about $\frac{7}{10}$ of Earth's surface. The rest is land. Use this information to determine how much of Earth's surface is land. Label the circle graph below.

watter

land

Who Is out on a Limb?

If you were in a forest, which bird would you expect to see up in the trees—a blue jay or an ostrich?

Active Reading As you read this page, underline the definition of *adaptation*.

Did you guess a blue jay? You are right! Blue jays are small and have feet that can grip tree branches. Ostriches are large. They have long legs and wide, strong feet. Blue jays have adaptations that help them live in trees, while ostriches do not. An **adaptation** is a characteristic that helps a living thing survive.

Ostriches live on grasslands. They have long, strong legs that enable them to run quickly in open spaces. Their brown color helps them blend in.

Prairie dogs have strong paws for digging burrows. Their brown color enables them to blend in with their environment.

A **physical adaptation** is an adaptation to a body part. Living things have different physical adaptations based on their specific environments. For example, plants and animals in open spaces have different physical adaptations than living things in forests.

In open spaces, grasses can bend in strong winds. Grassland animals have coverings to blend in with the grass. These animals may be able to run fast or have shovel-like paws for burrowing.

Living things in forests have physical adaptations to live in and around trees. Vines can climb up trees to help leaves reach sunlight they need to make food. Many forest animals can grip branches.

This blue jay's curved feet help it grip small branches. Its wings enable it to fly from branch to branch.

This sloth's long claws help it to hang from tree branches for most of its life. A sloth can even sleep without letting go of the branch.

▶ Describe the prairie dog's grassland adaptations that help it survive in its environment.

Thir brown color helps them to blend in with the dirt. Thir paws are strong for digging burrows. It tells mch a little in the box.

Who Can Go with the Flow?

Some living things swim upstream while others go with the flow. Which adaptations do living things need in different water environments?

Active Reading As you read these two pages, circle examples of fish adaptations. Underline how these adaptations help them survive in their environment.

Imagine you live in a constantly flowing stream of water. How could you stay in the same part of the stream without being carried away? Many fish that live in streams have smooth bodies and strong tails. These characteristics help fish swim against the current. Water plants have flexible stems that allow them to bend with the flow. Many water insects are able to hold on tightly to water plants. Other insects burrow into the soil at the bottom of the stream.

This fish has a smooth, streamlined body. Its body shape allows it to swim quickly in fast-moving water.

Elodea are very flexible plants, so flowing water is less likely to break them. If a piece of elodea is pulled off, though, the piece can sprout roots and start to grow in a new part of the stream.

© Houghton Mifflin Harcourt Publishing Company (bg) ©James Schwabel/Alamy Images; (b) ©blickwinkel/Alamy Images; (bc) ©Wildlife GmbH/Alamy Images

Plants in still water, such as ponds and lakes, have different adaptations. Some plants are tall and have strong stems, so they can grow above the water. Water lilies, have wide, flat leaves that float on the water's surface to take in sunlight.

Animals that live in lakes and ponds are excellent swimmers. Many are adapted to living in deep water with little light. Catfish have whiskers that sense chemicals in the water to help them find food in the dark. Some birds wade at the shore and hunt. Their long, thin legs look like the cattails, so fish do not see them until it's too late.

Cattails grow in relatively still, shallow water, such as the water of a pond. Their stems are strong and stiff. Cattails can grow to more than 3 m tall.

Pond turtles are strong swimmers. They are also able to hold their breath for long periods of time. Their dark color allows them to stay hidden in dark, muddy water.

▶ Explain how the adaptations of the *elodea* and of the cattail enable these plants to survive in their environments.

Elodea is a very flexible plant so flowing water is less likely to break. Cattails grow in shallow water their streams are strong and stiff.

Who Can Take the Heat?

Deserts are places that get very little rain. Some deserts are very hot. How do plants and animals live in such hot, dry places?

Active Reading As you read these two pages, circle the words or phrases that describe the adaptations of desert plants.

Desert plants and animals have physical adaptations that help them stay cool and conserve water. The leaves and stems of many desert plants have waxy coatings to minimize water loss. Many of these plants have very long roots to reach water that is deep underground. Some desert plants have wide root systems that can absorb lots of water when it rains. Desert animals have physical adaptations to keep cool. Some have short, thin fur, or no fur at all.

Many reptiles live in deserts. This lizard's scales help it keep water inside its body.

Jackrabbits have large ears. Their ears release body heat and help the hares stay cool.

A **behavioral adaptation** is something an organism does to help it survive. For example, most desert animals are active at night to avoid the heat of the day. An instinct is a type of behavioral adaptation.

An **instinct** is an inherited behavior an animal knows how to do without having to learn it. For instance, jackrabbits stay crouched in one position whenever they sense danger. This instinct helps them hide from predators.

Other behaviors help organisms survive in the desert. For example, some seeds of desert plants stay dormant, or inactive, until it rains. When it rains enough, the seeds grow quickly into plants that flower and make more seeds.

Saguaro cactus flowers open and release their fragrance at night and close the next day. It is cooler at night in the desert. As a result, the flowers do not wilt as quickly as they would during the day.

▶ Describe a living thing with adaptations that help it survive in the desert. Explain how each adaptation helps.

The saguaro catctus flowers open at night then they close the next day. This adapion helps by the animals there have no food without the catctus.

Who Can Take the Cold?

Polar environments are very cold places. How do plants and animals survive in cold places such as Antarctica and the Arctic?

Active Reading As you read these pages, circle the words or phrases that describe polar environments.

Temperatures in Antarctica rarely get above freezing—even in summer! Plants and animals that live there have adaptations to live in extreme cold. Emperor penguins have a thick layer of fat—a physical adaptation that keeps them warm on land and in the water. To protect themselves from very cold winds, male penguins huddle together in large groups. The behavior is an instinct that helps male penguins and their newly hatched baby penguins keep warm.

The Antarctic pearlwort grows close to the ground in the warmer, wetter parts of Antarctica.

Black feathers on the backs of emperor penguins absorb heat from the sun, which helps them keep warm.

The Arctic has extremely cold winters and very short summers. Arctic animals have thick fur and a layer of fat to keep in body heat. Some Arctic animals are often white in the winter, which helps them blend in with the snow. These characteristics are physical adaptations. Arctic animals also have behavioral adaptations. For example, many Arctic animals live in dens dug into the ground or snow during very cold months.

Most Arctic plants have short roots because the ground there is frozen the majority of the year. These plants produce seeds during the short summer when the ground isn't frozen. Most Arctic plants grow close to the ground, which helps protect them from strong, cold Arctic winds.

This prairie crocus has fuzzy hairs that cover its flowers and seeds. The hairs protect the plant from wind and trap heat from the sun.

▶ Compare the adaptations that help the desert jackrabbit and the Arctic hare survive in their environments.

Arctic hares tucked thir ears in to keep body heat. jackrabbit keep thir ears up to release body heat and to keep them cool.

Arctic hares grow white fur in winter to blend in with the snow. They sit with their paws, tails, and ears tucked in to keep from losing body heat.

Sum It Up!

When you're done, use the answer key to check and revise your work.

The outline below is a summary of the lesson. Complete the outline.

Summarize

I. Match each description to the living thing that has that adaptation.

A. flexible stem that bends in flowing water   Arctic hare

B. grows white fur in the winter   sloth

C. long claws to hang from tree branches   saguaro

D. flowers open at night when it's cooler   prairie dog

E. long claws for digging burrows   *Elodea*

II. Identify each adaptation described below as a physical adaptation or a behavioral adaptation.

A. An ostrich has long, strong legs. _____

B. An Arctic hare sits for hours to conserve heat. _____

C. A catfish has whiskers that sense chemicals in the water. _____

D. Male penguins huddle together to stay warm. _____

E. A fish has a smooth, streamlined body. _____

Answer Key: I. A. *Elodea* B. Arctic hare C. sloth D. saguaro E. prairie dog **II.** A. physical B. behavioral C. physical D. behavioral E. physical

Word Play

1 Complete the crossword puzzle.

Across

4. Desert animals are active at night to avoid the heat. Which type of adaptation is this?

5. Which type of behavior does an animal know how to do without having to learn it?

Down

1. What are all of the living and nonliving things in an area called?

2. A blue jay's small, curved feet help it grip branches. Which type of adaptation is this?

3. What is a body part or behavior that helps a living thing survive called?

Apply Concepts

2 Draw a circle around the plant that would most likely live in a forest. Describe an adaptation that enables this plant to survive in its environment.

_____

3 Snakes and lizards are rarely found living near polar environments. Explain why.

_____

_____

_____

4

This spider monkey lives in the treetops of a tropical rainforest. Which adaptations enable it to survive in its environment?

_____

5 Why is it better for an animal to know how to hide from predators because of an instinct than to have to learn how to hide from them?

_____

_____

_____

_____

_____

Take It Home!

Take a walk with your family through your neighborhood or a local park. Look at plants and animals, and point out adaptations that enable them to survive in their environments.

OHIO **4.SIA.2** Plan and conduct simple investigations; **4.SIA.3** Employ simple equipment and tools to gather data and extend the senses; **4.SIA.5** Communicate about observations, investigations and explanations; and

Name _____

Essential Question

Why Do Bird Beaks Differ?

Set a Purpose

Why do you think different birds have beaks with different shapes?

_____

_____

_____

_____

Write a statement summarizing what you plan to investigate.

_____

_____

_____

_____

What will you be modeling in this investigation?

_____

_____

_____

_____

Record Your Data

In the space below, make a table in which you record your observations.

Draw Conclusions

Did some beaks work for more than one kind of food? What might this suggest about the bird's ability to survive?

_____

_____

_____

_____

_____

Did one kind of beak work for eating all of the different foods?

_____

_____

_____

_____

Analyze and Extend

1. Which bird's beak would be best for eating flower nectar? Which beaks would be best for picking insects out of wood and worms out of sand?

_____

_____

_____

_____

_____

2. A toucan is a bird that eats very large, tough tropical fruit. What would you expect a toucan's beak to look like?

_____

_____

3. Look at the bird beaks below. Tell which tool in the investigation was most similar to each of the beaks.

hummingbird
_____

finch
_____

macaw
_____

shorebird
_____

woodpecker
_____

duck
_____

4. Think of other questions you would like to ask about how adaptations relate to the food an animal eats.

_____

_____

_____

182

OHIO 4.LS.1 Changes in an organism's environment are sometimes beneficial to its survival and sometimes harmful.

Essential Question

How Do Environmental Changes Affect Organisms?

Engage Your Brain!

Find the answer to the following question in this lesson and record it here.

A forest fire can change a landscape in a matter of minutes! Trees are burned, and animals run for shelter. How could a forest fire be a good thing?

_____

_____

_____

Active Reading

Lesson Vocabulary

List the terms. As you learn about each one, make notes in the Interactive Glossary.

_____

_____

Compare and Contrast

Many ideas in this lesson are connected because they explain comparisons and contrasts—how things are alike and different. Active readers stay focused on comparisons and contrasts when they ask themselves, How are these things alike? How are they different?

Change Comes Naturally

All environments change over time. Some changes happen slowly, while others occur quickly.

Over hundreds of thousands of years, mountains weather and erode. Rivers cut canyons into rock and change course through valleys and plains. Gradual changes like these affect the organisms that live in environments.

Weather patterns change over time as well. Like changes to the land, *climate changes* affect organisms. Throughout Earth's history, the average temperature has gone up and down many times.

An ice age happens when Earth's temperatures are colder than normal for a very long time. Large areas of land are covered with ice for thousands of years. During warmer climate cycles, ice melts and uncovers land.

During the last ice age, ice nearly 4 km thick covered much of North America. Because the ice held so much frozen water, the level of the oceans dropped and coastlines changed.

PACIFIC OCEAN

ATLANTIC OCEAN

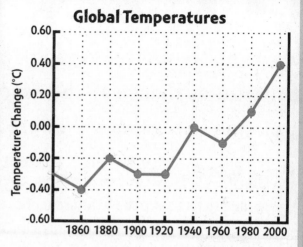

Do the Math!
Interpret a Graph

Global Temperatures

The graph shows average temperatures on Earth over time. Use the graph to describe temperature trends between 1900 and 2000.

well in 1900 it was 20° and it went up to 40° in the 2000.

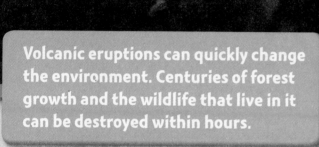

Volcanic eruptions can quickly change the environment. Centuries of forest growth and the wildlife that live in it can be destroyed within hours.

Earth is now in a warming cycle. Many scientists think this warming trend will continue and is in part linked to human activities. It is unclear how warming might affect the planet as a whole. As some areas become warmer, the organisms that inhabit those areas will move, adapt to the change, or disappear.

Many things can happen to change environments quickly as well. Heavy storms can cause floods that wash away land. Mudslides can destroy years of plant growth in minutes. Volcanic eruptions can be destructive, but they can also form entirely new land that will eventually be inhabited by plants and animals and become an ecosystem.

A *drought* occurs when little rain falls. Without water, plants and animals will disappear.

Next, Please!

Ecosystems change all the time, but the changes are often so slow that they are hard to notice.

Active Reading As you read these two pages, write numbers next to appropriate sentences to show the order of events.

The picture below shows how bare rock can change into an ecosystem filled with living things. The gradual change of organisms in an ecosystem is called **succession**. *Primary succession* begins on bare rock, such as after a volcano erupts. Dust settles in cracks in the rocks. The first organisms to colonize are called pioneer species. Lichens are common pioneers. They break down the rock as they grow, producing soil. When they die, their litter decays, adding nutrients to the soil.

As soil develops, plants can begin to grow. Mosses flourish, and they help produce more soil. The soil becomes thicker, and bigger plants take hold. Eventually, trees grow. A mature, stable community establishes itself.

It can take hundreds of years for a stable community to establish itself. Where water is plentiful, succession can happen more quickly. Even mature, stable communities continue to change.

Secondary succession occurs where an ecosystem has been disturbed, but soil is still present. Areas burned by forest fires undergo secondary succession. Secondary succession occurs more quickly than primary succession. The existing soil usually contains seeds and roots that sprout and grow after the fire is over. The first plants to grow tend to be hardy shrubs and grasses. Gradually, larger plants colonize the burned area. Animals also return. Eventually a stable ecological community re-establishes itself.

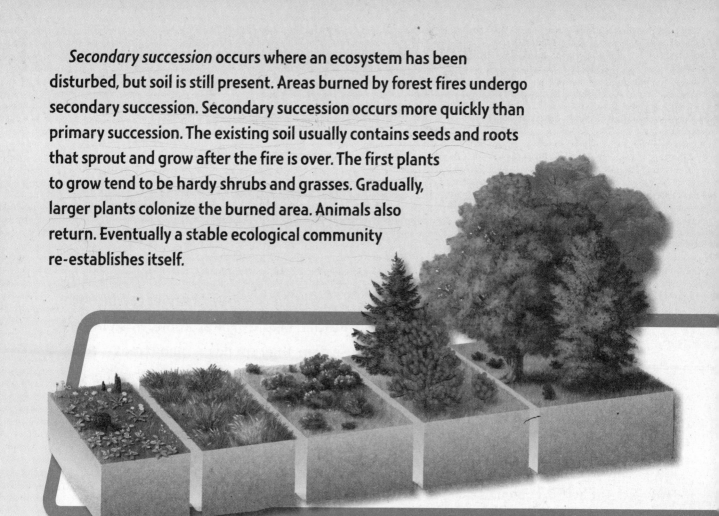

About Time

An area with no plants or animals returns to a grassy plain within a year. What kind of succession has occurred? Explain your answer.

secondary succession becuase durning arefire there is no plants and animals.

For Better or Worse

Living things change the places where they live. Is this a good thing or a bad thing? It depends on your point of view!

Organisms that live in an environment can cause huge changes. Changes can be both harmful and helpful. For example, when beavers make a dam, they cut down many trees—trees that provide food and shelter for other living things. In addition, the dam slows the flow of water, which affects animals that rely on faster-flowing water to live. On the other hand, the dams produce wetlands, which provide homes for other organisms.

Sometimes changes harm an ecosystem. They can even harm humans. When large numbers of algae in bodies of water reproduce rapidly, the algae release large amounts of harmful chemicals into the water and cause oxygen levels to drop. The resulting condition is known as red tide, which can kill fish and other wildlife and can poison people. When beaches experience red tides, officials post signs warning people to stay out of the water.

The algae that make up a red tide release harmful chemicals and use up oxygen that fish need to breathe.

Beavers change their environment by building dams across streams. The dams cause flowing water to back up and form ponds. These changes create environments where new plants and animals can establish themselves.

Contrast

Describe a way that the activities of beavers can be helpful to an ecosystem. Then describe one way in which their activities can be harmful.

Helpful	Harmful
_____	_____
_____	_____
_____	_____

Goats, sheep, and other grazing animals remove grass and other plants from an environment. When too many animals graze in an area, they eat grass faster than it can grow back.

Invasive Species

You may have seen a movie where space aliens invaded Earth. Invasions happen on Earth every day! Here's what happens when a new species moves into an environment.

Active Reading As you read these two pages, draw boxes around clue words or phrases that signal a main idea.

Sometimes the population of a species grows quickly after it is introduced into a new environment. This type of organism is called an *invasive species*. Invasive species take food and space away from *native species*, the organisms already living in an ecosystem. The factors that limit the growth of native species, such as predators, pests, and diseases, do not affect invasive species. The two species compete for resources. If no other species in the ecosystem can use the invasive species for food, there is no limit to its expansion. Invasive species often threaten less competitive organisms that have lived in an environment for a long time.

Populations of native harvester ants have been destroyed as invasive fire ants moved into harvester ant habitats and successfully competed with them for resources.

Zebra mussels are invasive to North America. They were accidentally carried into the Great Lakes in the hulls of ocean-going ships. Zebra mussels now grow in such large populations that they totally cover surfaces, block water outlets, and clog pipes in the lakes they have invaded.

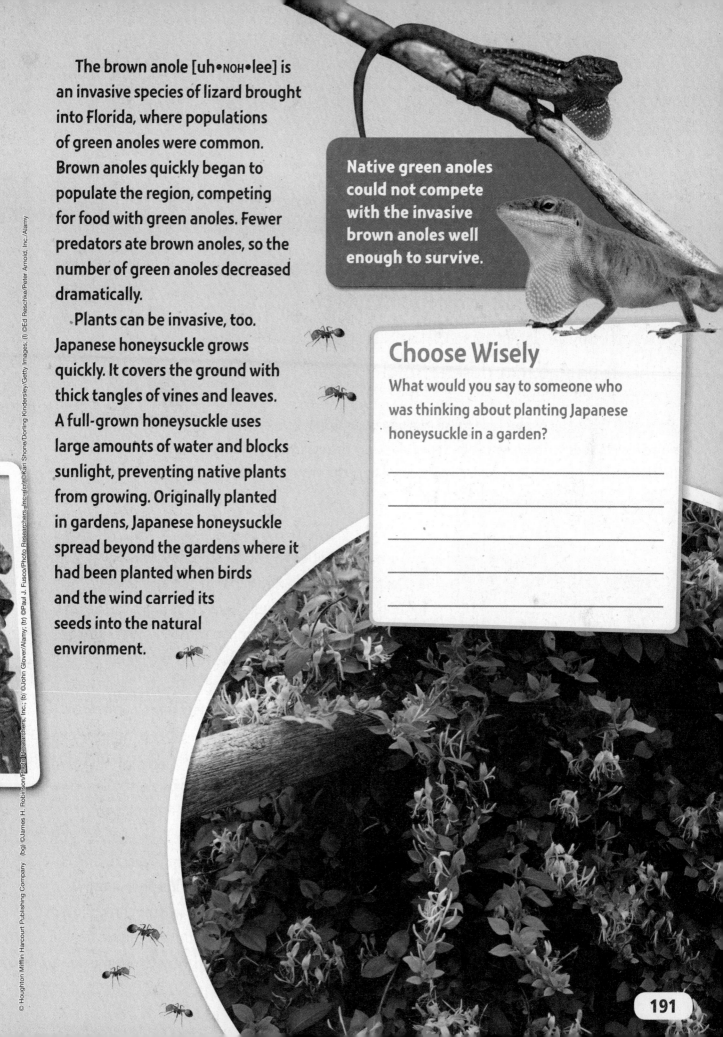

The brown anole [uh•NOH•lee] is an invasive species of lizard brought into Florida, where populations of green anoles were common. Brown anoles quickly began to populate the region, competing for food with green anoles. Fewer predators ate brown anoles, so the number of green anoles decreased dramatically.

Plants can be invasive, too. Japanese honeysuckle grows quickly. It covers the ground with thick tangles of vines and leaves. A full-grown honeysuckle uses large amounts of water and blocks sunlight, preventing native plants from growing. Originally planted in gardens, Japanese honeysuckle spread beyond the gardens where it had been planted when birds and the wind carried its seeds into the natural environment.

Native green anoles could not compete with the invasive brown anoles well enough to survive.

Choose Wisely

What would you say to someone who was thinking about planting Japanese honeysuckle in a garden?

_____

_____

_____

_____

_____

Humans Change the Environment

Humans are not outside of the environment, and we have a large impact on our ecosystems. The effects of humans on the environment can be both harmful and beneficial.

Active Reading As you read these two pages, draw brackets around sentences that describe ways in which people harm the environment. Underline sentences that describe ways people help the environment.

Human activities can harm an ecosystem. For example, people mine coal to produce energy for homes and businesses. Open-pit mining, as shown here, kills all the plants living in the area where the mine is dug. Animals that depend on the plants for food must move.

Highways can also disrupt ecosystems. Land must be cleared of plants and animals before a highway can be built. Often hills get leveled and valleys get filled in, blocking streams. Communities of plants and animals that lived in the ecosystem can no longer survive.

Humans produce a large amount of waste that is disposed of as trash. Most trash ends up in landfills. If landfills are not built properly, wastes can pollute soil and water. *Pollution* is the contamination of air, water, or soil by substances harmful to organisms.

Not all changes caused by humans are harmful. People work to protect their environment and to protect organisms from harm as a result of ecosystem change. Protecting ecosystems and the organisms living in them is called *conservation.*

People try to restore habitats and repair damaged ecosystems by replanting trees and cleaning up pollution. People also remove invasive plants and animals so native organisms can survive.

In addition, people try to help organisms affected by natural disasters. People care for animals injured or orphaned by these disasters.

What Can You Do to Help?

In the space below, list things that you can do to help the environment. Include things you already do and what you would like to do in the future.

> I picked up litter and I
> helped a dove but it was not
> anoth to help it.

Gone!

Some living things change when their environment changes. Some living things move to new places. Others do not survive.

Millions of years ago, Earth was covered with giant reptiles. Now most of those reptiles are extinct. **Extinction** happens when all the members of a certain species die. Giant reptiles, such as the *Tyrannosaurus rex* shown here, lived in a time in which Earth was warm. Over time, the environment cooled, and many of the reptiles could not survive.

Golden toads were once numerous in a part of the mountainous tropical forest of Costa Rica. Scientists think a period of drought that dried up the pools where the toads laid their eggs and where tadpoles matured caused a rapid population decline. The drought also allowed a fungus that harmed the toads to spread. Golden toads have not been seen since 1989 and are thought to be extinct.

The Tasmanian wolf lived in Australia and New Guinea. Ranchers believed the wolves killed sheep and cattle, but this was never proven. The Tasmanian wolf was hunted to extinction by the 1930s.

The dodo bird lived on an island in the Indian Ocean. Around 1600, people arrived on the island. They hunted the birds for food. They cut down the island's forests to make room for houses. Invasive species, such as cats and pigs brought by people, destroyed the dodo birds' nests. Within 80 years, dodo birds were extinct.

Time Traveler

If you could go back to the island of the dodo birds in 1600, what advice could you give to help conserve dodo birds?

_____

_____

_____

_____

_____

Today, people work to conserve habitats and protect organisms from extinction. Even so, many organisms are in danger of becoming extinct. As these organisms' environments continue to change, some will adapt, some will move, and some will not survive.

Sum It Up!

When you're done, use the answer key to check and revise your work.

Read the summary statements below. Each one is incorrect. Rewrite the part of the summary in blue so it is correct.

1

1. **Pollution is** all the living and nonliving things that affect an organism's life.

_____

2. **A natural event that causes the environment to change slowly is an** earthquake.

_____

3. **People can help conserve habitats by** mining, building landfills, and cutting down forests.

_____

_____

4. **Protecting ecosystems is an example of** extinction. _____

2 **The idea web below summarizes the lesson. Complete the web. Start with number 5.**

A gradual buildup of organisms in an environment that consists of bare rock is called 7. _____ succession.

A gradual buildup of organisms in an environment that has soil is called 8. _____ succession.

An environment can change 5. _____ or 6. _____.

A(n) 9. _____ is any nonnative plant or animal that takes over an environment.

An environment can be changed suddenly by a natural event such as a 10. _____ _____.

Name _____

Word Play

1 Use the clues to unscramble the words below.

1. iavinvse — i n v a s i v e : A nonnative animal that moves into a new place

2. ecnntavosroi — c o n s e r v a t i o n : Protecting ecosystems and the organisms living in them

3. nlpituloo — P o l l u t i o n : Litter on the ground or harmful chemicals in the water

4. tgurhdo — d r o u g h t : Occurs when no rain falls for a long period of time

5. consisuces — S u c c e s s i o n : The gradual change and buildup of organisms in an environment

6. galea — A l g a e : Organism that causes red tide when present in large numbers

7. vebera — b e a v e r : Can be helpful or harmful, depending on point of view

8. lonea — a n o l e : Brown lizard that has invaded some areas of Florida

9. vmetneonrin — e n v i r o n m e n t : Everything around an organism, such as other organisms, air, water, and land

10. txoniecnit — e x t i n c t i o n : Happened to dodo birds and Tasmanian wolves

11. navoolc — v o l c a n o : Can cause long-term environmental change by blowing dust and gases into the sky

Bonus: What kind of dinosaur accidentally smashes everything in its path?

_____   _____

Apply Concepts

2 Label each picture as a change caused by people, animals, or a natural event.

_____

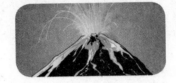
_____

_____

_____

_____

_____

3 Name four invasive species and describe their effect on ecosystems.

_____
_____
_____
_____
_____
_____
_____
_____

4 Draw one circle around animals that became extinct because of natural events. Draw two circles around animals that became extinct because of human activities.

5 In the first box below, draw a landscape that includes a river. In the second box, draw how the same landscape might look after a flood. Include captions explaining how the environment changed.

6 Fill in the graphic organizer below to describe how beavers change the environment. The first box is already completed.

Beavers build a dam in a stream.

↓

_____
_____

↓

_____
_____

Describe a way that people might be able to solve each environmental problem listed below.

7 Coal mining can harm habitats and cause pollution.

_____

_____

_____

8 Building a new highway destroys habitats and can lead to soil erosion.

_____

_____

_____

9 Waste from garbage in landfills can enter the ground and pollute soil and water.

_____

_____

10 Imagine that an orange tree frog eats only a certain type of small blue fly. A giant red fly starts moving into the tree frog's ecosystem. The red fly eats all the blue fly's food. In the space below, draw a flow chart that shows what might happen to the frog.

	→		→		→	

Bonus: How might orange frogs change because of the red fly? _____

_____

Take It Home!

Share what you have learned about conservation with your family.
Come up with at least four ways to help conserve resources at home.
Carry out your family's plan, and report the results to the class.

Meet the Tree-Planting Scientists

Wangari Maathai

Wangari Maathai was born in Kenya. Maathai started an organization that conserves Kenya's forests by planting trees. She recruited Kenyan women to plant native trees throughout the country. In 1977, this organization became known as the Green Belt Movement. The Green Belt Movement has planted more than 40 million trees. Maathai's work inspires other African countries to start community tree plantings.

Seeds from nearby forests are used to grow native trees.

Willie Smits

Willie Smits works to save orangutans in Indonesia. By clearing the forests, people are destroying the orangutan's habitat. The orangutan is endangered. Smits's plan helps both orangutans and people. Smits is growing a rain forest. The new forest gives people food and rainwater for drinking, so they protect it. The sugar palm is one of the trees planted. In 2007, Smits started using sugar palms to make sugar and a biofuel called ethanol. The sugar palms provide income for the community.

Sugar palms are fire-resistant. This protects the forest from fires.

Smits has rescued almost 1,000 orangutan babies. However, his goal is to save them in the wild.

Scientist saves the Day!

Read the story about the Florida scrub jay. Draw the missing pictures to complete the story.

The Problem: Florida scrub jays are endangered. They are found only in parts of Florida with shrubs and other short plants.

Fires kill tall trees that grow in the scrub jay's habitat. But people put out the fires, so the trees survive.

Trees are now growing, so there are fewer shrubs. The scrub jays can't live there.

The Solution: Scientists and firefighters start fires that can be kept under control. These fires kill the tall trees.

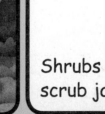

Shrubs grow and the scrub jays return.

Inquiry Flipchart page 25

OHIO **4.LS.1** Changes in an organism's environment are sometimes beneficial to its survival and sometimes harmful. **4.SIA.1** Observe and ask questions about the natural environment; **4.SIA.2** Plan and conduct simple investigations; **4.SIA.5** Communicate about observations, investigations and explanations; and

Name _____

Essential Question

How Does Drought Affect Plants?

Set a Purpose

What will you better understand about plants after doing this experiment?

_____
_____
_____
_____

State Your Hypothesis

Write your hypothesis, or testable statement.

_____
_____
_____

Think About the Procedure

What parts of your experiment stay the same for each test group?

_____
_____
_____

What part of the experiment did you change?

_____
_____
_____
_____

Record Your Data

Record your observations in the table below.

Plant Observations	
Cup A	
Cup B	
Cup C	
Cup D	
Cup E	

Draw Conclusions

Was your hypothesis supported? Why or why not?

_____

_____

_____

_____

What conclusions can you draw from this investigation?

_____

_____

_____

_____

_____

Analyze and Extend

1. What natural conditions did Cup A and Cup E represent?

_____

_____

_____

_____

2. Did the plants in the cups that got the most water do the best? What can you infer based on your results?

_____

_____

_____

_____

3. Suppose you are studying pea plants. You find that half of the individual pea plants are able to survive in mild drought conditions. Why might this data be important?

_____

_____

_____

_____

_____

4. How would you set up an experiment to test the following hypothesis: The amount of fertilizer does not affect how quickly plants grow. Draw and label a picture that shows your setup.

5. Think of other questions you would like to ask about how environmental conditions affect plants.

_____

_____

_____

_____

_____

S.T.E.M.
Engineering & Technology

Underwater Exploration

When you think of underwater exploration, you may think of scuba. The word *scuba* comes from the first letters of the phrase "**s**elf-**c**ontained **u**nderwater **b**reathing **a**pparatus." Scuba divers take everything they need with them; they are not connected to anything on the surface. Follow the timeline to learn how underwater diving equipment has changed over time.

1530s
Guglielmo de Lorena—Diving Bell
Diving bells are airtight containers opened at one end. De Lorena's diving bell rested over a diver's shoulders, allowing the diver to breathe the trapped air and to walk on the ocean floor. Ropes connected the diver to the surface.

1830s
Augustus Siebe—Diving Dress
A metal diving helmet is sealed onto a watertight canvas suit. An air hose and a cable connect the diver to the surface. In this closed-circuit system, used-up air is released into the suit. The diver controls when air is released.

1940s
Jacques Cousteau and Emile Gagnan—Aqua-Lung
This breathing system passes air to a diver from a tank carried on the diver's back. This is an open-circuit system that releases used-up air into the water. Divers can swim without any cables or hoses connecting them to the surface.

Critical Thinking

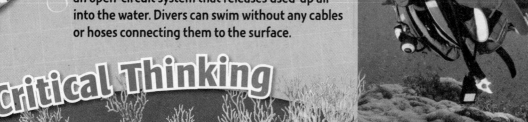

How are the first two types of diving equipment similar?

_____

_____

_____

S.T.E.M.
continued

Make Some History

Research another type of diving equipment. Describe how it works and where it should be placed on the timeline.

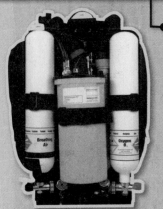

1960s
Rebreather

Rebreathers are closed-circuit systems. A diver breathes through a mouthpiece and used-up air is not released into the water. Instead, it is filtered to remove carbon dioxide and used again. This design feature extends the amount of time a diver can spend underwater.

1980s
ADS

Atmospheric Diving Suits (ADS) were developed for deep diving activities. They use rebreather technology and a hard suit that enable divers to safely dive to great depths. Modern ADS can work in water up to 610 m deep!

Design Your Future

What features do you think the next diving suit should have? What needs would those features meet?

Build On It!

Rise to the engineering design challenge—complete **Solve It: Getting Around a Dam** on the Inquiry Flipchart.

Name _____

Vocabulary Review

Use the terms in the box to complete the sentences.

adaptation
behavioral
  adaptation
environment
extinction
instinct
physical
  adaptation
succession

1. A characteristic that helps an organism survive is

    a(n) _____.

2. A behavior that an animal is born with is called

    a(n) _____.

3. All of the living and nonliving things that surround you make up

    your _____.

4. An adaptation to a body part is called

    a(n) _____.

5. Something an organism does to help it survive is called

    a(n) _____.

6. The disappearance of an entire species of organisms is known

    as _____.

7. The gradual change of organisms in an ecosystem is

    called _____.

Science Concepts

Fill in the letter of the choice that best answers the question.

8. Sharks can smell very small amounts of substances in ocean
    water. What does this physical adaptation enable the shark
    to do to survive in its environment?

    (A) sense water temperature

    (B) find a place to lay eggs

    (C) find a safe place to hide

    (D) find food that is far away

9. Which statement is most accurate?

Ⓐ All environments change in a way that is often gradual.

Ⓑ People cause all the changes in environments.

Ⓒ Succession is a cause of change in environments.

Ⓓ Competition is the main cause of change in ecosystems.

10. Which of these is an adaptation that allows a skunk to defend itself against predators?

Ⓐ its stripe

Ⓑ its odor

Ⓒ its tail

Ⓓ its size

11. In a science experiment, soil was placed in four different beakers. The diagram below shows the conditions of the soil for each beaker.

Soaked   Wet   Damp   Dry

   A   B   C   D

Which of the beakers models drought conditions?

Ⓐ Beaker A   Ⓒ Beaker C

Ⓑ Beaker B   Ⓓ Beaker D

12. A sloth's long claws are adapted for which activity?

Ⓐ digging burrows

Ⓑ running long distances

Ⓒ capturing prey

Ⓓ hanging from tree branches

13. A volcano erupts and covers the ground with lava that hardens into rock. As primary succession begins, which organism is likely to be the first to populate the area?

Ⓐ birds   Ⓒ lichens

Ⓑ snakes   Ⓓ bears

14. Sometimes a species that is introduced to an area grows quickly and crowds out organisms that were already living there. What is this introduced species called?

Ⓐ a native species

Ⓑ a protected species

Ⓒ an invasive species

Ⓓ a beneficial species

15. A new shopping center was built on a vacant lot. The table shows the numbers of plants before and after construction.

Plants	Before	After
flowers	500	1,000
grass	1,000	0
shrubs	260	50
trees	26	3

Which of these statements is true based on these data?

(A) Humans did not change the environment.

(B) There were fewer total plants before the shopping center was built.

(C) There were more kinds of plants before the shopping center was built.

(D) There were more kinds of plants after the shopping center was built.

16. Examine the beak on the bird below.

The beak's shape enables the bird to survive in its environment because the beak is adapted to which of these actions?

(A) tearing food

(B) eating small seeds

(C) getting flower nectar

(D) digging insects from bark

17. A farmer plants corn every year. One year, the farm experiences a drought and receives less rainfall than is normal during the growing season. Which of the following is the most likely result?

(A) The corn plants will not grow at all.

(B) The corn plants will be taller than usual.

(C) The corn plants will be shorter than usual.

(D) The corn plants will grow the same as usual.

18. Which is a physical adaptation that allows penguins and whales to survive in Antarctica?

(A) a thick layer of fat

(B) migration

(C) staying close to the warmer parts of Antarctica

(D) long flippers

19. Which of the following things signals that an ecosystem has become a stable community after years of succession?

(A) moss

(B) rocks

(C) soil

(D) trees

Apply Inquiry and Review the Big Idea

Write the answers to these questions.

20. How do a cardinal's body parts help it survive in the forest? Describe 3 adaptations.

_____

_____

_____

21. This picture shows organisms that live in a desert environment. Choose one of the organisms. Identify one of its physical adaptations, and describe how the adaptation helps the organism live in a desert environment.

_____

_____

_____

22. The graphic below shows the changes that occurred after a forest fire removed all the trees from a mountain meadow, leaving barren soil.

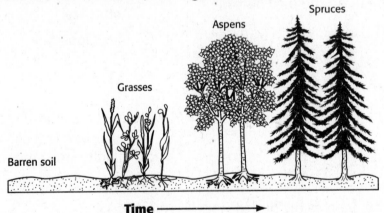

Describe what occurred at the different stages. Include how these changes affected the other organisms that live in the ecosystem.

_____

_____

_____

Earth's Living History

Big Idea

Fossils help us understand Earth's history.

OHIO 4.LS.1, 4.LS.2, 4.SIA.1, 4.SIA.5

I Wonder Why

These are shellfish fossils. Animals like these live in the ocean. Why were these fossils found on mountaintops? *Turn the page to find out.*

Here's why Fossils can tell scientists about past environments. Ocean, or marine, fossils found on mountaintops indicate that those areas were once covered by oceans. Over time the land changed, and the layers that contained the fossils rose above sea level.

In this unit, you will explore the Big Idea, the Essential Questions, and the Investigations on the Inquiry Flipchart.

Levels of Inquiry Key ■ DIRECTED ■ GUIDED ■ INDEPENDENT

Track Your Progress

Big Idea Fossils help us understand Earth's history.

Essential Questions

Now I Get the Big Idea!

Science Notebook

Before you begin each lesson, be sure to write your thoughts about the Essential Question.

OHIO **4.LS.2** Fossils can be compared to one another and to present day organisms according to their similarities and differences.

Lesson 1

Essential Question

What Are Fossils?

Engage Your Brain!

Find the answer to the following question in this lesson and record it here.

These animals no longer live on Earth. What can scientists learn about Earth's history by studying these animals?

_____

_____

_____

_____

Active Reading

Lesson Vocabulary

List the terms. As you learn about each one, make notes in the Interactive Glossary.

_____

_____

_____

Main Ideas

The main idea of a paragraph is the most important idea. The main idea may be stated in the first sentence, or it may be stated elsewhere. Active readers look for main ideas by asking themselves, What is this section mostly about?

Insects can get trapped in tree resin. Hardened resin is called amber. Insect parts and even whole insects are often preserved in amber.

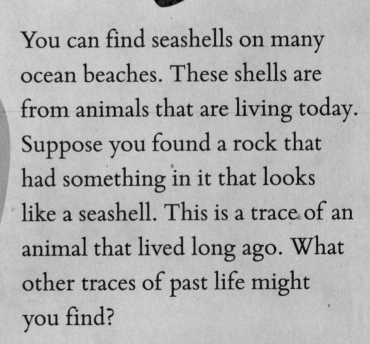

Traces of the Past

You can find seashells on many ocean beaches. These shells are from animals that are living today. Suppose you found a rock that had something in it that looks like a seashell. This is a trace of an animal that lived long ago. What other traces of past life might you find?

Active Reading As you read, underline each type of fossil discussed.

All living things contain the element carbon. Some plant tissues get preserved as *carbon films* in rock.

Footprints are examples of trace fossils. These features show that an animal was there, even though none of its parts were preserved.

The preserved remains or traces of a living thing is called a **fossil**. Fossils can be made of an organism's hard parts or its soft parts. Hard parts include bones, teeth, and shells. Soft parts are tissues such as skin and organs. Because bacteria quickly break down soft tissue, soft parts are rare as fossils. Soft-part fossils can be original tissue if it has been frozen or dried out as in a mummy. They can also be preserved as an impression in a rock.

Most fossils are found in sedimentary rock. One common way that fossils form is shown at right. Another way fossils form occurs as minerals, such as quartz, replace the shell or plant material that made up the organism. This is how *petrified* wood forms. Sometimes, the replacement is so perfect that even the bark and wood grain are visible.

These mold and cast fossils were made when a leaf was pressed into soft mud, leaving a hollow space called a **mold**. A **cast** can form if the mold is later filled with mud that hardens.

What Might You Leave Behind?

Draw a set of footprints or other trace that you might leave. Explain what part of your body would make the trace and what your trace fossil would tell future scientists.

_____

_____

Fossil Formation

1. An animal dies and settles on the bottom of a body of water.

2. Sediment buries the animal. Over time, the soft parts of the animal decay.

3. Hard parts are preserved in sediment as a fossil.

The plants and animals shown on these pages are fossils. Scientists study many types of fossils to help them learn about ancient life on Earth.

Fossil Features

Seed ferns were plants that lived on Earth long ago.

Scientists study fossils to see how animals and plants from long ago were the same and different.

Trilobites

trilobite art rendition and fossil from Caesar Creek State Park, Ohio

trilobite art rendition and fossil from Alnif, Morocco

These animals don't look exactly alike, but scientists put them in the same group, called trilobites. The animals both had exoskeletons and three body segments. Scientists know this by looking at their fossils.

When scientists find a fossil, they need a way to identify it. They can compare the fossil to other fossils. The scientists look at the fossil's physical characteristics to see if it is like other fossils.

Giant ground sloths once lived in North America. They ate bark and leaves stripped from trees by long claws. Scientists can tell they were mammals from the bones.

Brachiopods were small sea animals without backbones. They looked a little bit like clams.

Bryzoans were small sea animals without backbones. They lived in small groups and fed on tiny organisms that floated in the water.

Name That Fossil

Look at the fossils. Identify characteristics of each. Can you identify it as one of the fossils you have learned about?

Bryzoans where small sea animals without backbones.

seed ferns were plan

What Fossils Tell Us

Jawless fish

Armored fish

Fossils can tell us a lot about what life on Earth was like in the past.

Scientists who study fossils are called *paleontologists.* They study fossils to learn what life on Earth was like long ago. Fossils show that some types of plants and animals have changed a lot. Other plants and animals have hardly changed at all.

The woolly mammoth is related to modern elephants. It lived during the Ice Age, when the climate was very cold. Today's elephants live mostly in warm climates.

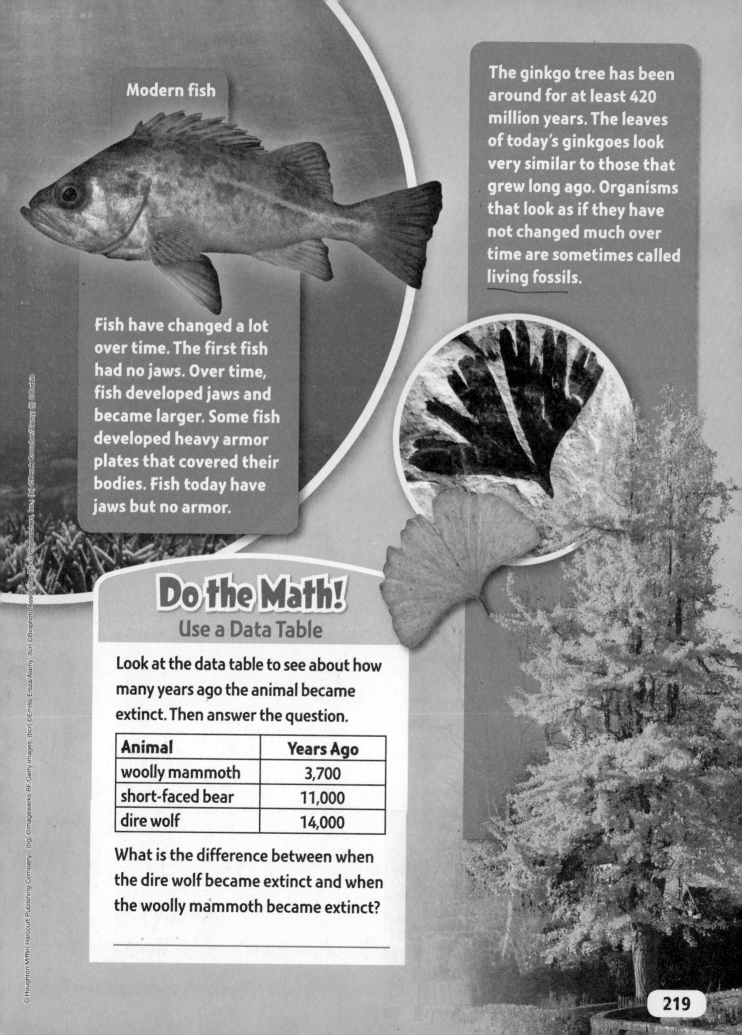

Modern fish

The ginkgo tree has been around for at least 420 million years. The leaves of today's ginkgoes look very similar to those that grew long ago. Organisms that look as if they have not changed much over time are sometimes called living fossils.

Fish have changed a lot over time. The first fish had no jaws. Over time, fish developed jaws and became larger. Some fish developed heavy armor plates that covered their bodies. Fish today have jaws but no armor.

Do the Math!
Use a Data Table

Look at the data table to see about how many years ago the animal became extinct. Then answer the question.

Animal	Years Ago
woolly mammoth	3,700
short-faced bear	11,000
dire wolf	14,000

What is the difference between when the dire wolf became extinct and when the woolly mammoth became extinct?

_____

When you're done, use the answer key to check and revise your work.

Complete the outline below to summarize the lesson.

Summarize

I. Traces of the Past

   A. Fossils are the preserved parts or traces of past life.

   B. How Fossils Form

      1. Organisms die and settle on the bottom of a lake or ocean.

      2. _____.

      3. _____.

   C. Kinds of Fossils

      1. preserved in amber or ice

      2. _____

      3. carbon film or trace fossil

II. Fossil Features

   A. Fossil identification

      1. Scientists identify fossils by comparing them to_____.

      2. _____ characteristics are compared to classify fossils.

   B. Examples

      1. Trilobites had three body segments and _____ .

      2. Scientists can tell the giant ground sloth was a _____ by looking at fossils of its bones.

      3. Bryozoans and brachiopods were both small sea animals without _____.

III. What Fossils Tell Us

   A. Scientists called paleontologists study fossils.

   B. How life has changed on Earth

Answer Key: I.B.2. Sediment buries the animal. I.B.3. Soft parts decay; hard parts are preserved. I.C.2. mold and cast fossils II.A.1 other fossils II.A.2 Physical II.B.1 exoskeletons II.B.2 mammal II.B.3 backbones

Name _____

Word Play

1 Read the summary statements below. Each statement is incorrect. Change the part of the statement in blue to make it correct. Use the word bank if you need help.

carbon film	~~fossil~~*	~~mold~~*	mud
paleontologist	petrified wood	trace fossil	

* Key Lesson Vocabulary

1. A paleontologist can be footprints preserved in rock. _trace fossil_

2. A cast forms when a shell leaves its shape in the mud. _mold_

3. A mummy is a scientist who studies fossils. _paleontologist_

4. The preserved remains or traces of a once-living organism is a mold.
   fossil

5. A fossil leaf that is made only of carbon preserved between two rock layers is called a fossil fuel. _carbon film_

6. A cast forms when minerals fills a mold and hardens. _mud_

7. Carbon film forms when minerals replace the plant material in a piece of wood.
   Petrified

Apply Concepts

2 Number the diagrams in the correct order to show how fossils can form.

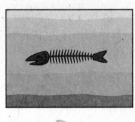      

____3____   ____2____   ____1____

3 Which would have a better chance of becoming a fossil: A fish that dies and settles to the ocean floor or a mouse that dies on the ground in a forest? Explain your answer.

_____

_____

4 What is a living fossil?

_____

_____

5 Choose one type of fossil. Draw a three-panel comic strip to show how the fossil forms. Write a description and labels for each picture to show how the fossil forms.

Take It Home!

Make one kind of fossil using a grape. Set up an area where you can leave the grape sitting undisturbed for several days. Examine the grape each day, and note any changes. When would you consider the grape a fossil?

OHIO 4.LS.2 Fossils can be compared to one another and to present day organisms according to their similarities and differences. 4.SIA.1 Observe and ask questions about the natural environment; 4.SIA.5 Communicate about observations, investigations and explanations

S.T.E.M.
Engineering & Technology

How It Works:

Walk This Way

Measuring the distance between fossil footprints gives scientists clues about how dinosaurs walked. Studying fossilized bones tells scientists how dinosaur joints moved. Scientists use these data with the aid of computers to see what a walking dinosaur would have looked like.

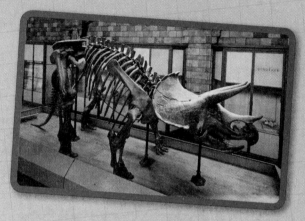

A computer model starts with a skeleton. Then virtual muscles are added. Finally scientists are able to animate *Triceratops* in motion.

Troubleshooting

Study the pictures of the walking *Triceratops* below. Describe how it moves.

_____

_____

_____

Before moving-picture cameras and computer technology, people began to study animal motion by finding ways to take rapid series of still photographs. They could look at the pictures in order to understand the animal's motion.

This famous set of images shows how a horse gallops. At one point in its stride, a horse has all four feet in the air. Write another detail that you observe about how the horse moves.

_____

_____

Research how a hummingbird flies. Draw separate images of a hummingbird in flight. How is high-speed video of hummingbirds shot?

_____

_____

_____

Build On It!

Rise to the engineering design challenge—complete **Make a Process: Design a Fossil Exhibit Hall** in the Inquiry Flipchart.

OHIO **4.LS.1** Changes in an organism's environment are sometimes beneficial to its survival and sometimes harmful. **4.LS.2** Fossils can be compared to one another and to present day organisms according to their similarities and differences.

Essential Question

What Was Ancient Earth Like?

Engage Your Brain!

Find the answer to the following question in this lesson and write it here.

This scene shows an environment on Earth millions of years ago. How are scientists able to hypothesize about what Earth looked like long ago?

_____

_____

_____

_____

Active Reading

Lesson Vocabulary

List each term. As you learn about each one, make notes in the Interactive Glossary.

_____

_____

_____

_____

Main Ideas and Details

In this lesson, you will read about Earth's ancient environments. Detail sentences throughout the lesson will provide information about this topic. The information may be examples, features, characteristics, or facts. Active readers stay focused on the topic when they ask, What fact or information does this sentence add to the topic?

How Rocks and Fossils Tell a Story

Sedimentary rock forms in layers. Many sedimentary rocks contain fossils. How can you tell the age of these layers and of the fossils within them?

You can learn about an area's history by studying its rocks and fossils. For example, you can tell how old the rock is compared to other rocks. You can also tell how living things and environments changed in that area over time. If you study rocks in different places, you can tell about large changes to Earth's surface and to life on Earth.

Imagine making a stack of newspapers in the order they were printed. When you look at the stack, you'll find the oldest paper on the bottom and the newest on the top. Rock layers work the same way. The oldest rock layers are at the bottom and the youngest rock layers are at the top. The *relative age* of a layer of rock is the age of that layer when you compare it to other layers—older, younger, or the same.

Each rock layer of the Grand Canyon formed at a different time in Earth's history and in a different environment.

Rock Layers of the Grand Canyon

The fossils in this layer of rock show that they were formed in an ocean.

This layer of rock is older than the layers above it. It contains a fossil imprint, or mold, of a plant.

Fossils form when sediment buries dead organisms. As a result, fossils are often found in sedimentary rocks. Scientists use fossils they find in rocks to help figure out the relative age of rock layers.

The *fossil record* is made up of all the fossils in Earth's rock layers. Fossils show how life on Earth has changed over time. So the *fossil record* contains information about Earth's history and the history of life on Earth.

Over time, movement of Earth's crust can cause layers of rock to become tilted. These movements can also lift rocks that were formed in the ocean to new positions high above sea level. The rock layers of the Grand Canyon were tilted and lifted millions of years ago.

Fossils like these are found in another layer of rock also formed in the ocean.

Relative Age

Suppose you find a fossil that looks like the second one from the top on this page. What can you say about its relative age?

_____

_____

_____

This layer of rock is one of the lower layers of the canyon, and is older than all of the rocks above. It contains fossils of trilobites, small animals like horseshoe crabs, that lived in ancient seas.

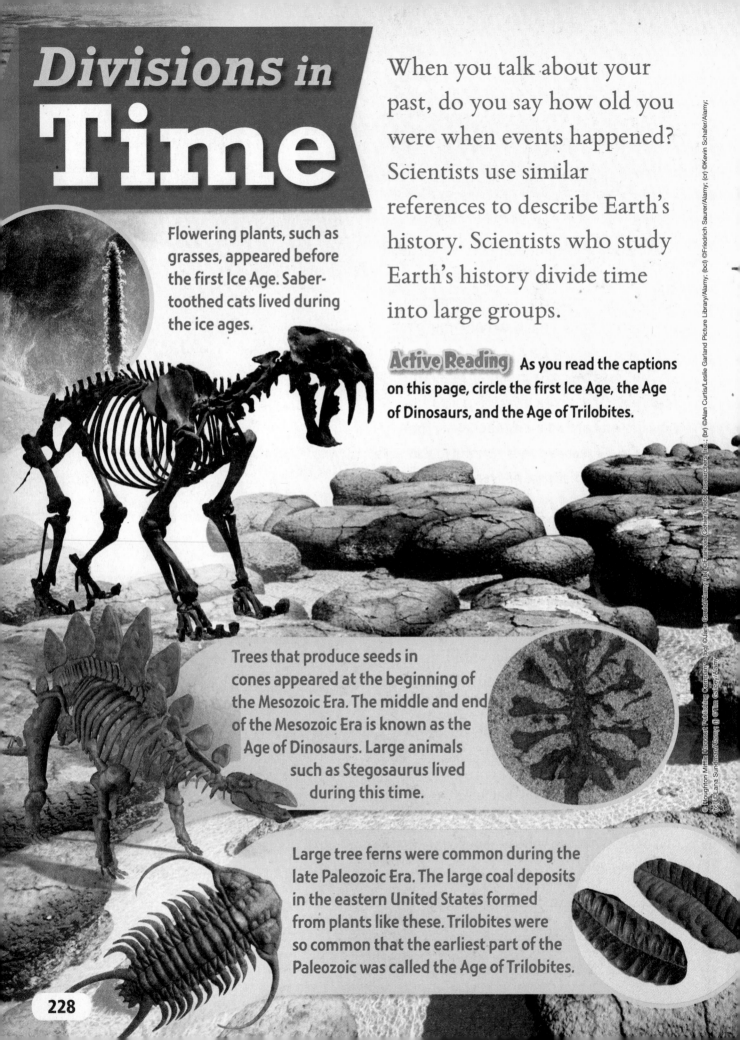

Divisions in Time

When you talk about your past, do you say how old you were when events happened? Scientists use similar references to describe Earth's history. Scientists who study Earth's history divide time into large groups.

Active Reading As you read the captions on this page, circle the first Ice Age, the Age of Dinosaurs, and the Age of Trilobites.

Flowering plants, such as grasses, appeared before the first Ice Age. Saber-toothed cats lived during the ice ages.

Trees that produce seeds in cones appeared at the beginning of the Mesozoic Era. The middle and end of the Mesozoic Era is known as the Age of Dinosaurs. Large animals such as Stegosaurus lived during this time.

Large tree ferns were common during the late Paleozoic Era. The large coal deposits in the eastern United States formed from plants like these. Trilobites were so common that the earliest part of the Paleozoic was called the Age of Trilobites.

All the rocks on Earth are a record of Earth's long history. Scientists developed the *geologic time scale* to divide Earth's history into manageable units. The fossils each unit contains define it.

Some fossils are more help than others. **Index fossils** help to identify a very short period of Earth's history. Index fossils must meet four requirements.

1. The organisms from which they formed lived during a short period of Earth's history.
2. The organisms must have had large populations so that many fossils formed.
3. The fossils must be widespread.
4. The fossils must be easily recognized.

Pterosaurs lived during the Mesozoic. These animals were not dinosaurs. They were flying reptiles. The largest pterosaur had a wingspan of at least 12 m (39 ft)!

Do the Math!
Read the Geologic Time Scale

Geologic Time Scale			
Cenozoic Era **65 mya–present**			Age of Mammals
146	Mesozoic Era	Cretaceous	
200		Jurassic	Age of Dinosaurs
251		Triassic	
299	Paleozoic Era	Permian	
359		Carboniferous	
416		Devonian	Age of Fishes
444		Silurian	
488		Ordovician	
542		Cambrian	
Precambrian time **4,600–542 mya**			1st life on Earth [stromatolites]

million years ago (mya)

Use the geologic time scale to answer the questions.

Which time interval was the longest?

_____

Which era was the shortest?

_____

How many years did each of the three eras last?

_____

_____

_____

How long did Precambrian time last?

_____

BIG
Changes
on Earth

Fossils tell about how life on Earth has changed over time. They also can give clues to how Earth's continents and landforms have changed.

Mesosaurus fossils are found in South America, Africa, Antarctica, Australia, and India.

Active Reading As you read these pages, underline details that provide evidence for continental drift.

Fossils can tell us about the relative ages of rocks. From fossils we can learn about changes in life through the divisions of geologic time. Fossils can also provide evidence about other larger changes to Earth's surface. Using fossils, you can identify areas of Earth that are now in different places than they once were.

Scientists have found the same type of fossil on both sides of the Atlantic Ocean. They are fossils of a small lizard-like reptile called *Mesosaurus* that lived in fresh water. At first, scientists thought that *Mesosaurus* swam from one side of the ocean to the other. But *Mesosaurus* was too small to have been able to swim across the salty Atlantic!

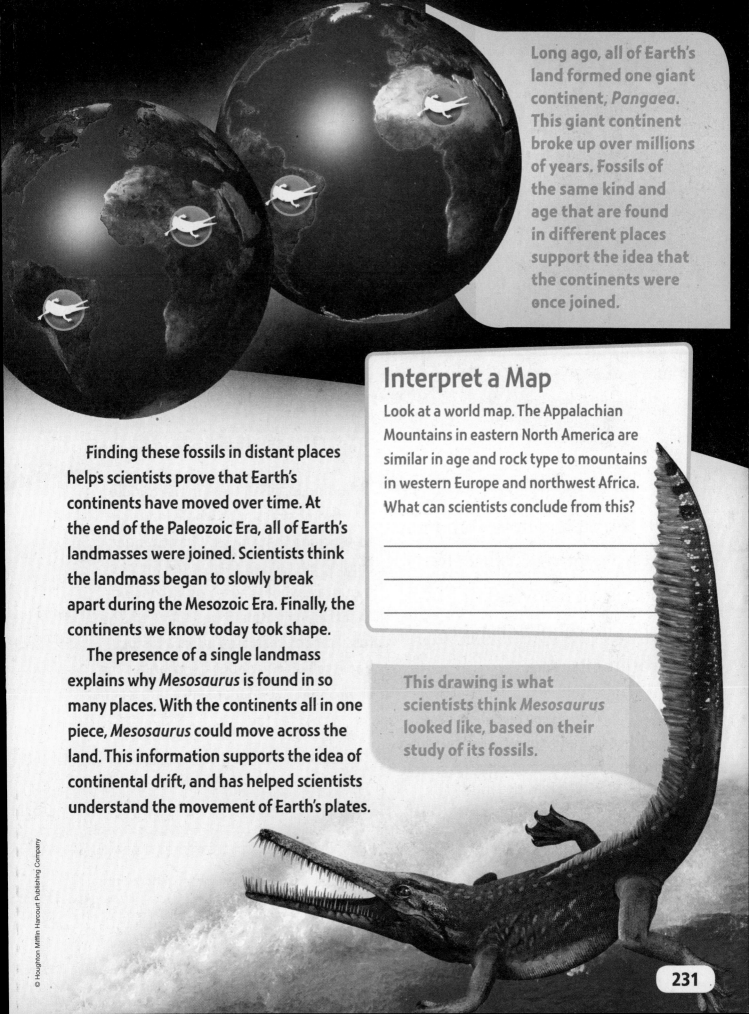

Long ago, all of Earth's land formed one giant continent, *Pangaea*. This giant continent broke up over millions of years. Fossils of the same kind and age that are found in different places support the idea that the continents were once joined.

Finding these fossils in distant places helps scientists prove that Earth's continents have moved over time. At the end of the Paleozoic Era, all of Earth's landmasses were joined. Scientists think the landmass began to slowly break apart during the Mesozoic Era. Finally, the continents we know today took shape.

The presence of a single landmass explains why *Mesosaurus* is found in so many places. With the continents all in one piece, *Mesosaurus* could move across the land. This information supports the idea of continental drift, and has helped scientists understand the movement of Earth's plates.

Interpret a Map

Look at a world map. The Appalachian Mountains in eastern North America are similar in age and rock type to mountains in western Europe and northwest Africa. What can scientists conclude from this?

_____

_____

_____

This drawing is what scientists think *Mesosaurus* looked like, based on their study of its fossils.

Changing Environments

The La Brea Tar Pits
40,000 years ago

You can use fossils to tell how old a rock layer is and how a landmass might have moved. What else can you learn from fossils? Fossils provide clues about changing environments, too.

Active Reading As you read these pages, turn each heading into a question in your mind, and underline sentences that answer it.

Rancho La Brea today

Finding fossils of trees in the middle of some grasslands would lead you to conclude that the land has changed. Finding a fossil sea snail at the top of a mountain would cause you to conclude that the environment has changed. The fossil record in an area is like a history book, telling you about the changes the environment in that area has undergone.

▶ Suppose you find a fossil seashell in the rocks in your local park. What does this tell you about the environment that was once there?

_____

_____

_____

The Devonian Sea 380 million years ago

Falls of the Ohio State Park today

The La Brea Tar Pits

The La Brea Tar Pits are located in Los Angeles, California, where tar still seeps from the ground. About 40,000 years ago, the area looked like the picture shown on the facing page. Scientists have collected fossils of thousands of plants and animals from the pits. Scientists know that those plants lived in a climate only a little wetter and cooler than it is today. In other words, the climate has not changed much in this area over the last 40,000 years.

Falls of the Ohio

Today the Falls of the Ohio is a state park in Indiana, tucked into a bend of the Ohio River where the land is flat and often dry. The summers are hot, and the winters are cold and snowy. But the rocks at the Falls of the Ohio State Park tell a different story. The rocks are filled with fossils of coral, clams, and other organisms that lived in shallow, warm, tropical seas. You can see on the map that Indiana is far from the ocean today. These fossils show that the climate in this area has changed a lot over the last 380 million years.

The Great Die Offs

When scientists look at the fossil record, they compare fossils to organisms living today. Scientists have discovered that many organisms have become extinct. There are times in Earth's history when a great many organisms became extinct all at once. How did this happen?

Active Reading As you read these pages, circle the possible causes of mass extinctions.

Sometimes only one species becomes extinct at a time. The passenger pigeon became extinct in 1914. Hunting and loss of habitat are likely causes. At several times during Earth's history, many species became extinct at the same time. These large events, caused by climate change, are called **mass extinctions**.

Worldwide volcanic eruptions can cause mass extinctions. These eruptions blow large amounts of ash and dust into the air. Sunlight is blocked, so plants can't grow. Other plants die when the ash settles on

Changing climate affects rainfall. Too much rain can cause flooding, which can destroy habitats. Too little rainfall means no plant growth and no water to drink. The result is death for many living things.

© Houghton Mifflin Harcourt Publishing Company   (bg) ©Martin Rietze/Westend61 GmbH/Alamy; (l) ©Stephen Ford/Alamy; (b) ©Andy Selinger/Alamy

them and smothers them. If plants die, the animals that eat them also die.

Objects from outer space can cause mass extinctions. At the end of the Mesozoic, an asteroid crashed into what is now Mexico. The impact sent huge amounts of dust into the air. The dust blocked out sunlight. Changes in climate occurred that were similar to those caused by large volcanic eruptions. These changes may have caused the extinction of many animals, including the last of the dinosaurs.

Summarizing Mass Extinctions

Fill in the chart to explain some causes of mass extinctions.

Cause	Effect	Result
volcanic eruption		
	flooding	
no rain		
	dust and ash in the air	

Volcanic ash can change climate.

Sum It Up!

When you're done, use the answer key to check and revise your work.

The statements below are incorrect. Replace the words in blue to correct each statement.

1. The units of the geologic time scale are defined the by the thickness of the rock layers. _____

2. The relative age of a fossil tells whether it is 1,000 years old or 1 million years old. _____
_____

3. Rocks that contain fossils of brachiopods, crinoids, and jawless fish formed in a desert environment. _____

4. The Age of Dinosaurs is known for the large number of animals, such as the saber-toothed cat, that were able to live in a cold environment.
_____

5. Index fossils must be found over a large area, be easily recognized, have lived during the Paleozoic, and have large populations.
_____

6. Support for continental drift includes different fossils found on the same continents. _____

7. Fossils of the reptile *Mesosaurus* are used to explain the movement of continents because this reptile lived in the desert.
_____

8. When volcanic eruptions send dust and ash into the air, increases in animal and plant populations can occur. _____
_____

Answer Key: 1. fossils that are in the rocks 2. younger or older than another fossil 3. ocean environment 4. Ice Age 5. lived during a geologically short period of time 6. the same, different 7. in fresh water and could not swim across salt water 8. mass extinctions

Name _____

Word Play

1 Use the clues to complete the puzzle.

Clues

Across

2. can be used to help identify the relative age of a rock layer
4. unit of time that contains the Age of Dinosaurs
6. occurs when many species die out at the same time
7. a geologic chart that divides Earth's history into units
8. common fossil animal from the Paleozoic

Down

1. used to describe if a fossil is older or younger than another fossil
3. all of the fossils in Earth's rock layers
5. giant continent that existed in Earth's past

fossil record	Mesozoic Era
geologic time scale	Pangaea
index fossil*	relative age
mass extinction*	trilobite

* Key Lesson Vocabulary

Apply Concepts

2 What does this fossil tell you about Antarctica's past environment?

_____

_____

_____

_____

3 The county is building a new road near your school. Bulldozers have dug up fossils of trees, leaves, and horses. Draw a picture of what the environment might have looked like when these plants and animals were living.

4 Place the following geologic time units in their correct order from oldest to most recent.

Cenozoic Era   Precambrian Time   Mesozoic Era   Paleozoic Era

_____

_____

5 What information in the picture supports the idea that Earth's continents have moved over time?

_____
_____

6 Read each description. Circle the fossil that is an index fossil.

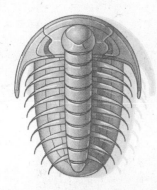

This animal lived for a short time during the late Paleozoic. Many of its fossils are found all over the United States.

This animal lived during the early and middle Paleozoic. Its fossils have only been found in a few parts of Indiana.

This tooth is from a shark that is living today. Many similar teeth have been found on the shores of Virginia.

7 Draw a three-panel comic strip that shows one way that a mass extinction might occur.

Cause	Effect	End Result

8 Which rock layer is the oldest? Which is the youngest? Explain how you know.

_____

_____

_____

_____

_____

_____

_____

Take It Home!

Take a walk with an adult around your neighborhood. Think about how the area might change over the next 5, 10, 50, 100, or 1,000 years. What clues would tell future paleontologists about how your area looks today?

Meet Some
Paleontology
Pioneers

Luis and Walter Alvarez

In 1980, a father-and-son geology team had an idea. They knew that dinosaurs may have become extinct around 65 million years ago when a huge asteroid hit Earth. To look for evidence of this, they looked at the layer of rock from that time period. The rock had a lot of the same chemical elements as asteroids. The Alvarezes hypothesized that an asteroid impact sent enough smoke and dust into the atmosphere to block out sunlight. Now many scientists agree with their idea.

Karen Chin

Karen Chin knows that we learn about animals by studying what they eat. That is why she studies the fossils of dinosaur dung! She learns a lot about dinosaurs this way. She can tell how they interacted with the plants and animals in their ecosystems. Dr. Chin was the first person to identify and study *Tyrannosaurus rex* poop! From her research, she could show that *Tyrannosaurus rex* ate *Triceratops*. And it didn't just eat meat from its prey. It ate bones and all.

Describe Dinosaurs

Look at each skeleton below. Answer the questions to compare and contrast the dinosaurs.

Stegosaurus

What do you think the plates on _Stegosaurus_'s back were for?

_____

_____

_____

Why do you think _Stegosaurus_'s tail was so long?

_____

_____

What do you think _Tyrannosaurus rex_ ate? Why do you think so?

_____

_____

_____

Tyrannosaurus rex

Why do you think _Tyrannosaurus rex_'s legs were longer than its arms?

_____

_____

_____

How do scientists find data to answer these questions?

_____

_____

_____

What do scientists learn from locations of dinosaur fossils?

_____

_____

_____

OHIO **4.LS.2** Fossils can be compared to one another and to present day organisms according to their similarities and differences. **4.SIA.1** Observe and ask questions about the natural environment; **4.SIA.4** Use appropriate mathematics with data to construct reasonable explanations; **4.SIA.5** Communicate about observations, investigations and explanations; and

Name _____

Essential Question

How Can Scientists Use Fossils?

Set a Purpose
What will you learn from this activity?

_____

_____

_____

State Your Hypothesis
Write your hypothesis or testable statement.

_____

_____

_____

_____

Think About the Procedure
Why is it important to examine the fossil symbols carefully?

_____

_____

How would the results change if only one fossil symbol was drawn on each card?

_____

_____

_____

Record Your Data
Record your results in the space below.

Sequence of Rock Layers (Oldest to Youngest)	Fossil Symbols
Youngest	
↑	
Oldest	▲ ★

Draw Conclusions

Use your card stack to order the fossils from oldest to youngest, according to when they last appeared in the rock record. Record your sequence on the lines below and in the chart.

_____

_____

_____

Oldest to Youngest	Fossil Symbols
Youngest	
↑	
Oldest	

Is the fossil $ older or younger than the fossil ♥?

_____

_____

_____

Analyze and Extend

1. Scientists use time-space relationships to compare rock layers around the world. What can you tell about the age of the fossil ✚ using this information?

   Fossil ○ is 25 to 50 million years old.
   Fossil ● is 75 to 110 million years old.

   _____

   _____

   _____

2. What has most likely occurred if a fossil that appeared in an older rock layer does not appear in a younger rock layer?

   _____

   _____

   _____

3. Suppose fossil # appeared in each rock layer. Would fossil # make a good index fossil? Explain.

   _____

   _____

   _____

4. What other questions do you have about how scientists use fossils?

   _____

   _____

   _____

Unit 5 Review

Name _____

Vocabulary Review

Use the terms in the box to complete the sentences.

> cast
> fossil
> index fossil
> mass extinction
> mold

1. The remains or traces of a plant or animal that lived long ago is

   a(n) _____.

2. An event that results in the dying off of many species is called

   a(n) _____.

3. An impression of an organism, formed when sediment hardens

   around the organism, is called a(n) _____.

4. A model of an organism, formed when sediment fills a mold and

   hardens, is a(n) _____.

5. A fossil of a type of organism that lived in many
   places during a relatively short time span is called

   a(n) _____.

Science Concepts

Fill in the letter of the choice that best answers the question.

6. Not every animal or plant becomes a fossil when it dies. Which event best helps a fossil form?

   (A) Water washes away dirt.

   (B) Animals eat the soft tissues.

   (C) Wind blows the dead organism away.

   (D) Sediment quickly buries the dead organism.

7. Josh read about a land animal whose fossils were found in similar rock layers in Africa and South America. What can he conclude from this discovery?

   (A) Animal fossils all look alike.

   (B) The landmasses were once joined.

   (C) The animals swam across the ocean.

   (D) The fossils formed in an ocean and washed ashore.

8. Nkomo found a piece of amber. Which object shown below would the amber most likely contain?

Ⓐ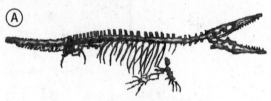

Ⓑ

Ⓒ

Ⓓ

9. Malaya was collecting fossils. She found one whose original material had been replaced by quartz. What type of fossil did she find?

Ⓐ trace fossil

Ⓑ carbon film

Ⓒ petrified wood

Ⓓ mummified body

10. Suppose you found fossils of sharks and other fish in a nearby forest. What could you infer about the area from these discoveries?

Ⓐ The area was once a desert.

Ⓑ The area was once an ocean.

Ⓒ The area was once a forest.

Ⓓ The area was once an ice field.

11. Which best describes an index fossil?

Ⓐ from a type of organism that lived over a long period of time

Ⓑ the oldest fossil in a layer

Ⓒ found in many places around the world

Ⓓ found in most rock layers

12. Which of the following organisms are most likely to become a fossil?

Ⓐ organisms with hard tissue that live in water

Ⓑ organisms with hard tissue that live on land

Ⓒ organisms with soft tissue that live in water

Ⓓ organisms with soft tissue that live on land

13. Fossils of ferns and reptiles have been found near Earth's poles. What does this tell us about Earth's past environments?

(A) Seas once covered areas at Earth's poles.

(B) The climate at Earth's poles used to be much warmer.

(C) Earth's poles used to be tilted directly toward the sun.

(D) The atmosphere at Earth's poles used to contain more oxygen.

14. Where might you expect to find a fossil of a woolly mammoth?

(A) in rock

(B) in a glacier

(C) in tree sap

(D) in a bog

15. What is a "living fossil"?

(A) a fossil that is easily identified

(B) an organism that is at least 100 years old

(C) a fossil that is well known in the scientific community

(D) a living organism that looks similar to its ancient ancestors

16. Study the rock layers in the diagram below.

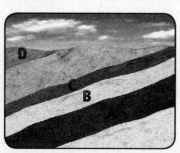

Which rock layer is probably the oldest?

(A) Layer A   (C) Layer C

(B) Layer B   (D) Layer D

17. Which life forms were common during the Mesozoic Era?

(A) dinosaurs   (C) tree ferns

(B) mammoths   (D) trilobites

18. Paul visited several western state capitals on his vacation. The map below shows the stops on his trip.

Paul said that he had found index fossils. Which one requirement for an index fossil had Paul completely satisfied?

(A) The fossil is from an organism that lived during a short period of Earth's history.

(B) The fossil is from an organism that had a large population.

(C) The fossil is widespread.

(D) The fossil is easily recognized.

Apply Inquiry and Review the Big Idea

Write the answer to these questions.

19. Leeza wanted to know the relative age of a fossilized bone she found. How can she use the rock layers shown below to help determine the bone's relative age?

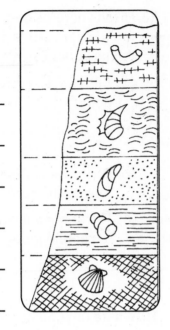

_____

_____

_____

_____

_____

20. Two fifth graders are planning to give a presentation about fossils to the class.

a. Ronda must explain how scientists use the fossil record to learn about ancient environments. Write at least two things that she should include in her presentation.

_____

_____

_____

_____

b. Gabe must explain how scientists use fossils found in areas such as the Grand Canyon to demonstrate how life forms have changed over time. Write three things that Gabe should include in his presentation.

_____

_____

_____

_____

UNIT 6
Matter

Big Idea

Matter has measurable physical properties that can be used to determine how matter is conserved, changed, and used.

OHIO 4.PS.1, 4.SIA.1, 4.SIA.4, 4.SIA.5

I Wonder How

Matter can take many forms. It can also be changed physically and chemically. How has this butter been transformed? *Turn the page to find out.*

Here's why It took 900 kilograms of butter to form this sculpture. The artist allows the butter to warm just enough to mold it and carve it. The butter is still butter; it has only been changed physically.

In this unit, you will explore the Big Idea, the Essential Questions, and the Investigations on the Inquiry Flipchart.

Levels of Inquiry Key ■ DIRECTED ■ GUIDED ■ INDEPENDENT

Track Your Progress

Big Idea Matter has measurable physical properties that can be used to determine how matter is conserved, changed, and used.

Essential Questions

Now I Get the Big Idea!

Science Notebook
Before you begin each lesson, be sure to write your thoughts about the Essential Question.

Essential Question

What Are Solids, Liquids, and Gases?

Engage Your Brain!

As you read the lesson, look for the answer to the following question and record it here.

Bottled water and the snow from this snow machine are both water. How are these forms of water different?

_____

_____

_____

_____

Active Reading

Lesson Vocabulary

List the terms. As you learn about each one, make notes in the Interactive Glossary.

_____   _____

_____   _____

_____   _____

Compare and Contrast

Many ideas in this lesson involve comparisons and contrasts—how things are alike and different. Active readers stay focused on comparisons and contrasts when they ask themselves, How are these things alike? How are they different?

What's the Matter?

This book is made of matter, and so are you. You might think that matter can be seen and felt. But did you know that air is matter also? What is matter?

Active Reading As you read these two pages, draw two lines under each main idea.

The large pencil has more matter than the smaller pencils. It has more mass and more volume.

Breathe in and out. Can you feel air hitting your hand? You can't see air, and you can't grab it. Yet air is **matter** because it has mass and it has volume. Matter cannot be created or destroyed. It might change form, but it is still matter.

Mass is the amount of matter in something. Each of the tiny particles that make up matter has mass, even though the particles are so small you cannot see them. **Volume** is the amount of space something takes up. When air is blown into a balloon, you can see that it has volume.

Name That Matter

Look at the matter in this picture.

1. What matter is soft and sticky?

_____

2. What matter is hard and sharp?

_____

Odor

Texture

Matter Has Properties

You might say that apple juice is gold in color, tastes sweet, and pours easily. These are properties of the juice, which means they are characteristics used to describe or identify it. All matter has properties.

All the properties shown on this page are physical properties. You can observe a physical property without changing the matter into a new substance. For example, texture is how something feels. In observing that sandpaper has a rough texture, you don't change the sandpaper.

Color

Comparing Stones

Complete the Venn diagram by comparing and contrasting the properties of the two stones.

More Properties

Color, texture, and odor are just a few physical properties. What are some other properties of matter?

As you read these two pages, circle common, everyday words that have a different meaning in science.

Temperature

Temperature is a measure of the energy of motion of the particles in matter. Melted glass has a very high temperature. Temperature can be measured by using a thermometer.

Volume

The food in the small bowl has less volume than the food in the large bowl because it takes up less space. Many tools can be used to measure volume.

Mass

A bowling ball and a basketball have about the same volume. The bowling ball has a greater mass because it contains more matter. Mass can be measured by using a balance.

Density

Density is found by dividing the mass of an object by its volume. The density of the gas in this balloon is less than the density of the air around it. That is why the balloon "floats" in air.

Do the Math!
Use Division

Use the data to find the density of each of these foods.

Determining Densities of Foods			
Food	Mass (g)	Volume (cm³)	Density (g/cm³)
gelatin	75	100	
pudding	90	100	
whipped cream	50	100	

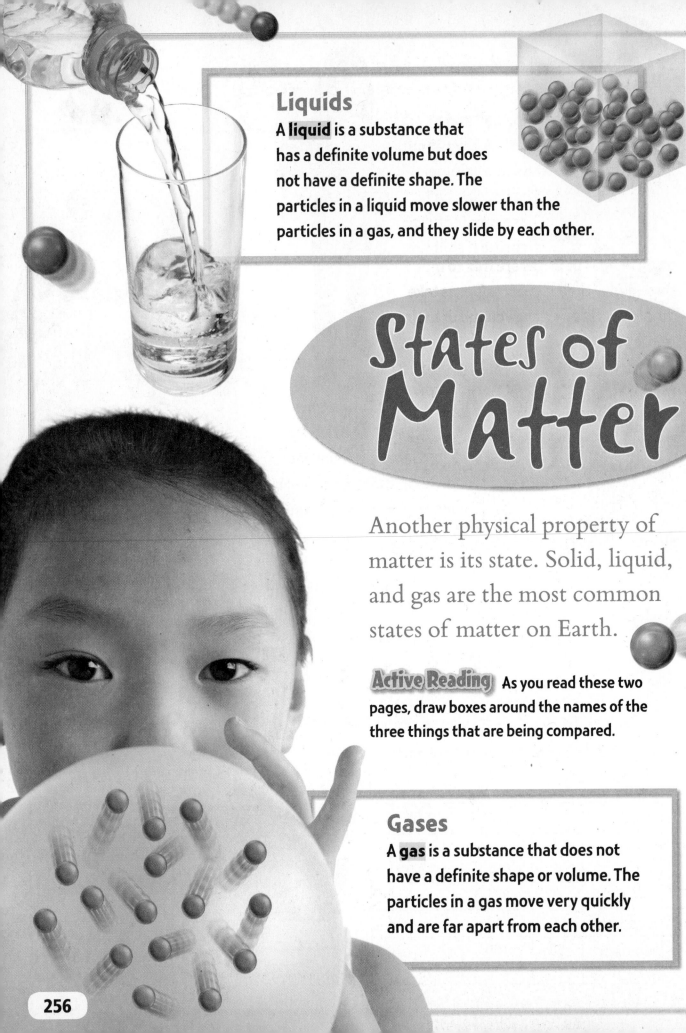

Liquids

A **liquid** is a substance that has a definite volume but does not have a definite shape. The particles in a liquid move slower than the particles in a gas, and they slide by each other.

States of Matter

Another physical property of matter is its state. Solid, liquid, and gas are the most common states of matter on Earth.

Active Reading As you read these two pages, draw boxes around the names of the three things that are being compared.

Gases

A **gas** is a substance that does not have a definite shape or volume. The particles in a gas move very quickly and are far apart from each other.

Matter is made of tiny particles. The particles in solids, liquids, and gases have different amounts of energy. The amount of energy affects how fast the particles move and how close together they are.

The shape and volume of something depends on its state. Because each particle in a gas is affected little by the other particles, gas particles are free to move throughout their container. Gases take both the shape and the volume of their container.

Particles in a liquid cannot move as freely. A sample of a liquid keeps the same volume no matter what container it is in. However because the particles slide by each other, a liquid takes the shape of its container.

The particles in a solid do not move from place to place, so solids keep the same shape and volume.

Solids

A **solid** is a substance with a definite shape and volume. The particles in a solid are very close to each other. They don't move from place to place. They just vibrate where they are.

The bubbles in the tank are a _____.

The water is an example of a _____.

The castle is a _____.

A Matter of Temperature

On a hot day, an ice cube melts. This change is caused by a change in temperature. When matter changes state, the type of matter is not changed.

Active Reading As you read these two pages, draw one line under a cause. Draw two lines under the effect.

When matter takes in or releases energy, its temperature changes. When enough energy is taken in or released, matter can change state.

When a gas releases energy, its temperature goes down until it *condenses*, or changes to a liquid. When a liquid releases energy, its temperature goes down until it *freezes*, or changes to a solid.

When a solid takes in energy, its temperature rises until it *melts*, or changes to a liquid. When a liquid takes in energy, its temperature rises until it *evaporates*, or changes to a gas. Evaporation and boiling are similar—both turn liquids into gases. Evaporation is slower and happens only at a liquid's surface. Boiling is faster and happens throughout the liquid.

When a solid absorbs enough energy, the solid melts, changing to a liquid.

When a liquid absorbs enough energy, the liquid *boils*, or rapidly changes to a gas.

© Houghton Mifflin Harcourt Publishing Company

When a gas releases enough energy, the gas condenses, changing to a liquid. Particles of water vapor condense and form raindrops and dew.

The temperature at which a certain type of matter freezes or melts is the same. The temperature at which a type of matter condenses or boils is also the same. For water, the melting and freezing points are 0 °C. The condensation and boiling points are 100 °C. Evaporation can happen at temperatures below the boiling point.

When a liquid releases enough energy, the liquid freezes, changing to a solid. Dripping water that freezes can form icicles.

Lava is hot, melted rock that erupts from a volcano. Lava releases energy as it cools and becomes solid rock.

▶ Complete this graphic organizer.

As a solid takes in energy, its temperature _____. Eventually, it will _____, changing to a _____.

If the liquid takes in enough _____, it will _____, changing to a _____.

Properties of Solids, Liquids, and Gases

Each different material has its own unique properties. However, properties can change depending on the state of the material.

Active Reading As you read these two pages, find and underline facts about each state of matter.

Each state of matter has different physical properties. Liquids and gases both flow, moving from place to place. Gases can expand, taking up more space, or compress, taking up less space. Solids have definite textures.

Liquid water flows much more quickly than honey.

Liquids
All liquids flow from one place to another. Different liquids may flow at different rates.

Solids

Although clay and a wooden table are both solids, each one feels different. All solids have a shape, but the shape of some solids can be changed easily.

Gases

A lot of gas has been compressed in this tank. It is under high pressure. Compressed gas from the tank expands, filling many balloons.

▶ Complete this main-idea-and-details graphic organizer.

Main Idea
_____

Liquids	Gases	_____
Motor oil and milk _____ at different rates.	When you push on the sides of a balloon, the gas inside is _____.	Glass and sandpaper have different _____.

When you're done, use the answer key to check and revise your work.

Read the summary statements below. Each one is incorrect. Change the part of the summary in blue to make it correct.

1. A property is a characteristic of matter that is used to determine the state of the matter.
_____

2. A sample of ice has a volume of 1.0 cm³ and a mass of 0.9 g. The density of the ice is 1.1 g/cm³.
_____

3. The particles in a solid are close together, but they can slide past each other.
_____

4. A solid changes to a liquid during a process known as freezing.
_____

5. Solids and liquids can be compressed when put under pressure.
_____

6. The mass of an object can be measured by using a measuring cup.
_____

Summarize

Read the properties below. Write *S* for solid, *G* for gas, and *L* for liquid. Some properties may have more than one answer.

7. Has a definite texture and shape _____

8. Can melt _____

9. Can freeze _____

10. Can boil _____

11. Takes the volume of its container _____

12. Can condense _____

13. Can flow _____

14. Takes the shape of its container _____

15. Has a definite volume _____

Answer Key: 1. describe or identify matter 2. 0.9 g/cm³ 3. liquid 4. melting 5. Gases 6. balance
7. S 8. S 9. L 10. L 11. G 12. G 13. L, G 14. L, G 15. S, L

Word Play

Name _____

1 Use the clues below to fill in the words in the puzzle.

1. To squeeze a gas into a smaller space
2. A physical property that describes how something feels
3. The state of matter that keeps its shape and volume when it is placed in a different container
4. The measure of the energy of motion of particles of matter
5. Anything that has mass and volume
6. What happens to a liquid when it releases enough energy
7. Calculated by dividing mass by volume
8. The state of matter that has particles that slide by each other
9. The amount of space something takes up
10. The state of matter that expands to fill its container

Read down the squares with red borders. The word you find will complete the riddle below.

Perry the porcupine's portrait perfectly portrayed his pestering personality and prickly __ __ __ __ __ __ __ __ __ __ __ __.

Apply Concepts

2 Tell what property each of the following tools is used to measure.

_____   _____   _____

3 Complete these descriptions of the different states of matter.

_____		*Solids*
_____	*Particles are closer together and move past each other.*	*Particles are very close and vibrate in place.*
Examples: air; helium in balloons; oxygen in a tank	*Examples:* _____	*Examples:* _____

4 Fill in the name of the processes (such as freezing) that are represented.

a _____   b _____

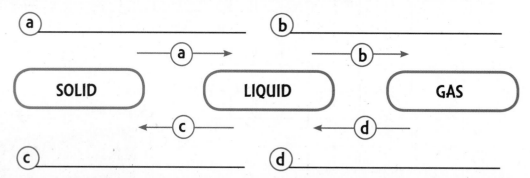

c _____   d _____

Take It Home!

Play a game of 20 Questions with members of your family. Have them choose a simple item that you can see in the room. Try to guess what the item is by asking yes/no questions about the item's properties.

S.T.E.M.
Engineering & Technology

Baby, It's Cold Inside
Refrigeration

Have you ever thought about how refrigeration has changed the way we live? We can store foods without having them rot as quickly. Spoiled foods can make people ill.

1920s
In the 1920s, electric refrigerators became available for home use. The inside of this refrigerator stayed cold without needing blocks of ice. It used an electric motor and a gas compressor to remove heat from its wooden or metal box.

1800s
People put food on blocks of ice to keep it cold. The ice was cut from lakes or ponds, packed in straw, and stored in warehouses. This ice had to be replaced often.

1900s
By the early 1900s, many homes had iceboxes. Ice was placed in the bottom to cool the air inside the box. It became easier to cool food for longer periods of time until it could be used. These iceboxes were like coolers we use today but larger.

Critical Thinking

In addition to slowing food spoilage, what is another advantage of refrigerating food?

another advantage is that less people will get sick from spoil food.

Make Some History

If you look closely, you will find that many of your home appliances have an *Energy Star* label. Do research to find out more about this label. Draw the Energy Star label in the space below on the timeline. Then, describe what it is and when it was first used on refrigerators.

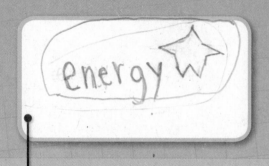

It is a volunteer labbing program that designed and promote engergy effecthos. It first used on refrige in 1996.

2010s

Today's refrigerators are larger but use less energy. They have electronic controls that can be adjusted to set different parts of the refrigerator at different temperatures. Some modern refrigerators can alert people when a particular food supply is running low!

Design Your Future

Other household appliances help you save time. Think about a computer. Describe how it helps you collect and analyze information. Then, explain what you would do to improve its design.

_____

_____

_____

Build On It!

Rise to the engineering design challenge—complete **Improvise It: Build a Rubber Band Scale** on the Inquiry Flipchart.

OHIO **4.PS.1** The total amount of matter is conserved when it undergoes a change. **4.SIA.5** Communicate about observations, investigations and explanations; and

Name _____

Essential Question

How Does Water Change?

Set a Purpose
What can you learn from this experiment?

_____

_____

Think About the Procedure
Why do you dry the bag in Step 2?

_____

_____

Where did the moisture on the outside of the bag come from?

_____

_____

Make a Prediction
Write your prediction from Step 3.

_____

_____

_____

Record Your Observations
In the space below, draw a table to record the masses that you measured.

Draw Conclusions

Was your prediction correct? Explain.

_____

_____

_____

_____

_____

_____

Analyze and Extend

1. Why was the mass of the bag not important in this activity?

_____

_____

_____

2. What properties of water changed during this activity? What properties did not change?

_____

_____

_____

_____

3. What do you predict would happen to the mass if you put the bag from Step 5 in the freezer and then found the mass after the water changed to ice?

_____

_____

_____

4. Suppose you poured the water from Step 5 into a container and measured its volume. If you froze the water, would its volume change or stay the same? Explain.

_____

_____

_____

5. What other questions would you like to ask about how water changes during a physical change? What experiments could you do to answer the questions?

_____

_____

_____

_____

_____

OHIO **4.PS.1** The total amount of matter is conserved when it undergoes a change.

Lesson **3**

Essential Question

How Does Matter Change?

Engage Your Brain!

As you read the lesson, look for the answer to the following question and record it here.

A piece of iron can change in different ways. How is iron bending different from iron rusting?

_____

_____

_____

Active Reading

Lesson Vocabulary

List each term. As you learn about each one, make notes in the Interactive Glossary.

_____

_____

_____

_____

Main Idea and Details

Detail sentences give information about a topic. The information may be examples, features, characteristics, or facts. Active readers stay focused on the topic when they ask, What fact or information does this sentence add to the topic?

Inquiry Flipchart p. 34 — Observe Some Chemical Changes/Shhhh! Secret Messages

269

Classifying Change

▲ Slicing apples and cracking eggs are physical changes.

When an apple pie cooks, chemical changes occur. Cooked apples do not have the same properties as a raw apple.

Matter has properties, but matter also undergoes changes. How many different ways does matter change?

Active Reading Each visual on these two pages has an empty bubble. Write a *C* if the visual shows a chemical change. Write a *P* if it shows a physical change.

Matter has physical properties that can be observed without changing the type of matter. Matter can also change in ways that do not affect the type of matter. These changes are called **physical changes**.

When you sharpen a pencil, the pencil goes through a physical change. The wood shavings and bits of graphite don't look like a pencil any more. But the wood is still wood, and the graphite is still graphite.

▲ Slicing a pie is another physical change.

▲ The properties of the ash and gases that form when wood burns are different from the properties of wood.

▲ When iron rusts, it undergoes a chemical change.

Matter has other properties that cannot be observed without changing the identity of the matter. These properties are chemical properties. For example, you don't know if a type of matter will burn unless you burn it. When matter burns, it changes identity.

In the same way, **chemical changes** result in a change in the identity of matter. When a strawberry rots, it undergoes chemical change. The rotten strawberry's properties are quite different from those of a fresh strawberry. A chemical **reaction** is the process in which new substances are formed during a chemical change.

◄ When you eat apple pie, chemical changes in your body digest the food.

▶ Place a *P* by each physical change and a *C* by each chemical change.

Change	Type
Bacteria decompose leaves.	
A newspaper turns yellow in sunlight.	
Water evaporates.	
Gasoline burns in a car engine.	

Swelling
and Shrinking

Why do you think many car owners use one tire pressure in summer and another one in winter? When temperature differs, volume often differs.

Active Reading As you read this page, draw two lines under each main idea. Circle an example of matter expanding when it becomes warmer.

Most matter expands when the temperature goes up and contracts when the temperature goes down. Some kinds of matter expand and contract more than others. People may run hot water over the metal lid of a glass jar. This expands the lid so that it's easier to take off the jar.

One exception is water. It expands when it freezes. Because ice takes up more volume than the same amount of liquid water, ice is less dense than water. That's why ice floats in a glass of water. In winter, ice first forms at the surface of a lake.

Frozen Water
Volume = 1.09 L

Liquid Water
Volume = 1.00 L

One of water's unique properties is that it expands when it freezes.

Sometimes water flows into cracks in rocks and freezes. The expanding water makes the cracks in the rock larger and breaks large rocks into smaller pieces.

Expansion Joints

▶ Explain why bridges have expansion joints in them.

_____

_____

_____

_____

◀ This photo shows the same balloon at two different temperatures. The size of a sample of gas depends on its temperature. The gas in a balloon expands when it is warmed. The gas compresses when it is cooled.

Temperature = –80 °C
Volume = 1.9 L

Temperature = 35 °C
Volume = 3.0 L

273

Tampering with Temperature

When a burner on a stove is really hot, it glows red. A change in color is just one way temperature can affect matter.

Active Reading As you read this page, underline examples of how temperature affects physical changes in matter.

Some physical changes, such as tearing a piece of paper, are not affected by temperature. Other physical changes happen faster or slower at different temperatures. How quickly a change occurs is called the rate of change.

For example, ice on a lake will melt if the air temperature is above 0 °C. It will melt even faster if the air temperature is warmer. In the same way, water condenses more quickly on the outside of a very cold soft drink can than it does on a cool can.

Hot! Hot! Hot!
As iron is heated, it glows red or yellow.

WOW! This metal rod has been heated to more than 500 °C (932 °F).

OUCH! The filament of a light bulb is made of a metal called tungsten. It is glowing because it is heated to 2,500 °C!

Do the Math!
Graph Data

The data table shows how long it takes identical ice cubes to melt when placed in equal amounts of water at different temperatures. Make a line graph of these data.

Temperature of water (°C)	Melting time of ice (sec)
14	450
19	300
27	170
42	140
48	90
70	25

When grass and the air around it cool at night, water vapor in the air might condense, forming dew. As morning sunlight warms the air, the dew evaporates. In this photograph, the grass in the shade is wet but the grass in the sun has dried.

Adding it Up!

What happens to the mass of substances during physical or chemical changes?

As you read these pages, underline examples of conservation of mass.

75 grams

110 grams

During physical and chemical changes, matter may change its appearance or its identity. In either type of change, the total mass of the matter before and after the change remains the same. This is called **conservation of mass**. To *conserve* means "to save."

For example, as water boils, it seems to disappear. However, the total mass of the particles of water vapor in the air equals the mass of the water that boiled away. Suppose you tear a 100-gram cardboard box into pieces. The total mass of all the pieces will also be 100 grams. The mass of the cardboard box stays the same. In this example, however, the volume of the cardboard box changes because tearing it into pieces causes it to lose its shape.

90 grams

The total mass of the mixed salad is the sum of the masses of the vegetables in it.

▶ **What is the mass of the salad?**
_____

During this chemical reaction, the flask is sealed. Nothing can enter or leave, so the final mass equals the starting mass.

A chemical change turns one kind of matter into another. However, the mass of the matter stays the same. It can be tricky to compare, though. First, you must collect and measure the mass of everything you begin with. Then, you must collect and measure the mass of everything you are left with.

When wood burns, it combines with oxygen from the air. Burning produces ashes, smoke, and other gases. The mass of the wood and oxygen equals the mass of the ashes, smoke, and gases that are produced.

Do the Math!
Solve Problems

In a physical change, sugar is dissolved in water to form sugar water. In a chemical change, iron combines with oxygen to form rust. Fill in the missing values in the table.

Physical Change	Mass (grams)
sugar	125
water	
sugar water	198
Chemical Change	
iron	519
oxygen	23
rust	

Faster or Slower?

Temperature affects the rate at which chemical changes occur, too. Read to find out how.

Active Reading As you read this page, circle two clue words or phrases that signal a detail such as an example or an added fact.

cold water

warm water

An effervescent antacid tablet reacts more quickly with warm water than it does with cold water.

Increasing temperature often speeds up the rate of a chemical change. For example, increasing oven temperature speeds up the chemical changes that occur when a cake bakes or a potato cooks.

Decreasing temperature usually slows down the rate of chemical change. This is why food stays fresh longer when it is kept cool. Also, unused batteries stay charged longer when kept in the refrigerator.

The chemical changes that make food spoil are slowed down by keeping the food in the refrigerator.

Fevers

You feel awful. Your head hurts, and you have a fever. Why might having a fever be a good thing?

When you have a fever, your temperature rises above your normal body temperature (about 37 °C). A low fever is between 38 °C and 39 °C. A high fever is greater than 40 °C. Low fevers help the body fight disease. High fevers can cause severe problems.

Temperature can increase for many reasons. For example, certain bacteria have materials that your brain identifies as harmful. The brain sends out signals that cause an increase in the chemical changes that produce energy. Your temperature increases. Bacteria cannot survive at this higher temperature.

Do the Math!
Use a Number Line

On the number line below, plot the following values in °C.

a. normal body temperature

b. a slight fever

c. a high fever

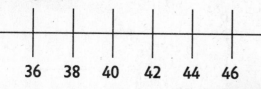

36 38 40 42 44 46

When you're done, use the answer key to check and revise your work.

The outline below is a summary of the lesson. Complete the outline.

I. Matter undergoes changes.

   A. One type of change is a (1) _____.

      1. Matter does not change identity.

      2. Example: (2) _____

   B. (3) _____

      1. Matter changes identity.

      2. Example: (4) _____

II. Temperature affects matter.

   A. When temperature increases,

      1. the speed of a chemical change (5) _____.

      2. the rate of melting and boiling (6) _____.

   B. When temperature decreases,

      1. the speed of a chemical change (7) _____.

      2. the rate of freezing or condensing (8) _____.

III. During physical or chemical changes, the total mass of matter (9) _____.

Tell whether each change is a physical change or a chemical change.

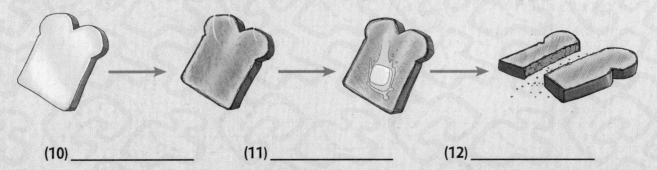

(10) _____   (11) _____   (12) _____

Name _____

Word Play

1 It's easy to get tongue-tied when talking about how matter changes. Look at the statements below. Switch the red words from one sentence to another until each statement makes sense.

A. In a chemical change, the identity of matter does not change. _____

B. Water will melt faster on a very cold soft drink can than it will on a cool soft drink can. _____

C. Another name for a chemical change is a chemical property. _____

D. Ice will condense more slowly in cold water than in warm water. _____

E. In a physical change, the identity of the matter changes. _____

F. When water freezes, its mass decreases. _____

G. A reaction of matter will stay the same during a physical change. _____

H. When water freezes, it contracts. _____

Challenge The words in the boxes below are jumbled. Put them in the correct order to make a meaningful sentence.

changes are rusting and chemical burning
_____
_____

is physical and mass changes in chemical conserved
_____
_____

2 Each of the pictures shows a change. Write a *P* by the pictures that show physical changes and a *C* by the pictures that show chemical changes.

3 Make a list of physical changes and chemical changes that you observe or see the effects of in your school.

Physical Changes

_____

_____

_____

_____

_____

_____

_____

_____

_____

Chemical Changes

_____

_____

_____

_____

_____

_____

_____

_____

_____

4 What would make each of the following processes happen faster? On each line, write *increase in temperature* or *decrease in temperature*.

Ice cream melting

_____

Boiling water to cook potatoes

_____

Water condensing on
the outside of a glass

_____

Water freezing
overnight on a street

_____

5 Explain what is happening in these pictures. Tell whether the changes are physical or chemical.

_____

_____

_____

_____

_____

_____

6 Why is it important to follow the instructions on this jar of food?

_____

_____

_____

_____

_____

_____

7 Draw a picture of a chemical reaction. Then explain what happens and why mass is conserved during the reaction.

_____

_____

_____

_____

_____

_____

8 Explain why most sidewalks have built-in cracks every few feet.

_____

_____

_____

_____

_____

9 Explain what happens in a campfire.

Wood is made of cellulose, lignin, and other substances.

↓

The wood is set on fire, and a _____ change occurs.

↓

The cellulose and lignin are changed into other substances, including _____ and _____.

Take It Home! Ask an adult to help you practice taking the temperature of someone in your family. Determine whether any of your family members have a fever. Explain to family members why people get fevers.

OHIO **4.PS.1** The total amount of matter is conserved when it undergoes a change. **4.SIA.4** Use appropriate mathematics with data to construct reasonable explanations; **4.SIA.5** Communicate about observations, investigations and explanations; and

Name _____

Essential Question

What Is Conservation of Mass?

The **law of conservation of mass** says that you cannot make or destroy matter. You can change matter into a new form. However, the new form will have the same amount of mass as the old form.

Set a Purpose

What do you expect to show in this experiment?

_____

_____

_____

_____

Think About the Procedure

How can you change the object?

_____

_____

_____

_____

Record Your Data

Make a table in which you record your results.

Was the mass of the whole object the same as the mass of the object broken apart?

_____

_____

_____

Draw Conclusions

How is this investigation a good example
of the law of conservation of mass?

_____

_____

_____

_____

_____

_____

_____

_____

Analyze and Extend

1. Write the law of conservation of mass
   in your own words. Can you think of
   another example of this law?

_____

_____

_____

_____

_____

_____

_____

2. Scientists often have to be creative
   when planning investigations. What is
   another way that you could show the
   law of conservation of mass?

_____

_____

_____

_____

_____

_____

_____

_____

_____

3. What other questions would you like
   to ask about the law of conservation
   of mass?

_____

_____

_____

_____

_____

_____

_____

Essential Question

What Are Mixtures and Solutions?

Engage Your Brain!

As you read the lesson, look for the answer to the following question and record it here.

How are a smoothie and a salad alike? How are they different?

_____

_____

_____

_____

Active Reading

Lesson Vocabulary

List each term. As you learn about each one, make notes in the Interactive Glossary.

_____

_____

Problem and Solution

Ideas in this lesson may be connected by a problem-solution relationship. Active readers mark a problem with a *P* to help them stay focused on the way information is organized. When multiple solutions are described, they mark each solution with an *S*.

Matter Mix-Up

A box of colored pencils. A basket of footballs, tennis balls, and hockey pucks. A toy box full of toys. All these things are mixtures. But what is a mixture?

Active Reading As you read the next page, draw two lines under the conclusion. Draw one line under each fact that leads to the conclusion.

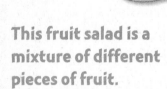

This fruit salad is a mixture of different pieces of fruit.

Look at the mixtures on these pages. They have a few things in common. First, two or more substances or objects were combined. The fruit salad has several types of fruit. The laundry pile has several types of clothing. Second, each type of matter in a mixture keeps its own identity. The peach in the fruit salad is the same type of matter as it was before it was mixed into the fruit salad. The jeans in the laundry pile are still jeans.

By now, you've probably figured out that a **mixture** is a combination of two or more substances that keep their identities. The parts of a mixture don't undergo a chemical change. Making a mixture is a physical change.

A carbonated beverage is a mixture of water, gases, and other ingredients.

▶ These clothes are all jumbled together. How do you know this pile of laundry is a mixture?

_____

_____

_____

Find a Solution!

In some mixtures, it's easy to see the individual pieces that are mixed together. In other mixtures, small parts are very evenly mixed. What are these special mixtures?

Active Reading As you read these two pages, underline lesson vocabulary words each time they are used.

Each bite of fruit salad contains different combinations of fruit. You can separately taste peaches and different kinds of berries. But what do you notice when you drink a glass of lemonade? Every sip tastes the same. This is because lemonade is a solution. A **solution** is a mixture that has the same composition throughout.

When food coloring is added to water, the two liquids evenly mix, forming a solution.

A solution forms when one substance *dissolves* in another. When something dissolves, it breaks up into particles so tiny they can't be seen even with a microscope. These particles then evenly mix with the other part of the solution. Not everything dissolves. If you put a rock and salt in water, the rock won't dissolve, but the salt will.

Solutions are commonly liquids, such as the mixture of the different liquids that make up gasoline. But not all solutions are liquids. Air is a solution of different gases. Tiny particles of nitrogen, oxygen, and other gases are evenly mixed in air. Brass is an example of a solid solution formed from solid copper and solid zinc.

A mixture of sand and water forms where waves wash over the sand. Such a mixture is not a solution.

Ocean water itself is a solution. It contains several different dissolved substances.

▶ What makes a solution different from other mixtures?

_____

_____

Separating Mixtures

Suppose you really don't like olives. How are you going to get them off that deluxe pizza your friend ordered? Sometimes you need to separate the components of a mixture.

Mixtures are not always easy to separate. But since mixing is a physical change, each component in a mixture keeps most of its physical properties. Physical properties such as color, size, melting point, boiling point, density, and ability to dissolve can be used to separate mixtures. Separating a mixture can be very simple. Or it can involve several, complex steps when one method is not enough.

Density

Every substance has its own density. A less-dense substance will float on a denser substance. Objects will float in water if they are less dense than water. They will sink if they are denser than water.

▶ What property was used to separate the items on this tray?

_____

When One Isn't Enough

sieve/mesh screen

A sieve or mesh screen has holes that matter can pass through. Matter that is smaller than the holes passes through the mesh screen while matter that is larger than the holes stays above the mesh screen.

magnetic force

A magnet attracts matter that contains iron, separating it from the other parts of the mixture.

filtration

A filter works like a mesh screen with very tiny openings, or pores. Only the smallest bits of matter—like water particles and dissolved particles of salt—can pass through the pores.

evaporation/boiling

Boiling is when a liquid rapidly changes to a gas at the boiling point of the liquid. Evaporation also changes a liquid to a gas, but it occurs at temperatures below the boiling point. During these processes, only the liquid particles leave the solution. Dissolved particles stay behind.

A magnet takes away bits of iron.

Water is added. Then the filter removes the soil.

The water is boiled away. Only salt is left behind.

Proportions and Properties

When you make lemonade, it's important to get the amounts of lemon and sugar right. If it's too sweet or too sour, it doesn't taste right. How do proportions affect the properties of a mixture?

Mixtures of metals are called *alloys.* The properties of the alloy depend on how much of each metal is in the mixture. Chemists first decide on the properties they need their alloy to have. Then they decide how much of which metals will give them those properties.

Steel is an alloy. It is made from iron and other substances. Different substances give steel different properties. For example, adding chromium will make steel shiny. Metals such as nickel and titanium can keep it from rusting. Carbon is often added to steel to make it stronger. Other substances help steel used in tools stay sharp or keep from wearing down.

To make an alloy, metals and other elements are melted together and then allowed to harden.

► For each steel object on this page, list at least two properties that the steel must have.

Kettle

Sculpture

Steel Building Frame

Do the Math!
Use Graphs

Compare and contrast the metals and other substances in stainless steel and tool steel by making two circle graphs.

Substance	Stainless Steel %	Tool Steel %
Iron	74	94
Chromium	18	0
Nickel	8	1
Carbon	0	1
Other	0	4

When you're done, use the answer key to check and revise your work.

Write *S* if the photo and caption describe a mixture that is a solution.
Write *M* if they describe a mixture that is NOT a solution.

_____ (1) When you combine ingredients to make a sandwich, each ingredient keeps its identity. You could easily separate them.

_____ (2) Soft drinks are made by dissolving a gas and other ingredients in water. The dissolved particles are much too small to be seen.

_____ (3) The solid bits of orange pulp do not dissolve in the liquid. Because the pulp particles are large, they will eventually settle out.

_____ (4) Particles of several different gases make up air. Air on one side of a room is just like the air on the other side.

Summarize

Fill in the missing words to tell how to separate mixtures.

To sort the items in your junk drawer, you'd use observable (5) _____

such as size, color, shape, and (6) _____ attraction. But how would you separate

table sugar, sand, and pebbles? Because the pebbles are (7) _____

than the grains of sugar and sand, you could remove them using a sieve, or mesh (8) _____.

You could then add water and shake until the sugar (9) _____.

If you poured this mixture through a coffee (10) _____ into a beaker, the

(11) _____ would be left on the filter, but the sugar solution would pass

through. Adding heat would cause the water to (12) _____ , leaving solid sugar

behind.

Answer Key: 1. M 2. S 3. M 4. S 5. properties 6. magnetic 7. larger 8. screen 9. dissolves 10. filter 11. sand 12. evaporate or boil

Name _____

Word Play

1 Complete the crossword puzzle. Use the words in the box if you need help.

Across

1. Another name for a mesh screen
4. Type of change that doesn't involve the formation of a new kind of matter
5. Tool that attracts objects that contain iron
6. What an object that is less dense than water will do when placed in water
7. Object used to separate very small particles from a mixture
8. The amount of matter in a given volume

Down

1. A physical property; for example, round, square, rectangular, or flat
2. Process by which a liquid changes slowly to a gas
3. Kind of mixture that has the same composition throughout
5. A combination of two or more substances that keep their individual identities

| sieve | shape | evaporation | solution* | physical |
| magnet | mixture* | float | filter | density |

* Key Lesson Vocabulary

Apply Concepts

2 Circle the substances below that are solutions.

brass trumpet

trail mix

shells

sandwich

drink from a mix

3 Make a list of solid mixtures in your classroom.

_____   _____

_____   _____

_____   _____

_____   _____

_____   _____

4 Draw and label a diagram to show how you would separate each mixture.

5 Answer these questions in terms of what you know about mixtures.

a. How would changing the proportions of substances in an alloy change its properties?

_____

_____

_____

b. Why is it possible to use physical properties to separate a mixture?

_____

_____

c. Recycling help us conserve resources. Draw a line connecting each piece of garbage in a mixed bag with the bin it should be thrown in.

(milk jug)   (soup can)   (envelope)   (cardboard box)

(soda can)   (water bottle)   (broken pencil)

[Garbage]   [Plastic]   [Aluminum and Tin]   [Paper]

6  Salt seems to disappear when it is poured into water. Use the terms *mixture, solution,* and *dissolve* to explain what happens.

_____

_____

_____

7 Tell how you would use one or more of these tools to separate the mixtures.

Rice from dried soup mix

_____

_____

_____

_____

_____

Salt from saltwater

_____

_____

_____

_____

_____

Nails from gravel

_____

_____

_____

_____

_____

8 Tell what would happen if you stirred each of these cups faster.

_____   _____

_____   _____

_____   _____

_____   _____

_____   _____

Water and Sugar

Water and Sand

Share what you have learned about mixtures with your family. With a family member, identify examples of mixtures at mealtime, or in places in your home.

Take It Home!

300

Name _____

Essential Question

How Do Substances Change When They Form a Solution?

Set a Purpose

What will you learn from this investigation?

_____

_____

_____

Think About the Procedure

What physical properties will you observe during the investigation?

_____

_____

_____

Making detailed observations and accurate measuring are important science skills. Why don't you have to subtract the mass of the beaker to find out whether the mass of the liquid-solid mixture has changed?

_____

_____

_____

Record Your Data

Record your data for the first half of the investigation in the table below. Then use a computer to draw a table to record your data for the investigation's second half.

Liquid-Solid Mixture		
Substance	**Volume (mL)**	**Mass (g)**
water		
powdered drink mix		
water and powdered drink mix		

Draw Conclusions

How did the appearance of the water, alcohol, and powdered drink mix change when they formed a solution?

_____

_____

_____

_____

_____

_____

_____

_____

_____

_____

_____

Were there any observable changes in the mass or volume of the substances after they formed a solution? Explain.

_____

_____

_____

_____

_____

Analyze and Extend

1. How do you know when a solution forms? How could you prove that the powdered drink mix and the alcohol are still present in the solution?

    _____

    _____

    _____

2. Matter is made of tiny particles. Use indirect (inferred) evidence to explain any changes in the volume of the water-alcohol solution.

    _____

    _____

    _____

    _____

3. Would you classify powdered drink mix as soluble or insoluble in water? What about alcohol? Explain.

    _____

    _____

    _____

4. Think of other questions you would like to ask about what happens to properties when a substance dissolves.

    _____

    _____

    _____

    _____

Meet the Atomic All-Stars

Marie Curie

Marie Curie worked as a scientist in France. She discovered that some elements are radioactive. That means energy radiates, or comes out, of the elements. In 1903, Marie Curie became the first woman ever to win a Nobel Prize. In 1911, she won another. She is one of the most famous female scientists of all time.

In some of Marie Curie's early work on radioactivity, she studied this type of uranium mineral, known as pitchblende.

Inés Triay

Inés Triay is a scientist who works with radioactive materials, too. She works to clean up dangerous wastes that are produced when radioactive elements are used in nuclear power plants. In 2009, President Barack Obama assigned Triay to an important job in the U.S. Department of Energy. She is head of the team that properly disposes of nuclear waste.

The symbol on this sign warns of radioactivity that could be dangerous to your health.

Complete a Timeline

Fill in the boxes with information about Marie Curie and Inés Triay. For each entry you add, draw a line to the correct location on the timeline.

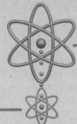

1898 Marie Curie discovers two new radioactive elements, called radium and plutonium.

1908 Hans Geiger invents a tool now called the "Geiger counter." It measures radioactivity.

1896 Marie Curie's teacher, Henri Becquerel, first discovers radioactivity.

_____

_____

_____

_____

1951 For the first time, electricity is generated using radioactive elements.

1934 Marie Curie dies from a disease caused by radiation. No one knew that radioactivity can be very bad for human health.

_____

_____

_____

_____

1979 Two scientists, Godfrey Hounsfield and Allan McLeod Cormack, win the Nobel Prize in Medicine for the C.T. scan machine. It uses small amounts of radiation and takes pictures of the inside of the human body.

How did Marie Curie's work lead to improved health care?

_____

_____

_____

_____

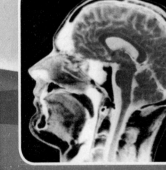

Name _____

Vocabulary Review

Use the terms in the box to complete the sentences.

> chemical changes
> conservation of
>   mass
> gas
> liquid
> matter
> mixture
> physical changes
> solution

1. Matter that has a definite volume but no definite shape is

   a(n) _____.

2. A mixture that has the same composition throughout is called

   a(n) _____.

3. Changes in one or more substances that form new and different

   substances are called _____.

4. Anything that has mass and takes up space is

   called _____.

5. Changes in which the form or shape of a substance changes
   but the substance still has the same chemical makeup are

   called _____.

6. Matter without a definite volume or shape is called

   a(n) _____.

7. The law that states that matter cannot be made or destroyed

   is called the law of _____.

8. A combination of two or more different substances in
   which the substances keep their identities is called

   a(n) _____.

Science Concepts

Fill in the letter of the choice that best answers the question.

9. Which graph shows how the volume of a gas changes as the temperature of the gas increases?

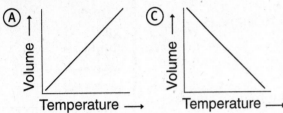

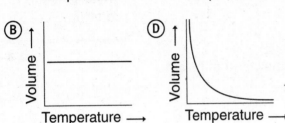

10. Which of the following is a physical property of matter?

Ⓐ the ability to burn

Ⓑ the ability to rust

Ⓒ the ability to decay

Ⓓ the ability to dissolve

11. Which of the following physical changes is not an example of a change in state?

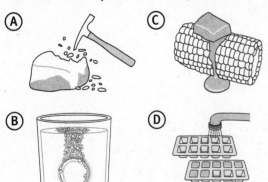

12. Carlo mixes sand, salt, and iron filings. What tools could Carlo use to separate the mixture?

Ⓐ a magnet and a beaker of water

Ⓑ a thermometer and a hot plate

Ⓒ a balance and a hand lens

Ⓓ a sieve and a pair of tweezers

13. Nadia has a mixture of oil and water. She wants to remove most of the oil from the mixture. How can she do this?

Ⓐ use a magnet to attract the oil

Ⓑ pour the mixture through a sieve

Ⓒ stir the mixture until the oil dissolves

Ⓓ let the oil float to the top and skim it off

14. An engineer is making a mixture of metals to make steel for the frame of a building. Which two properties should the steel have?

Ⓐ shiny and easily shaped

Ⓑ strong and slightly flexible

Ⓒ shiny and magnetic

Ⓓ magnetic and resistant to rust

15. This diagram shows what happens when water changes state.

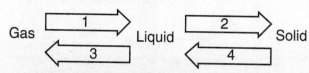

Which statement is true?

Ⓐ Temperature increases in Step 1 and Step 2.

Ⓑ The energy of the molecules decreases in Steps 3 and 4.

Ⓒ The mass of the water stays the same between any two steps.

Ⓓ The mass of the water changes between any two steps.

16. Daniel puts water, sugar, and yeast into a balloon. He knows that yeast will react with sugar and water. He measures the mass of the balloon and its contents. He puts the balloon in a warm place for two hours. Then he measures the mass again. He repeats his experiment three times to get more data. Predict how the mass of the balloon will change.

Ⓐ It will increase.

Ⓑ It will decrease.

Ⓒ It will stay the same.

Ⓓ It has no mass.

17. Which of these correctly describes how water changes state?

Ⓐ Liquid water melts to form ice.

Ⓑ Liquid water boils to form water vapor.

Ⓒ Ice condenses to form liquid water.

Ⓓ Water vapor melts to form liquid water.

18. Peter places six balls of modeling clay on one side of a balance. He places plastic cubes on the other side. It takes 41 plastic cubes to balance the modeling clay. He then removes the clay, shapes it into a dinosaur, and puts it back on the balance. How many cubes will Peter most likely need to balance the dinosaur?

Ⓐ 35 cubes

Ⓑ 38 cubes

Ⓒ 41 cubes

Ⓓ 47 cubes

19. Lia dissolves sugar in water. She says that the sugar must have changed into another substance because it disappears. Which of the following could you use to support or contradict Lia's claim?

Ⓐ Add sugar in different amounts of water to see if the same thing happens.

Ⓑ Add different amounts of sugar to water to see if it all disappears.

Ⓒ Let the water evaporate to show that the sugar is still present.

Ⓓ Heat the sugar-water mixture to see if it produces bubbles.

20. The rate at which a solid dissolves in a liquid depends on many factors. Which of these properties does not affect the rate at which a solid dissolves?

Ⓐ temperature of the liquid

Ⓑ the size of the solid

Ⓒ whether or not the liquid is stirred

Ⓓ the color of the solid

Apply Inquiry and Review the Big Idea

Write the answer to these questions.

21. Kym tested how quickly 10 g of sugar dissolved in 1 L of water at different temperatures. A graph of her results is shown here. What were Kym's variables? Based on her graph, do you think she correctly labeled her beakers of water? Why or why not?

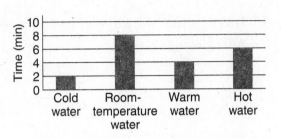

_____

_____

_____

22. Frank was learning about states of matter in science class. He made some drawings but forgot to label them. His drawings are shown below.

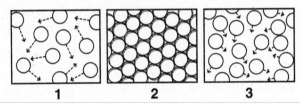

Describe what each of Frank's drawings shows.

_____

_____

_____

23. Mia is having a picnic. She will provide orange juice, unsweetened tea, and sodas. She plans to make peanut butter sandwiches and trail mix. She will also make some gelatin with bananas in it. Which picnic items are mixtures? Which are solutions? Explain your choices.

_____

_____

_____

_____

Forms of Energy

Big Idea

Energy exists in many forms that can be transferred between objects.

OHIO 4.PS.2, 4.SIA.4, 4.SIA.5, 4.SIA.6

I Wonder Why

This surfer lets many waves go by him before choosing one to ride. Why?
Turn the page to find out.

Here's Why The best waves have a lot of energy. Surfers use the energy from these waves to get a nice, long ride to shore.

In this unit, you will explore the Big Idea, the Essential Questions, and the Investigations on the Inquiry Flipchart.

Levels of Inquiry Key ■ DIRECTED ■ GUIDED ■ INDEPENDENT

Track Your Progress

Big Idea Energy exists in many forms that can be transferred between objects.

Essential Questions

Now I Get the Big Idea!

Science Notebook

Before you begin each lesson, be sure to write your thoughts about the Essential Question.

OHIO **4.PS.2** Energy can be transformed from one form to another or can be transferred from one location to another.

Lesson **1**

Essential Question

What Are Some Forms of Energy?

Engage Your Brain!

Find the answer to the following question in this lesson and record it here.

How does this person use energy to ride the river's rapids?

_____

_____

_____

_____

Active Reading

Lesson Vocabulary

List the terms. As you learn about each one, make notes in the Interactive Glossary.

_____ _____

_____ _____

_____ _____

_____ _____

Main Idea and Details

In this lesson, you'll read about different kinds of energy. Active readers look for main ideas before they read to give their reading a purpose. Often, the headings in a lesson state the main ideas. Preview the headings in this lesson to give your reading a purpose.

What Is Energy?

All the lights in your house need energy. So do the refrigerator and washing machine. Can you name three other things in your home or school that use energy?

Active Reading As you read these two pages, find and underline a definition of *energy*. Then circle two sources of energy.

What do you and a car have in common? You both need energy. Gasoline is the car's source of energy. This car won't go anywhere if it runs out of gas.

▶ Draw lines to match each item on the left with its source of energy.

Name something that uses electricity as a source of energy.

_____

_____

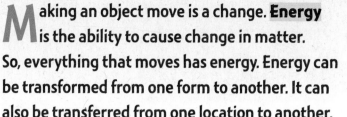

Making an object move is a change. **Energy** is the ability to cause change in matter. So, everything that moves has energy. Energy can be transformed from one form to another. It can also be transferred from one location to another.

Where does energy come from? You can see some sources of energy on these pages.

Where does this toy get its energy?

_____

_____

This man needs energy to run. Where do you think he gets it? Runners eat healthful foods such as trail mix so they will have plenty of energy.

Get Moving!

Have you ever been on a roller coaster? When roller coaster cars climb a hill, they seem to stop at the top for just a moment. Then they speed down to the bottom. How does energy make this happen?

Active Reading As you read these two pages, find and underline the definition of *mechanical energy*. Then draw circles around the two parts of mechanical energy.

Something in motion, such as the girl on the pogo stick, has kinetic energy. **Kinetic energy** is the energy of motion. Something at the top of a hill, such as a roller coaster car, has potential energy. **Potential energy** is the energy something has because of its position or condition. **Mechanical energy** is the total potential energy and kinetic energy of an object.

As the roller coaster cars climb to the top of a hill, they gain potential energy. The higher the cars go, the more potential energy they have. As the cars go down a hill, their potential energy decreases because it changes to kinetic energy. The roller coaster cars have more kinetic energy when they move faster. At each point along the ride, the mechanical energy of the cars is the sum of their potential and kinetic energies.

The girl pushes the pogo stick's spring down. The spring now has potential energy. When the spring spreads out, the pogo stick goes up and has kinetic energy.

This roller coaster goes fast because of mechanical energy. That's good, because a slow roller coaster isn't much fun!

© Houghton Mifflin Harcourt Publishing Company   (br) ©Jason Smalley/Wildscape/Alamy; (t) ©Corbis; (c) ©Jason Smalley/Wildscape/Alamy

▶ Everything in the left column has potential energy. Tell what happens when the potential energy of each object changes to kinetic energy. Then explain how to differentiate between potential energy and kinetic energy on the lines below.

A ball sits on top of a hill	
A person stretches back a rubber band	
Someone gets ready to throw a paper airplane	

_____

_____

_____

_____

_____

Flash and Boom!

You see lightning flash across the sky. You hear a boom so loud it makes your heart pound. These are two forms of energy.

Light energy is made and used in different ways. Light is a form of energy that can travel through space. Plants use light from the sun to make food. The same energy from the sun allows us to see. Some light allows us to see colors. Another source of light energy is electricity. If we couldn't use electricity to produce light energy, it would be hard to work or play at night.

Another form of energy is sound. Sound is made when something moves back and forth. This back-and-forth motion is called *vibration*. Sound can move through gases, liquids, and solids. Sound cannot move through space, as light can. We cannot see sound, but we can hear it. Sound is described in different ways. *Pitch* describes how high or how low a sound is. Loud sounds have more energy than quiet sounds. Can you think of an example of a loud, high-pitched sound?

Do the Math!
Solve Real-World Problems

How far away was that lightning strike? As soon as you see a flash of lightning, count the seconds until you hear thunder. Then divide the number of seconds by 5. This number gives you the approximate distance in miles.

35 seconds _____

20 seconds _____

40 seconds _____

Lightning can be hotter than the surface of the sun. Lightning makes the air around it expand quickly. This expansion causes the boom of thunder.

► Describe how each member of this musical group produces sound. Write your answers in the spaces provided.

► How are light and sound alike? How are they different?

Energy at Home

Do you think you could do without energy for one day? Without chemical energy, you couldn't mow the lawn. Without electrical energy, you couldn't power your MP3 player.

Active Reading As you read these two pages, draw a circle around a use of chemical energy. Draw a box around a use of electrical energy.

Many things use chemical energy and electrical energy. **Chemical energy** is a form of energy than can be released by a chemical change. Chemical energy from food gives us energy. Most cars run on gasoline, a source of chemical energy. Have you ever warmed yourself by a campfire? Fire is the release of chemical energy.

Electrical energy is a form of energy that comes from electric current. Electrical energy provides the energy for most of the devices you use, such as computers and televisions. Anything plugged into a wall outlet uses electrical energy.

Where does electricity come from? In most cities, electricity is generated using the chemical energy released during the burning of fossil fuels such as coal and natural gas. The sun and wind can also be used to generate electricity.

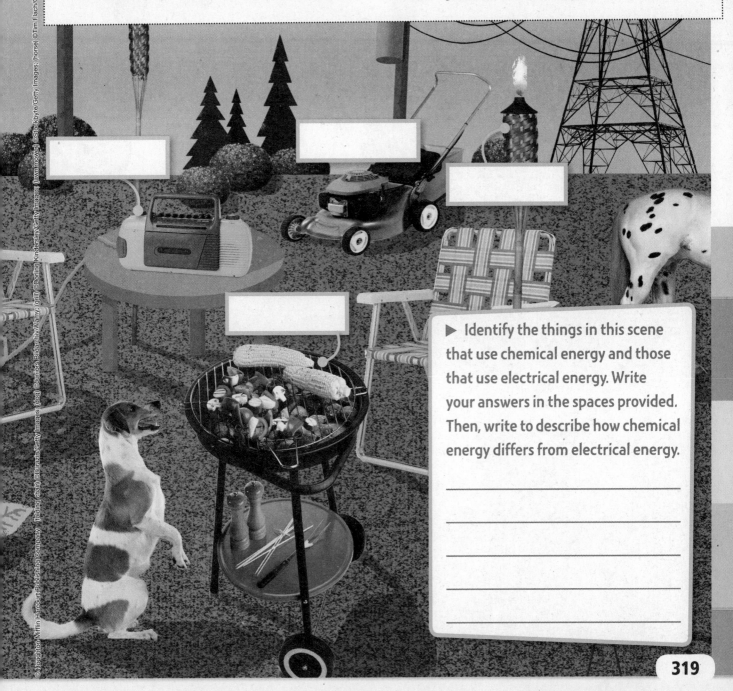

▶ Identify the things in this scene that use chemical energy and those that use electrical energy. Write your answers in the spaces provided. Then, write to describe how chemical energy differs from electrical energy.

_____

_____

_____

_____

_____

Some Like it Hot!

Rub your hands together quickly and then press them against your face. Your hands and face feel warm. Why?

Active Reading As you read these two pages, underline the definition of *thermal energy* and circle an example of it.

Cool hands become warm when rubbed together. A toaster oven makes freshly toasted bread feel hot. An ice sculpture melts. All these changes involve the transfer of heat.

You know that kinetic energy is the energy of motion. The particles that make up a substance are always moving. These moving particles make your rubbed hands or toast feel warm. **Thermal energy** is the total kinetic energy of the particles in a substance. The faster the particles in a substance move, the more thermal energy the substance has. Temperature is a measure of the average kinetic energy of the particles of an object.

Heat is energy that moves between objects at different temperatures. It moves from warmer objects to cooler objects. Many objects around us, such as a toaster or a campfire, give off heat.

Look at the picture of the sculptor. She is using a blowtorch on a piece of metal. As she does this, the particles in the metal being touched by the torch begin to vibrate faster and faster. The metal's thermal energy is transferred, or moved, along it. As the thermal energy moves, the metal becomes heated.

Differentiate Between Heat and Thermal Energy

Write to describe how heat and thermal energy differ.

_____

_____

_____

_____

_____

_____

_____

Particles in a solid vibrate, or move back and forth, quickly. As the metal is heated, the particles move faster, which causes heat to be felt.

Energy Can Change Forms

Can you read by the light of chemical energy? Can you use electrical energy to make something move? You can do both of these things, and more.

Active Reading As you read these two pages, draw a line under two examples of energy changing forms.

Chemical energy changes into light energy in a glow stick.

Energy can transform, or change, from one form to another. Electrical energy changes to light energy when you turn on a light switch. You may also feel the heat given off by some light bulbs. Chemical energy in gasoline changes to mechanical energy when a driver presses on the gas pedal to drive.

Glow sticks have a glass tube inside them. The glass tube has chemicals inside it. When you bend the glow stick, the tube breaks. The chemicals in the tube mix with other chemicals in the glow stick. When they mix, light energy is given off.

A remote control sends radio waves to the remote-controlled car. Radio waves are another form of energy, similar to light energy. The radio waves change to electrical energy to tell the motor what to do—start, stop, or go faster. The car also has batteries inside it. The batteries change chemical energy to electrical energy to move the car.

This plant transforms light energy from the sun into chemical energy for food.

Energy Changing Forms

Draw a picture to show another way energy can transform. Write a caption that describes how the two forms of energy in your picture differ.

_____

_____

Sum It Up!

When you're done, use the answer key to check and revise your work.

Use information in the summary to complete the graphic organizer.

Summarize

Energy is the ability to cause change in matter. Making an object move is a change. Kinetic energy is the energy of motion. Potential energy is the energy something has because of its position. The mechanical energy of an object is the sum of its kinetic and potential energies. Light energy enables plants to make food and helps us see. Sound energy is caused by a vibrating object. Thermal energy is the total kinetic energy of the particles in a substance. Heat is energy that moves between objects at different temperatures. Energy can be transformed from one form to another or can be transferred from place to place.

Cause   **Effect**

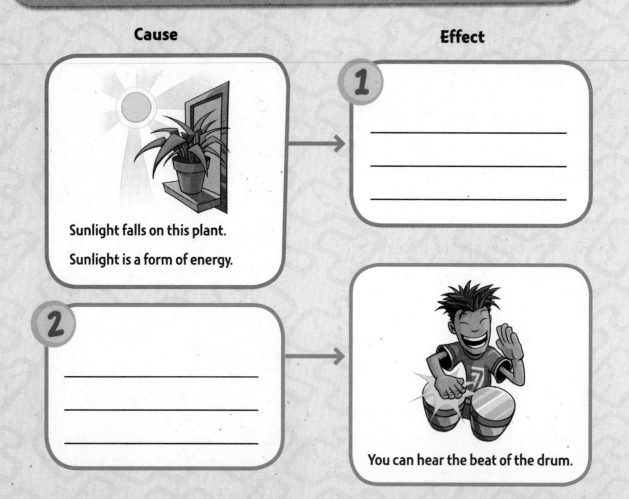

Sunlight falls on this plant.

Sunlight is a form of energy.

You can hear the beat of the drum.

Answer Key: 1. The plant captures light energy from the sun and uses it to make food. **2.** The drum heads vibrate to make sound.

Name _____

Word Play

1 Choose words from the box to complete the Forms of Energy word web.

Forms of Energy

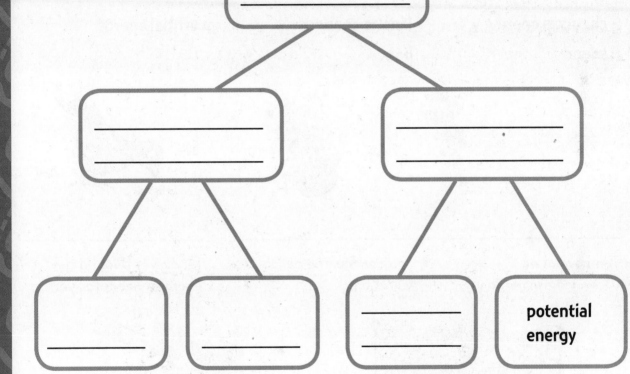

potential energy

| energy* | chemical energy* | mechanical energy* |
| kinetic energy * | food | gasoline |

* Key Lesson Vocabulary

Apply Concepts

2 How are kinetic energy and potential energy different?

_____

_____

_____

3 Use the words from the box to label each picture. Each term will be used once.

chemical energy	kinetic energy	potential energy
sound	light	

_____

This boy has an
up-and-down motion.

_____

You can feel the cello's
vibrations.

_____

Food gives this bird the
energy it needs to live.

_____

The roller coaster cars go to
the top of the hill and stop
for a moment.

_____

You can carry these glow
sticks in the dark so people
can see you.

4 A light bulb changes electrical energy into two other forms of energy. Identify these forms of energy and tell how they differ from one another.

_____

_____

_____

_____

5 Which of these objects has potential energy? How do you know?

_____

_____

_____

  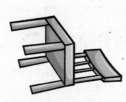 

6 Describe how sound energy is produced when you strike the top of a drum.

_____

_____

_____

_____

7 Many forms of energy are around us and within us. Write three paragraphs in the form of an e-mail to a friend or family member describing some ways you use energy in a typical day. Tell your reader where the energy comes from and how it transforms into other forms of energy.

_____

_____

_____

_____

_____

_____

_____

_____

_____

_____

_____

_____

_____

_____

_____

_____

Take It Home!

Share what you have learned about forms of energy with your family. With a family member, discuss how you use different forms of energy around your house.

Inquiry Flipchart page 39

Name _____

OHIO **4.PS.2** Energy can be transformed from one form to another or can be transferred from one location to another. **4.SIA.4** Use appropriate mathematics with data to construct reasonable explanations; **4.SIA.5** Communicate about observations, investigations and explanations; and **4.SIA.6** Review and ask questions about the observations and explanations of others.

Essential Question

Where Does Energy Come From?

Set a Purpose
What will you learn from this investigation?

_____

_____

_____

_____

_____

_____

Think About the Procedure
How does repeating Step 3 increase the reliability of your results?

_____

_____

_____

Record Your Data
In the space below, construct a simple table to record and organize your data. Be sure to use numerals.

Draw Conclusions

Analyze your data to construct a reasonable explanation. What did you observe in this investigation?

_____

_____

_____

Analyze and Extend

1. Why do you think the ball traveled farther when it was pushed by the fully compressed spring?

_____

_____

_____

2. When you compressed the spring, it gained potential energy. What was the source of this energy?

_____

_____

_____

3. What happened to the spring's potential energy when you let go of the ball?

_____

_____

_____

4. Scientists explain that the further a spring is compressed, the more potential energy it has. Analyze why squeezing the spring halfway affects the distance the ball travels.

_____

_____

_____

_____

_____

5. Did each group in the class have the same results from the investigation? Why or why not?

_____

_____

_____

_____

_____

6. Think of other questions you would like to ask about energy and how it changes form.

_____

_____

_____

_____

8 THINGS YOU SHOULD KNOW ABOUT Geothermal Technicians

1 *Geothermal* means heat from inside of Earth. Volcanoes, geysers, and hot springs are all sources of geothermal energy.

2 Geothermal energy is a *green energy*, which means that it is renewable, and it does not pollute the environment.

3 At geothermal energy stations, machines called *generators* convert geothermal energy into electrical energy.

4 Geothermal technicians may work inside, using computers to monitor energy production.

5 These technicians may work outside, installing and repairing equipment used to capture geothermal energy.

6 Geothermal technicians read blueprints and technical drawings as part of their work.

7 These technicians work with geothermal engineers to design and install geothermal systems.

8 To be a geothermal technician, you must complete high school as well as a special set of training courses.

Show What You Know About Geothermal Technicians

Answer the five questions about geothermal technicians.

1 What type of energy do these technicians work with, and where does it come from?

_____

_____

_____

_____

2 What do geothermal technicians do when they work outside?

_____

_____

_____

3 Why is geothermal energy green energy?

_____

_____

_____

4 What are some natural sources of geothermal energy?

_____

_____

_____

 5 Would you like to work as a geothermal technician? Why or why not?

_____

_____

_____

 Think About It!

Would you want to heat your home using geothermal energy? Explain.

_____

_____

_____

OHIO 4.PS.2 Energy can be transformed from one form to another or can be transferred from one location to another.

Essential Question

What Are Conductors and Insulators?

Engage Your Brain!

Find the answer to the following question in this lesson and record it here.

How can these dogs stay warm in such cold weather?

_____

_____

_____

_____

_____

Active Reading

Lesson Vocabulary

List the terms. As you learn about each one, make notes in the Interactive Glossary.

_____

_____

_____

_____

Cause and Effect

Some ideas in this lesson are connected by a cause-and-effect relationship. Why something happens is a cause. What happens as a result of something else is an effect. Active readers look for effects by asking themselves, What happened? They look for causes by asking, Why did it happen?

Go with the Flow...of Heat

A pan in the oven gets very hot. But if you pick it up with an oven mitt, your hand stays cool. Why?

Active Reading As you read these two pages, circle lesson vocabulary each time it is used.

Heat moves through some materials very easily. In the example above, heat from the oven moved easily into the pan. But heat from the pan did not pass through the oven mitt. A material that allows heat to move through it easily is called a **conductor**. Many heat conductors also conduct electricity well.

For the most part, solids are better conductors of heat than liquids or gases are. That's because the particles that make up a solid are packed closely together. They vibrate, but don't move apart much. Heat can move quickly from one particle to another.

Glass

Glass does not conduct heat well. If you pour boiling water into a metal bowl, the outside of the bowl quickly gets hot. A glass bowl gets warm more slowly.

Stone

Marble does not conduct heat as well as metals do. But it can still conduct heat away from your body. That's why marble feels cool when you touch it.

Metal

Metals are great heat conductors. Some metals conduct heat better than others do.

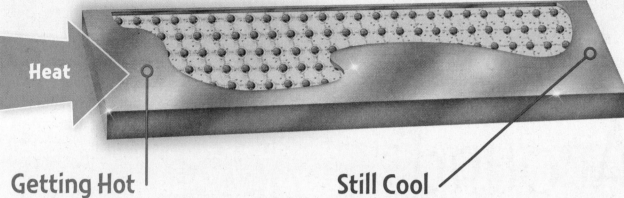

Heat

Getting Hot

This diagram shows the particles of a metal bar. The particles on this end are hot. This end was placed over a flame, but the other end wasn't.

Still Cool

The particles on this end aren't hot yet, but they will be soon. In metals, heat moves from particle to particle very easily.

▶ Imagine you touched the handles of all four spoons. Circle the spoon handle that would be the hottest. Then explain your choice.

_____

_____

_____

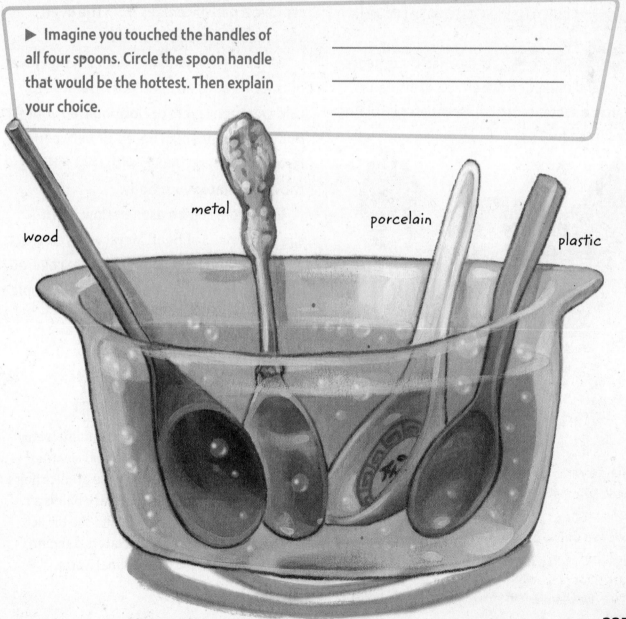

wood

metal

porcelain

plastic

Turn the Heat Around

Wearing gloves insulates your hands. The gloves trap heat near your skin.

Not all materials are conductors. Heat does not move easily—or at all—through some materials.

Active Reading As you read these pages, find and underline two effects of insulators. Circle a sentence that differentiates insulators from conductors.

Materials that do not conduct heat well are called **insulators**. Oven mitts are insulators. They are made of materials that are poor conductors of heat. When you remove a pan of cookies from the oven, your hands don't get burned.

Gases can be good insulators. A thin layer of trapped air is an excellent insulator. In cold weather, layers of clothing trap your body heat near you. There's air between the layers of clothing. Along with the clothing, the air insulates your body.

Insulators can be used to slow down the movement of heat. Metal wires conduct electricity and heat. Most wires are covered in rubber to insulate them and keep people safe from the electricity and heat.

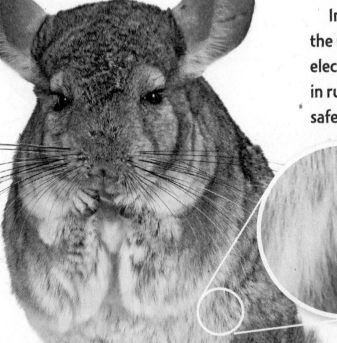

Hair as an Insulator

Most furry animals stay warm in cold weather. Fur is made of thick hairs. Around each hair is air. The air and the fur act as insulators, keeping the animal warm.

Why Does a Thermos Work?

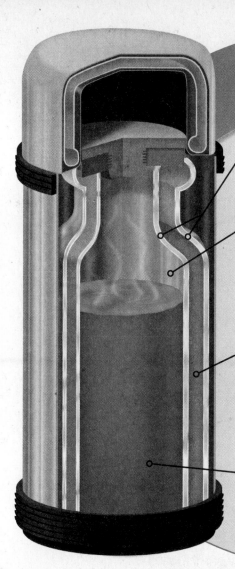

Glass lining
A layer of glass holds the tea. Glass does not conduct heat very well.

Reflection
Even in a vacuum, radiation can move energy. The facing sides of the layers are coated in silver, which act like a mirror. It reflects some heat back.

Vacuum
There is a vacuum between the inner and outer glass layers of the bottle. The vacuum keeps conduction or convection from taking place.

Still Hot
With the conduction, convection, and radiation slowed down, the tea stays hot for a long time!

▶ Although the straw house is not the sturdiest, a straw house can be well insulated. Why?

_____

_____

Heat Proofing a Home

All across the United States, people are trying to conserve, or save, energy. It's good for the environment, and it saves money. Heat proofing a home is one way that people can conserve energy.

When the weather is hot, you want to keep heat from coming into your home. When the weather is cold, you want to keep heat from leaving your home. It costs money to cool and heat a home! There are different ways to slow the flow of heat into or out of a house. Some things need to be done while the house is being built. Others can be done to an existing home. Insulating a home saves money. It also helps conserve energy.

Answer Key: 1. conductor 2. insulator 3. insulator 4. conductor 5. insulator 6. conduct 7. insulate 8. conduction, convection, and radiation 9. radiation

1 Insulation

Insulation is blown inside the walls of a house. Insulation keeps heat from traveling through to the attic.

2 glass panes

2 Windows

These windows have two panes of glass to limit conduction. They also have a coating that limits heat radiation.

3 Pipes

Hot pipes radiate heat from water into the air. Wrapping them keeps the heat from escaping.

4 Soil

Soil is a great insulator. Basements are usually cool, even in the summer.

Do the Math!

Solve Real-World Problems

The Ogburn family wants to heat proof their house. They can save about $800 a year by adding insulation. Wrapping the water pipes will save an additional $5 each month. Buying new, energy-efficient windows will save them about $2,000 every year.

1. How much money will wrapping the water pipes save the Ogburns in a year?

_____

2. About how much more money will replacing the windows save each year than wrapping the water pipes?

_____

3. Write an equation to calculate how much all three things will save the Ogburns in a year.

_____

Bonus!

If new windows cost $10,500, pipe insulation costs $100, and adding insulation costs $400, in how many years will the savings pay for the cost of these home improvements?

_____
_____
_____

Sum It Up!

When you're done, use the answer key to check and revise your work.

Write the vocabulary term that describes each material.

1

metal cube

_____

2

a knit hat

_____

3

rubber bands

_____

Draw a box around the correct answer or answers.

[4] Heat moves easily through it.	insulator	conductor	
[5] Heat does not move easily through it.	insulator	conductor	
[6] Solids often do this to heat.	insulate	conduct	
[7] A thin layer of trapped air can do this to heat.	insulate	conduct	
[8] Which forms of heat transfer do insulated bottles prevent?	conduction	convection	radiation
[9] Wrapping hot water pipes prevents which form of heat transfer?	conduction	convection	radiation

Answer Key: 1. conductor 2. conductor 3. insulator 4. insulator 5. conductor 6. insulate 7. insulate 8. conduction, convection, and radiation 9. radiation

Word Play

1 Use the clues to help you write the correct word in each row. Some boxes have been filled in for you.

A. ☐ I N ☐ ☐ ☐ ☐
B. I N ☐ ☐ ☐ ☐ ☐ ☐
C. I N ☐ ☐
D. ☐ ☐ ☐ C
E. ☐ ☐ ☐ C
F. ☐ ☐ ☐ M ☐
G. ☐ M ☐ ☐
H. ☐ M ☐ ☐
I. ☐ ☐ ☐ ☐ ☐ M

A. Some of them have two panes of glass.

B. It can be blown inside walls.

C. It slows the transfer of heat.

D. It's the opposite of answer C.

E. The silver layer of an insulated bottle does this to radiated heat.

F. Because of natural insulation, it's often the coolest part of a house.

G. It's an excellent conductor.

H. It does not conduct as well as metals do.

I. It makes conduction and convection impossible.

Apply Concepts

2 You are going to make a kitchen spoon. It will be used to stir hot liquids. Circle the material that will be warmest when you touch its handle.

cotton

metal

plastic

wood

3 Many people are building "green" houses, which use very little energy. Some of these houses are partially or completely underground. Why?

_____

_____

_____

4 How would you design a lunchbox that could keep hot food hot or cold food cold? Sketch a diagram of the box.

Take It Home!

Look around your kitchen with your family. Find two things that conduct heat and two things that are heat insulators.

342

OHIO **4.PS.2** Energy can be transformed from one form to another or can be transferred from one location to another. **4.SIA.5** Communicate about observations, investigations and explanations; and

Name _____

Essential Question

How Do Conductors and Insulators Differ?

Set a Purpose
What do you think you will learn from this experiment?

_____

_____

_____

_____

_____

State Your Hypothesis
Write your hypothesis, or testable statement.

_____

_____

_____

_____

_____

Think About the Procedure
What is the tested variable?

_____

_____

_____

_____

Which things must be the same in each setup?

_____

_____

_____

_____

_____

Record Your Observations

Use the space below to construct a chart to organize, examine, and evaluate the data you collected.

Draw Conclusions

Which material did heat move through more quickly?

_____

_____

Differentiate between conductors and insulators. Which material is a conductor? Which is an insulator? How do you know?

_____

_____

_____

_____

Analyze and Extend

1. On which knife did the butter melt faster? On that knife, which pat of butter melted faster?

_____

_____

_____

2. Write a hypothesis about which knife would lose heat faster. Then plan an experiment to test your hypothesis.

_____

_____

_____

_____

_____

_____

_____

3. What other materials could you test this way?

_____

_____

_____

4. What other questions would you like to ask about conductors and insulators?

_____

_____

_____

OHIO **4.PS.2** Energy can be transformed from one form to another or can be transferred from one location to another. **4.SIA.5** Communicate about observations, investigations and explanations; and

How It Works:
Piezoelectricity

This gas lantern has a tool that changes kinetic energy from an impact into electrical energy. Electrical energy produced this way is called *piezoelectricity*, or electricity from pressure!

Quartz is a piezoelectric material.

Gas Chamber

You don't need a match to light this lantern! It has a piezoelectric igniter. The igniter is a tool made up of a small, spring-loaded bar and a piezoelectric material.

Piezoelectric Igniter

When this red button is pushed, the bar strikes, or impacts, the piezoelectric material.

Piezoelectric Circuit

Force

Electric Spark

Piezoelectric Material

Force

The bar's force squeezes the piezoelectric material, producing electric charges that flow as an electric current. Inside the lantern's gas chamber, the current jumps between two conductors, causing an electric spark. The spark ignites the gas. *Voilà!* Light and heat are produced.

Troubleshooting

Why might a lantern not light up when a piezo igniter is pushed?

_____

_____

_____

These solar cells transform, or change, solar energy into electrical energy. Electrical energy is changed into heat and light inside the home.

Show How It Works

The gas lantern shows some ways that energy changes take place. Kinetic energy changes into electrical energy, which ignites the natural gas. Chemical energy stored in the gas changes into heat and light. Identify different forms of energy and their sources in your classroom or home. In the space below, draw and describe how energy from one of these sources is transformed.

Suppose that popcorn kernels are being cooked over a campfire. Differentiate between the forms of energy being used and how they are being transformed.

Build On It!

Rise to the engineering design challenge—complete **Design It: Solar Water Heater** on the Inquiry Flipchart.

Name _____

Vocabulary Review

Use the terms in the box to complete the sentences.

> conductor
> chemical energy
> energy
> heat
> insulator
> kinetic energy
> mechanical energy
> potential energy

1. The energy of motion is _____.

2. The energy something has because of its position or condition is _____.

3. The energy that moves between objects of different temperatures is _____.

4. The ability to cause a change in matter is _____.

5. The total potential energy and kinetic energy of an object is _____.

6. A form of energy that can be released by a chemical change is _____.

7. A material that allows heat to move through it easily is a(n) _____.

8. A material that does not let heat move through it easily is a(n) _____.

Science Concepts

Fill in the letter of the choice that best answers the question.

9. When turned on, the radio display lights up and you hear sound. How does light energy differ from sound energy?

   (A) Light energy is measured by pitch.

   (B) Light energy is made from vibrations.

   (C) Light energy can travel through space.

   (D) Light energy can only be found during the day.

10. Niko jumps on a trampoline. The pictures below show him at different points during jumping.

1   2   3   4

   At which point does Niko have the most potential energy?

   (A) Point 1   (C) Point 3

   (B) Point 2   (D) Point 4

11. Energy can change form. Which picture shows electrical energy changing into heat energy?

(A)

(C)

(B)

(D)

12. Ang has a pogo stick like the one shown at right. When he jumps on it, the spring squeezes toward the ground and then moves back to its starting position.

   The potential and kinetic energies of the spring are forms of which type of energy?

   (A) chemical energy

   (B) electrical energy

   (C) magnetic energy

   (D) mechanical energy

13. Objects that vibrate make energy. Which type of energy results from vibrations that travel through the air?

   (A) sound   (C) potential

   (B) chemical   (D) electrical

14. Rachel tests how quickly different materials change temperature. She heats each one the same way and constructs a table to examine and evaluate her data.

Material	Starting Temperature (°C)	Temperature After Five Minutes (°C)
1	19	37
2	19	48
3	19	31
4	19	42

   Which material is the best insulator?

   (A) Material 1   (C) Material 3

   (B) Material 2   (D) Material 4

15. Which type of energy change takes place as a car burns fuel to race down a track?

Ⓐ electrical energy to light energy

Ⓑ kinetic energy to potential energy

Ⓒ chemical energy to kinetic energy

Ⓓ mechanical energy to kinetic energy

16. Kendra is jumping rope. What happens when she twirls the jump rope?

Ⓐ She gives it thermal energy.

Ⓑ She gives it chemical energy

Ⓒ She gives it kinetic energy.

Ⓓ She gives it electrical energy.

17. Nancy says that mechanical energy enables her clothes dryer to operate. Which form of energy listed below can Nancy use to correct her statement?

Ⓐ heat energy

Ⓑ electrical energy

Ⓒ thermal energy

Ⓓ chemical energy

18. A scientist measures the average kinetic energy of the particles of an object. What is he measuring?

Ⓐ heat

Ⓑ current

Ⓒ insulation

Ⓓ temperature

19. Jaden has many things on his desk at home as shown in the picture below.

Which material was most likely used because it is a good insulator?

Ⓐ copper used for the coins

Ⓑ metal used for the computer

Ⓒ steel used for the paper clips

Ⓓ rubber used for the lamp cord

20. This picture shows a pot of water heating on a stovetop.

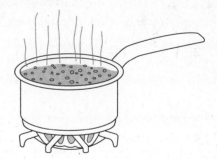

Which statement explains what happens to the water in the pot?

Ⓐ The water temperature decreases inside the pot.

Ⓑ The water will freeze when enough heat is added.

Ⓒ Heat is transferred from the water in the pot to the burner.

Ⓓ Heat is transferred from the burner to the pot and then to the water.

Apply Inquiry and Review the Big Idea

Write the answers to these questions.

21. Louis knows there are many forms of energy that can be observed in different systems. Study the picture to the right. Describe the different forms of energy present.

_____

_____

_____

_____

22. Long underwear that is worn in extreme cold is called thermal underwear. From what you know about how heat moves, how do you think this underwear, as well as other clothing, helps keep people warm?

_____

_____

_____

23. Misa puts thermometers in four boxes that are exactly alike. She covers each box with a top made of a different material. Then, Misa leaves the boxes outside on a hot, sunny day. Explain which thermometer should show the highest temperature after two hours.

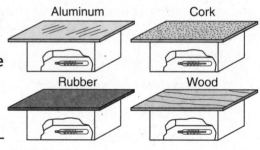

_____

_____

_____

24. Mr. Lewis wants to put insulation around the pipes in his basement to keep heat from escaping. He measures 6 m of pipe in one area and 5 m of pipe in another area. If insulation costs $9.00 per meter, how much will Mr. Lewis spend for the cost of insulation? _____.

Electricity

Big Idea

Electric currents and magnets can be used for many purposes.

OHIO 4.PS.2, 4.SIA.1, 4.SIA.5

I Wonder Why

Electrical energy is important to modern society. How does electricity reach homes and businesses? *Turn the page to find out.*

Here's Why Generating stations transform potential and kinetic energy into electrical energy. Electrical energy travels over the electric grid. This grid is a system of steel towers, conductors, and insulators that carries electricity from generating stations to our homes and businesses.

In this unit, you will explore the Big Idea, the Essential Questions, and the Investigations on the Inquiry Flipchart.

Levels of Inquiry Key ■ DIRECTED · ■ **GUIDED** ■ INDEPENDENT

Track Your Progress

Big Idea Electric currents and magnets can be used for many purposes.

Essential Questions

Now I Get the Big Idea!

Science Notebook

Before you begin each lesson, be sure to write your thoughts about the Essential Question.

OHIO **4.PS.2** Energy can be transformed from one form to another or can be transferred from one location to another.

Lesson **1**

Essential Question

What Is Electricity?

Engage Your Brain!

Find the answer to the following question in this lesson and record it here.

How does electricity get from a generating station to homes and businesses?

_____

_____

_____

_____

Active Reading

Lesson Vocabulary
List the terms. As you learn about each one, make notes in the Interactive Glossary.

_____

_____

_____

Main Idea and Details
In this lesson, you'll read about electricity. Active readers look for main ideas before they read to give their reading a purpose. Often, the headings in a lesson state the main ideas. Preview the headings in this lesson to give your reading a purpose.

All About Electricity

Batteries, like the one in this cordless drill, contain stored energy that is turned into electricity.

Think about how you use electricity every day. What kind of things would be hard to do if you didn't have electricity?

Active Reading As you read these two pages, find and underline the definition of *electricity*.

Electricity is more than just a plug in a wall socket. **Electricity** is a form of energy. We use it in our homes and in businesses to do many things. Electricity allows us to warm and cool our homes. It allows us to heat water for showers and to clean our clothes. We use it to cook food and to keep food cold to preserve it.

Businesses such as shopping malls and schools use electricity for heating, cooling, and light. They use it to run computers and copy machines. Businesses use electricity to keep offices clean and to provide services to their customers. Many stores sell devices, such as smartphones and MP3 players, that need electricity to operate.

Electricity is used by cars, trucks, and trains.

Electricity isn't just found in your home. You can see it in nature, too. Lightning is a giant electrical spark, or discharge, produced by a thunderstorm.

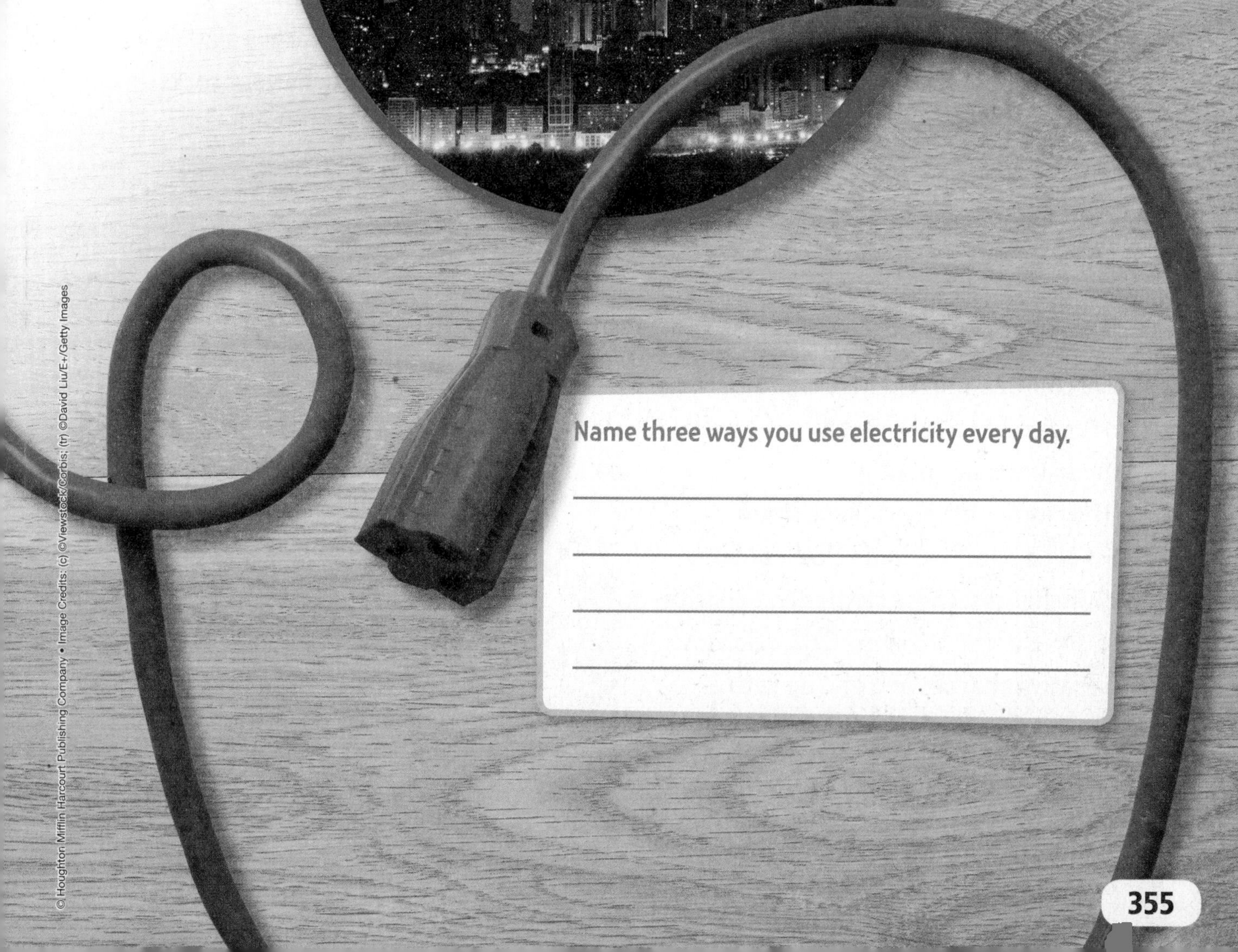

Name three ways you use electricity every day.

_____

_____

_____

_____

So Static

Have you ever pulled your sweater out of the clothes dryer and found your socks stuck to it? What causes that?

The reason your socks stick to your sweater is static electricity. **Static electricity** is an electrical charge that builds up on an object. Static electricity results from invisible changes in matter.

Before you put socks and a sweater in a dryer, they don't stick together. The socks and the sweater have the same number of positive charges and negative charges. The charges cancel each other out, so the socks and the sweater are neutral.

In the clothes dryer, your socks rub against other clothes. Some clothes gain negative charges. These clothes end up with a negative electrical charge. Other clothes lose negative charges and end up with a positive electrical charge.

Objects with opposite charges attract, or pull, each other. That's why your socks stick to your sweater. Objects with the same charge repel, or push away, each other.

Charged objects tend to become neutral again. It can happen quickly, for example during the crackle of tiny sparks between a charged sweater and a sock. It can happen slowly as charges move into the air from a balloon or comb.

Objects with the same charge repel each other. Objects with opposite charges attract each other.

The negatively charged comb picks up the positively charged paper. Electrically charged objects can attract or repel each other from a distance.

Suppose a piece of hair that has a positive charge comes close to a comb that has a negative charge. Would the objects attract or repel each other?

_____

_____

Static electricity can cause your hair to stand on end!

Get with the Flow

What kind of electricity makes your television work and your lights turn on?

Active Reading As you read these two pages, find and underline two facts about current electricity.

Another form of electricity is current electricity. **Current electricity** is a steady stream of charges. In current electricity, an electric current moves through a material, such as a copper wire. The path an electric current follows is a *circuit*. Look at the picture of the circuit to see how an electric current moves.

We use current electricity for cooking food, lighting a room, and producing sound. How does current electricity get to our homes?

A generating station produces a flow of electric charges. The station then sends the current along wires to homes and businesses, where people use it to run machines and lights. The wires may be on poles or buried below ground.

An electric current follows a circuit. When a circuit is working, charges flow around it without starting or stopping. For any electrical machine to work, the circuit must be complete, or closed.

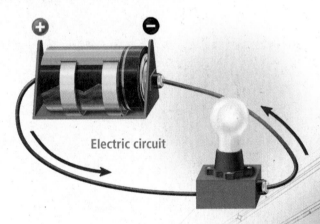

Electric circuit

Wires from this generating station connect to the wall sockets in homes.

Explain how current electricity moves from a generating station to your home.

_____

_____

_____

Ingenious Electricity

You know how electricity helps us do everyday things. How is electricity being used in new technology?

When you get older, instead of a gasoline station, you may need a place to plug in your car! Electric cars have motors that use batteries instead of gasoline. Scientists are working on ways to make electric cars better. At The Ohio State University, professors and students are working on electric cars that are much faster than regular cars! The Venturi Buckeye Bullet can travel in a straight line at speeds over 495 km/h (about 300 mph).

Electric companies are working on ways to help customers conserve electricity with the help of . . . electricity! One electric company in Ohio is testing "smart" meters that customers use to track their energy needs. The meters show how much electricity a customer uses during a month. The information on the meter can be shared with the electric company.

Electricity can also be generated in other ways. Some people install solar panels on the roof of their home. The panels convert energy from the sun into electricity.

The new version of the Venturi Buckeye Bullet being developed at The Ohio State University with Venturi engineers will be faster than most regular cars.

Do the Math!
Solve Real-World Problems

Read the paragraph, and answer the questions.

Some of the exhibits at the Great Lakes Science Center in Cleveland help power the center. The solar panel display can produce about 31 kilowatts of energy—enough to light the center for an hour. The wind turbine at the center can produce up to 225 kilowatts if the wind is blowing fast enough!

How many kilowatts would it take to light the center for three hours? Write an equation.

_____

The wind turbine can produce up to 225 kilowatts. For how many hours could this light the center? Round your answer to the nearest tenths place.

_____

You can use electricity to conserve energy in your home. Smartphones can control some kinds of thermostats. This allows you to have more control over how energy is being used.

Solar energy often is used to heat swimming pools. Small wind turbines can be installed in a front yard or on a roof. Wind energy moves the turbine, which powers a generator. The generator turns energy into electricity.

Wind turbines make electricity for this home.

When you're done, use the answer key to check and revise your work.

Draw a line to match the words in Column A to their definitions in Column B.

Column A

(1) static electricity

(2) circuit

(3) current electricity

Column B

a. An electrical charge that builds up on an object

b. A steady stream of charges

c. A path along which electric charges flow

Summarize

Fill in the missing words to tell about electricity.

Electricity is a form of (4) _____ we use to do many things. We use it to

warm and cool our homes and to prepare food. Static electricity is an electrical (5) _____

that builds up on an object. Objects with the (6) _____ charge move

away from each other. Objects with (7) _____ charges pull together.

Another form of electricity is current electricity. In current electricity, an (8) _____

moves through a material such as a copper wire. We use current electricity for cooking food,

lighting a room, and producing sound.

Answer Key: 1. a, 2. c, 3. b, 4. energy, 5. charge, 6. same, 7. opposite, 8. electric current

Name _____

Word Play

1 Look at the picture and the word clues. Write the answer to each clue on the blanks.

1.

$\underline{\ }\ \underline{\ }\ \underline{\ }\ \underline{\ }\ \underline{\ }\ \underline{\ }$
$\overset{\bigcirc}{\underset{1}{\ }}\ \underline{\ }\ \underline{\ }\ \underline{\ }\ \underline{\ }\ \underline{\ }$

makes socks stick together.

2.

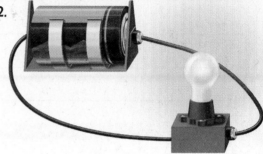

An electric current follows a

$\underline{\ }\ \overset{\bigcirc}{\underset{2}{\ }}\ \underline{\ }\ \underline{\ }\ \underline{\ }\ \overset{\bigcirc}{\underset{3}{\ }}$.

3.

Two objects with

$\overset{\bigcirc}{\underset{4}{\ }}\ \underline{\ }\ \overset{\bigcirc}{\underset{5}{\ }}\ \underline{\ }\ \underline{\ }\ \underline{\ }\ \underline{\ }$ — charges

repel each other.

4.

We use current electricity to

$\underline{\ }\ \underline{\ }\ \underline{\ }\ \overset{\bigcirc}{\underset{6}{\ }}\ \underline{\ }$ our homes.

Look at the letters in the circles. Match the letter with the number below each space to solve the riddle.

Where can we see electricity in nature? We can see it in

$\underline{\ }\ \underline{\ }\ \underline{\ }\ \underline{\ }\ \underline{\ }\ \underline{\ }\ \underline{\ }\ \underline{\ }\ \underline{\ }$.
$\ \ \ 1\ \ \ 2\ \ \ 5\ \ \ 6\ \ \ 3\ \ \ 4\ \ \ 2\ \ \ 4\ \ \ 5$

Apply Concepts

2 Explain why the clothes are sticking together.

_____

_____

_____

_____

_____

_____

3 Describe how an electric current moves through a circuit.

_____

_____

_____

_____

_____

4 How are static electricity and current electricity alike? How are they different?

_____

_____

_____

_____

_____

Name ______________________________

5 **Fill in the blanks to complete the sequence graphic organizer.**

A generating station produces a flow of charges.

↓

____

____

↓

____

____

6 **Name an example of how electricity can help conserve energy.**

____

____

____

____

____

____

____

____

____

7 Draw a line from each picture to its description.

static electricity	circuit	generating station current

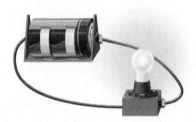

8 Suppose the generating station around where you live couldn't produce current electricity for your neighborhood. What are some other ways people can produce electricity at home?

_____

_____

_____

_____

_____

_____

Take It Home! Discuss with your family what you have learned about electricity. Walk around your home, and point out examples of electricity. Identify the kinds of electricity you point out.

Inquiry Flipchart page 44

OHIO **4.PS.2** Energy can be transformed from one form to another or can be transferred from one location to another. **4.SIA.5** Communicate about observations, investigations and explanations; and

Name _____

Essential Question

How Do Electric Charges Interact?

Set a Purpose

What do you think you will observe during this activity?

_____

_____

_____

_____

Think About the Procedure

Why do you rub only one balloon in Step 2?

_____

_____

_____

Why do you rub both balloons in Step 3?

_____

_____

_____

_____

Why is this activity not an experiment?

_____

_____

_____

_____

Record Your Observations

Draw and label diagrams to show what happened during Steps 2 and 3.

Draw Conclusions

What caused the balloons to act the way they did in Steps 2 and 3?

_____

_____

_____

_____

_____

_____

Analyze and Extend

1. **What do you think happens when you rub a balloon with a wool cloth?**

_____

_____

_____

2. **What happens when objects with opposite charges are near one another? Give an example that you have seen in your everyday activities.**

_____

_____

_____

_____

3. **What happens when objects with similar charges are near each other? Give an example that you have seen.**

_____

_____

_____

4. **Look at the pictures of balloons below. Each picture shows the charges on one balloon. Look at the way the pairs of balloons are interacting, and draw the charges on the second balloon.**

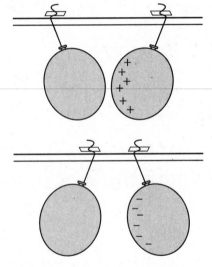

5. **What other questions would you like to ask about using electric charges? What investigations could you do to answer your questions?**

_____

_____

_____

_____

OHIO **4.PS.2** Energy can be transformed from one form to another or can be transferred from one location to another. **4.SIA.5** Communicate about observations, investigations and explanations; and

Name _____

Essential Question

What Is an Electric Circuit?

Set a Purpose

What will you learn from this investigation?

_____

_____

_____

Think About the Procedure

Did the order in which you arranged the parts make a difference? Explain.

_____

_____

_____

_____

Was the procedure an experiment? Why or why not?

_____

_____

_____

Record Your Data

In the space below, draw your circuit that worked. Label each part, and describe how the parts were connected.

Place a check mark next to the materials that enabled the bulb to light up.

Paper clip _____

Wood craft stick _____

Pencil lead _____

Draw Conclusions

How can you build a circuit?

_____

_____

_____

_____

_____

Analyze and Extend

1. Why is it helpful to have a switch in a circuit?

_____

_____

_____

2. Why would a circuit not work when a wire is replaced with a cotton string?

_____

_____

_____

3. Look at the first part of the word *circuit*. Why do you think what you built is called a circuit?

_____

_____

_____

4. Look at the picture below. Draw lines to show how three wires could be connected to make the bulbs light up.

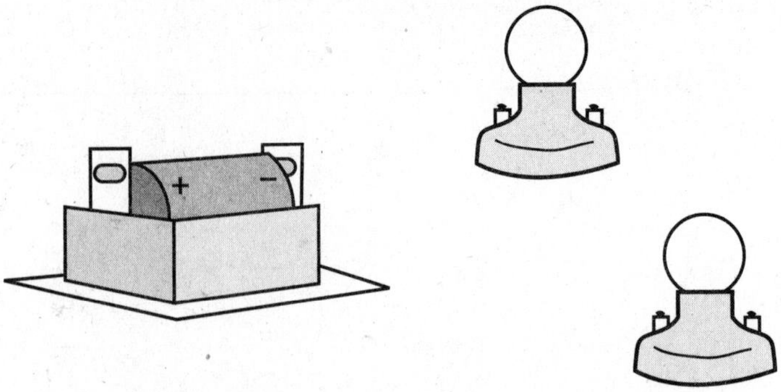

5. Each part of a circuit has a different job. Write the name of each part that performs the jobs listed below.

- Source of current   _____

- Carries current   _____

- Turns circuit
  on and off   _____

- Changes electrical
  energy to light   _____

6. What other questions would you like to ask about electric circuits? What investigations could you do to answer the questions?

_____

_____

_____

_____

_____

370

OHIO **4.PS.2** Energy can be transformed from one form to another or can be transferred from one location to another.

Essential Question

What Are Electric Circuits, Conductors, and Insulators?

Engage Your Brain!

Find the answer to the following question and record it here.

This picture shows the inside of a robot. What do the dark lines have to do with the robot's operation?

_____

_____

_____

Active Reading

Lesson Vocabulary
List the terms. As you learn about each one, make notes in the Interactive Glossary.

_____ _____

_____ _____

_____

Compare and Contrast
When you compare things, you look for ways in which they are alike. When you contrast things, you look for ways in which they are different. Active readers stay focused by asking themselves, How are these things alike? How are these things different?

Inquiry Flipchart p. 46 – Compare Two Circuits/Bright Lights

It's Shocking!

Working around electric utility lines is dangerous! How does a line worker stay safe?

Active Reading Draw a box around the sentences that contrast conductors and insulators.

Even on a hot day, a worker who repairs electric utility lines must be bundled up in protective clothing. The thick gloves, the bulky boots, and the hard plastic hat are heavy; however, these clothes protect the worker from an electric shock!

The rubber and plastic used in the protective clothing do not allow electric charges to flow through them. A material that resists the flow of electric charges is called an **insulator**. Electric charges flow easily through metals and some liquids. A material that readily allows electric charges to pass through it is called a **conductor**.

This worker's clothing is made up of insulators. The clothing will not allow electric charges to flow through it if the worker accidentally touches the wrong wires.

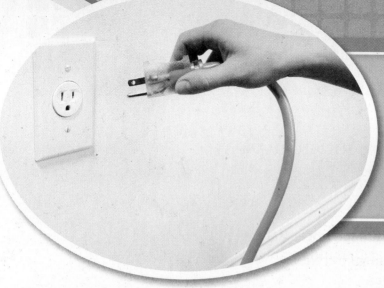

The parts of a plug that you hold and the covering on the wire are insulators. The metal prongs that go into the outlet are good conductors.

Electrical appliances work when electric charges flow through them. The parts that carry electric charges are made from conductors. Insulators are wrapped around the conductors to make appliances safe to handle.

► Label the parts of the wire as a conductor or an insulator.

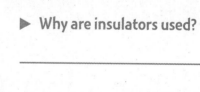

► Why are insulators used?

_____

_____

_____

_____

_____

_____

_____

A Path to Follow

If the wiring in a lamp does not change,
why isn't the lamp on all of the time?

Draw a box around the sentences that tell you
how a closed circuit and an open circuit are different.

When you go to school and back home, your path is a loop. A **circuit** is a path along which electric charges can flow. For an electrical device to work, the circuit must form a complete loop. This type of circuit is called a *closed circuit*. There are no breaks in its path.

What happens if a loose wire gets disconnected? The path is broken, and charges cannot flow. This type of circuit is called an *open circuit*. Many circuits have a switch. A switch controls the flow of charges by opening and closing the circuit.

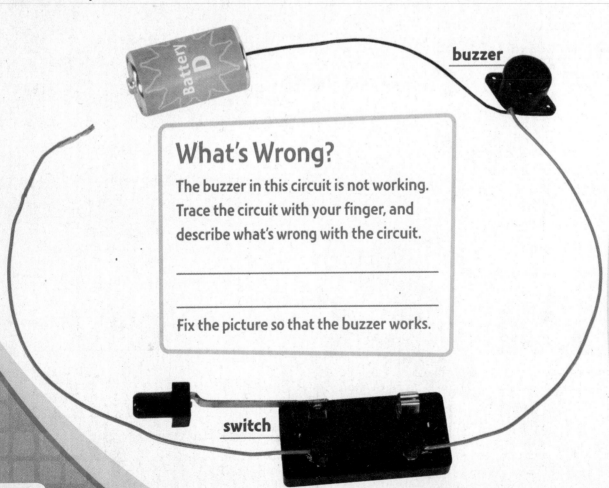

buzzer

What's Wrong?

The buzzer in this circuit is not working. Trace the circuit with your finger, and describe what's wrong with the circuit.

_____

_____

Fix the picture so that the buzzer works.

switch

Open Circuit

When the switch in a circuit is open, the circuit is not complete. Electric charges cannot flow, so the light stays off.

Closed Circuit

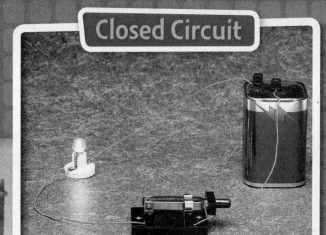

When the switch is closed, the circuit is complete. Electric charges can flow through it to light up the bulb.

▶ The filament in a light bulb is a tiny wire. It is part of the circuit. If the filament breaks, the circuit will be _____.

filament

Who Needs a Map?

To travel from point A to point B, you usually take the shortest route. What if one of the roads on that route is blocked? Simple! You just take another road. What would happen if there were only one road between point A and point B?

Active Reading Underline the sentences that compare series circuits and parallel circuits.

Series Circuits

In a series circuit, electric charges must follow a single path. The charged particles move from the battery's positive terminal to its negative terminal.

▶ Draw arrows to show how charges flow in this circuit.

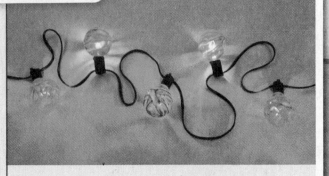

If one light bulb in a series circuit burns out, all of the lights go out, because the circuit is broken.

Suppose that the television and all the lights in a room are part of the same circuit. What would happen if one of the light bulbs burned out? It would depend on how the circuit is wired.

A **series circuit** has only one path for electric charges to follow. If any part of the path breaks, the circuit is open. Nothing works!

A circuit with several different paths for the charges to follow is called a **parallel circuit**. If one part of the circuit breaks, the charges can still flow along the other parts.

Color a Complex Circuit

1. Look at the circuit below. Color the bulb or bulbs that should be lit.
2. Draw an X on the switch that is open. Draw an arrow above the closed switch.

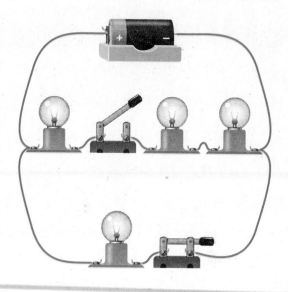

Parallel Circuits

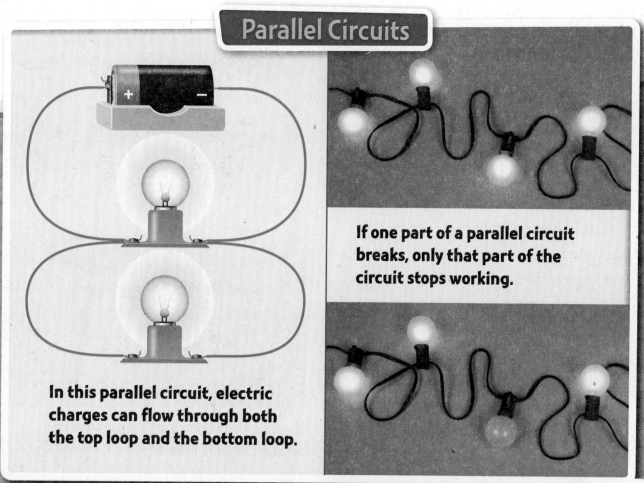

In this parallel circuit, electric charges can flow through both the top loop and the bottom loop.

If one part of a parallel circuit breaks, only that part of the circuit stops working.

Circuit Overload!

television
3 amps

Some house fires are caused by overloaded electrical wiring. How can you use electrical appliances safely?

hair dryer
12.5 amps

As electric charges flow through conductors, they produce heat. Insulation protects the materials around these conductors from the heat—up to a point! If the conductor gets too hot, the insulation can melt.

Wow!

This wire got so hot that it melted the insulation around it. It could have started a fire.

To protect against fires, a fuse or a circuit breaker is added to each circuit. Fuses and circuit breakers are switches that work automatically. They open if charge flows too quickly through a circuit. The flow stops and the wires cool, which prevents a fire.

Circuit overload takes place when too many devices in one circuit are turned on. Each device needs a certain flow of charge. This flow of charge, or current, is measured in units called *amperes*, or amps.

Circuit breakers open when the number of amps is greater than a certain value. Suppose the value for a breaker is 15 amps. The breaker will open if all plugged devices draw more than 15 amps.

Never plug more appliances into a circuit than it is designed to handle!

Should You Plug It In?

Draw a line connecting the hair dryer to one of the outlets in the power strip. Then connect the other devices you could use at the same time without overloading a 15-amp circuit breaker.

With power strips like this one, it's possible to plug many devices into a single wall outlet. **That could be a big mistake!**

lava lamp
0.5 amp

laptop computer
1.5 amps

clothes dryer
42 amps

This panel contains circuit breakers. Each breaker allows a certain number of amps of electric current to pass through one circuit.

Do the Math!
Solve Word Problems

1. How many times as much current does a television need than a lava lamp?

   _____

2. Circuit breakers are made in increments of 5 amps. What size breaker would you need for a circuit with a television, two laptops, and a lava lamp?

   _____

Sum It Up!

On each numbered line, fill in the vocabulary term that matches the description.

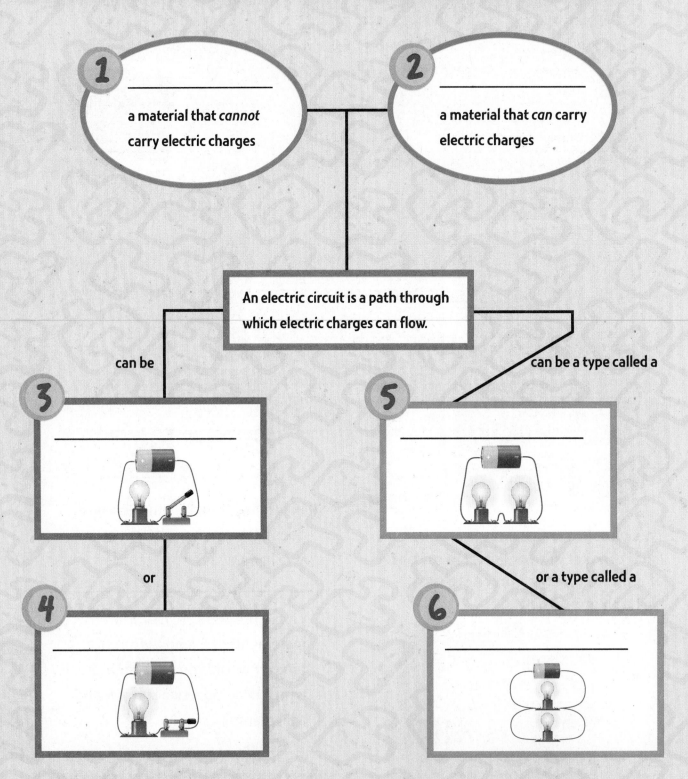

1 _____
a material that *cannot* carry electric charges

2 _____
a material that *can* carry electric charges

An electric circuit is a path through which electric charges can flow.

can be

3 _____

or

4 _____

can be a type called a

5 _____

or a type called a

6 _____

Name _____

Word Play

1 Unscramble the scrambled word in each sentence. Write the unscrambled word after the sentence. The first one is done for you.

A.	In some circuits, electrical energy is transformed into light energy by a light **lubb**.	Ⓑ U _L_ B 6
B.	The wires in a circuit are made of a material that is a **doortuccn**.	_ _ _ _ _ _ _ _ _ ◯ 10
C.	A path that an electric current can follow is an electric **icurict**.	_ _ _ ◯ _ ◯ _ 4 5
D.	A circuit in which electric charges can follow several different paths is called a **rallpale** circuit.	_◯_ _ _ _ _ _ _ 8
E.	If a wire is disconnected, the circuit is an **enop** circuit.	_ _ ◯ _ 9
F.	The covering on electric plugs and around wires is made of an **rainulost**.	◯_ _ _ _ _ _ _ _ ◯ 2 7
G.	A circuit in which all the devices are connected in a single path is a **ressie** circuit.	_ _ ◯ _ _ _ 3
H.	When a light is on, it is part of a **scolde** circuit.	◯_ _ _ _ _ _ 1

Solve the riddle by writing the circled letters above in the correct spaces below.

Riddle: What is another name for a clumsy electrician?

A _ _ _ _ C _ I _   B _ E _ K _ _ _
    1 2 3   4 5   6 7   8   9 10

Apply Concepts

2 Draw a closed series circuit with two light bulbs, a battery, and a switch. What would happen if one of the light bulbs blows out?

_____

_____

_____

_____

3 Explain what causes an overloaded circuit. How can you prevent an overloaded circuit?

_____

_____

_____

_____

_____

4 Write the word _conductor_ or _insulator_ on each of the lines. Then infer which type of material is inside the holes in the outlet. Explain your answer.

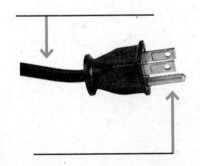

_____

_____

_____

_____

_____

5 Suppose you are building a series circuit using a small battery and a small light bulb, and you run out of wire. What everyday objects could you use to connect the battery to the light bulb? Explain.

_____

_____

_____

6 Identify each lettered part of the circuit, and explain what each part does.

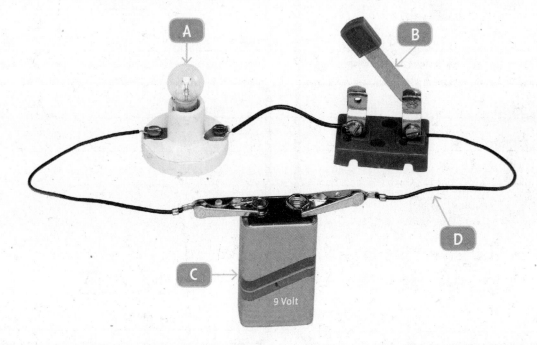

A _____

B _____

C _____

D _____

7 Study each of the following circuits.

- Make a check mark to show whether the circuit is open or closed.

- Draw the missing parts needed to make the open circuits work.

- Label each circuit as a series circuit or a parallel circuit.

 open

 closed

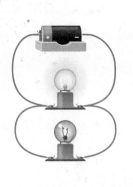

 open

closed

open

closed

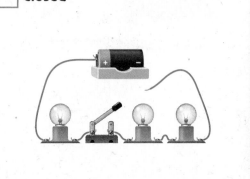

 open

closed

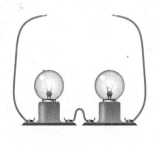

Take It Home!

Discuss with your family what you have learned about circuits. Gather some electrical devices and explain how they use electricity. Try flipping some switches in your home, and explain whether they are series circuits or parallel circuits.

Ask an Electrician

Q. Do electricians make electricity?

A. No. Electricity is produced in energy stations and carried to buildings through wires. Electricians work with wires to make sure the electricity moves safely.

Q. Don't electricians worry about electric shocks when they work?

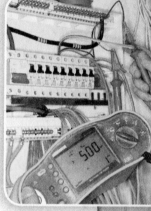

A. Electricians must always turn off electricity to the wires they are working on. Electricity can be dangerous and safety is an important part of the job.

Q. What kind of training do you need to be an electrician?

A. Most electricians learn from experienced electricians while they are attending classes. During this period, they are called an apprentice.

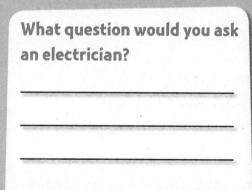

Now It's Your Turn!

What question would you ask an electrician?

_____

_____

_____

_____

Untangle the Wires!

For each circuit, explain what would happen
when the switch at the bottom is closed.

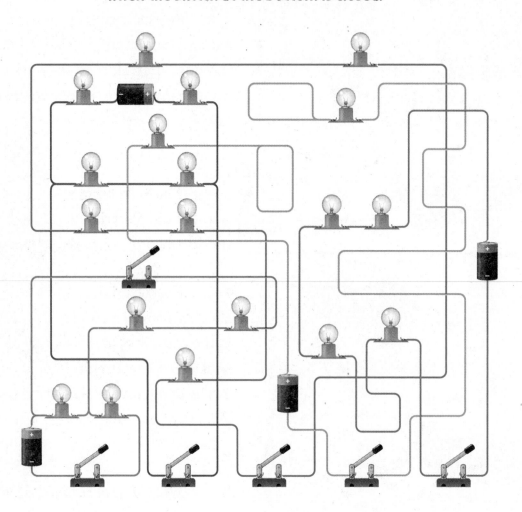

Red: _____

Purple: _____

Green: _____

Orange: _____

Blue: _____

OHIO **4.PS.2** Energy can be transformed from one form to another or can be transferred from one location to another.

Lesson **5**

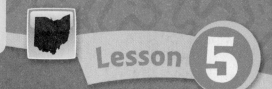

Essential Question

How Do We Use Electricity?

Engage Your Brain!

Find the answer to the following question in this lesson and record it here.

What types of energy is electricity being changed into in this picture?

_____

_____

_____

Active Reading

Lesson Vocabulary

List the terms. As you learn about each one, make notes in the Interactive Glossary.

_____

_____

_____

_____

Cause and Effect

Some ideas in this lesson are connected by a cause-and-effect relationship. Why something happens is a cause. What happens as a result of something else is an effect. Active readers look for effects by asking themselves, What happened? They look for causes by asking, Why did it happen?

Inquiry Flipchart p. 47 – Build an Electromagnet/Is There Current?

387

Electricity
Has Many Uses

How did your day start? Did an alarm clock wake you? Did you turn on a light? Did you eat something out of the refrigerator? Yes? Then you used electricity!

Active Reading As you read these two pages, draw a box around the sentence that contains the main idea.

Think of all the things in your home or school that use electricity. What do they do? Devices that use electricity change electrical energy into other types of energy, such as light or heat. We use electricity to heat our homes and cook our food. We also use it to light our rooms and to keep foods cold.

A computer changes electrical energy into light, sound, and heat. When you turn on a computer, you see pictures and hear sounds. You feel heat coming off of it. A computer can be plugged into an electrical outlet. It can also run on batteries. How do the objects on these pages change electrical energy?

a ceiling fan

a television and a video game system

Many electrical devices have electric motors. An **electric motor** is a machine that changes electrical energy into energy of motion. An electric fan uses an electric motor to move air. A refrigerator uses an electric motor to keep foods cold. What other objects in your home have electric motors? Any electric device that makes motion probably does.

an electric stove

a hair dryer and a light

Making a Better Change

A light bulb produces heat and light. Why would an engineer want to reduce the amount of heat a light bulb produces?

_____

_____

_____

Magnets and Magnetism

You can feel the force between two magnets. You feel magnets pull together, and you feel them push apart. How do magnets work?

Active Reading As you read these two pages, underline words or phrases that describe what causes magnets to push or pull.

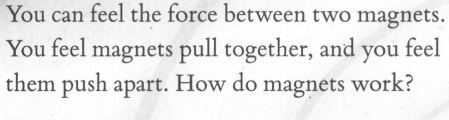

Each flat surface on a ring magnet is either an *N* pole or an *S* pole.

Magnets have been used for thousands of years. A **magnet** is an object that attracts iron and a few other metals. People make magnets, but they are also found in nature. Magnets are found in many common things.

Magnetism is a physical property of matter. Magnets push and pull because of their magnetic field. A *magnetic field* is the space around the magnet where the force of the magnet acts.

Each magnet has two ends, or *poles*. A magnetic pole is the part of a magnet where its magnetic field is the strongest. One end is called the *south-seeking* pole, or *S* pole. The other is the *north-seeking* pole, or *N* pole.

Two *N* poles or two *S* poles are similar, or like, poles. If you place the *N* poles of two magnets near each other, they repel, or push away. Two *S* poles push away, too. Like poles repel each other.

An *N* pole and an *S* pole are unlike poles. If you place unlike poles of two magnets near each other, they attract, or pull toward each other.

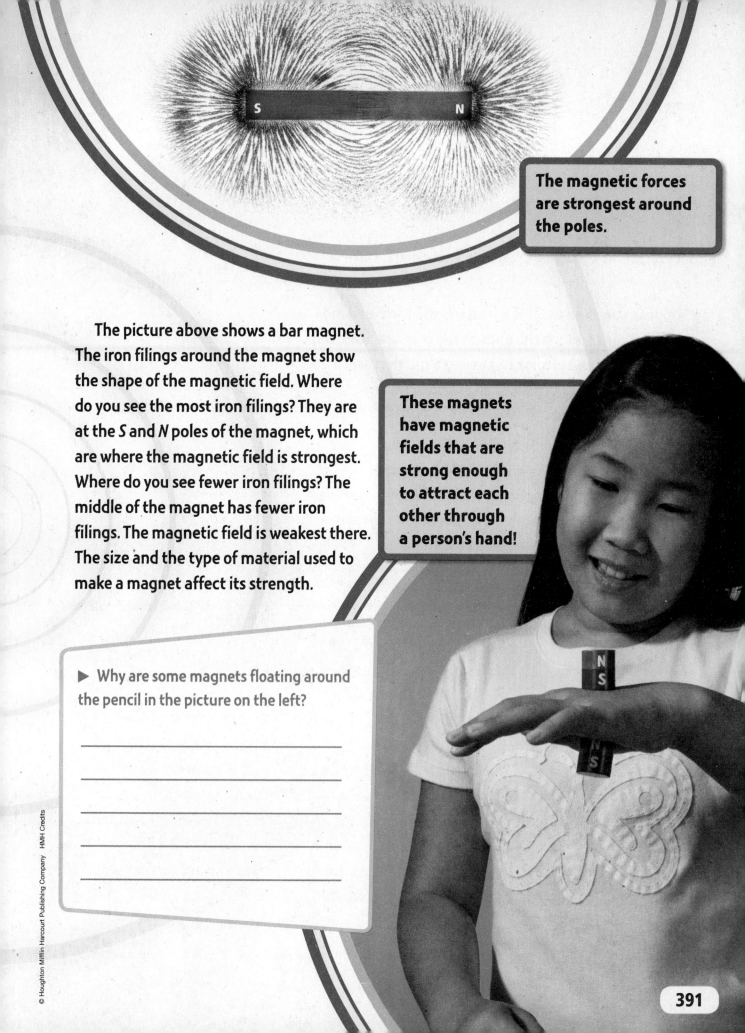

The magnetic forces are strongest around the poles.

The picture above shows a bar magnet. The iron filings around the magnet show the shape of the magnetic field. Where do you see the most iron filings? They are at the *S* and *N* poles of the magnet, which are where the magnetic field is strongest. Where do you see fewer iron filings? The middle of the magnet has fewer iron filings. The magnetic field is weakest there. The size and the type of material used to make a magnet affect its strength.

These magnets have magnetic fields that are strong enough to attract each other through a person's hand!

▶ Why are some magnets floating around the pencil in the picture on the left?

_____

_____

_____

_____

_____

Electromagnets

Electricity and magnetism are related.
One can produce the other.

Active Reading As you read this page, circle the sentence that explains how magnetism produces an electric current.

Suppose you slide a coil of wire back and forth around a bar magnet. When the ends of the wire are attached to a light bulb, the bulb lights! Moving a magnet and a wire near each other produces an electric current.

Turning the handle on the device below turns a coil of wire inside three U-shaped magnets. Electric charges flow through the wire and the bulb lights. On the picture on the right, an electric current is used to make a magnet.

hand-cranked light bulb

battery electromagnet

SUPER HEAVY DUTY LANTERN BATTERY

If magnets produce electricity, can electricity make magnets? Yes! Wrapping a coil of current-carrying wire around an iron coil such as a nail makes a magnet. You can use this magnet to pick up small iron objects such as paper clips. A device in which current produces magnetism is called an **electromagnet**.

Huge electromagnets are used in junkyards. They separate iron and steel objects from other objects. The operator swings the electromagnet over a pile of junk. He turns on the current. All the iron pieces are attracted to the magnet. The operator then swings the magnet over a container and turns off the current. The magnetism stops, and the iron drops into the container.

Electromagnets have become very important and useful. Today, every electric motor contains at least one electromagnet. You can also find electromagnets in telephones, doorbells, speakers, and computers. Doctors can use electromagnets to take pictures of the inside of the body.

junkyard electromagnet

What Are the Parts of an Electromagnet?

List the parts of an electromagnet. Then draw an electromagnet in the space provided.

_____

_____

_____

_____

Generating Electricity

We use electricity every day. How does it get to our homes and schools?

Active Reading As you read, circle the resources used to make electricity.

hydroelectric dam

Electricity generating stations, also known as energy stations, may use water, coal, or atoms to produce the electricity you use.

Inside a hydroelectric [hy•droh•ee•LEK•trik] dam, the mechanical energy of falling water is used to turn generators, which change mechanical energy into electrical energy.

windmills

Windmills have been used to grind grain or pump water. Today, wind turbines generate electricity.

Suppose you spin a magnet inside a coil of wire. A current begins to flow through the wire. You've made a **generator**, a device that converts mechanical energy to electrical energy. Huge generators in energy stations produce electricity that travels through wires to homes, schools, and businesses.

Some energy stations use falling water or wind to turn generators. Other stations convert sunlight, or solar energy, into electrical energy. These resources are called renewable resources, because they can be replaced quickly.

Most energy stations burn coal or other fuels to heat water. The water rises as steam, which turns the generators. Coal is a nonrenewable resource that will eventually run out. That's why it's important for us to conserve, or use less, electricity.

Do the Math!
Solve a Problem

Sam's electric bill was $200 for the month of June. The air conditioner accounts for $\frac{1}{2}$ of the bill, and the water heater accounts for $\frac{1}{5}$ of the bill. How much did it cost to run each appliance in June?

When you're done, use the answer key to check and revise your work.

Use information in the summary to complete the graphic organizer.

Summarize

Electricity is used and produced in many ways. Electrical devices change electrical energy into other types of energy, such as heat, light, and sound. Many devices, including fans and refrigerators, have electric motors that change electrical energy into energy of motion. Electricity and magnetism are related. Magnets produce a magentic field. A magnetic field can be used to produce an electric current. An electric current may also be used to make an electromagnet. An electromagnet can be used in a generator at an energy generating station. A generator changes energy of motion into electrical energy. Energy generating stations produce the electrical energy we use. We need to conserve electricity because some resources used by energy generating stations will run out.

1 Main Idea:

_____

_____

2 Detail: Electrical devices convert

_____

_____

_____

_____

3 Detail: Magnetism and electricty are related because

_____

_____

_____

_____

4 Detail: An electromagnet can be used in a generator at an energy generating station to produce

_____

_____

_____

Name _____

Word Play

1 Unscramble each of the clues to form a word or a phrase from the word bank. Copy each letter in a numbered cell to the cell below with the same number.

TECGARLOETNEM

RECLICTE ROOTM

TORRAGEEN

ONECREVS

REECUSROS

GANETM

CICLETERTIY

Word Bank

conserve
electricity
electric motor
electromagnet
generator
magnet
resources

This lesson is about [1][2][3][4][5] [6][7][8][9][10][11].

Apply Concepts

2 Draw a common electrical appliance. Then explain how it changes electrical energy to other forms of energy.

_____

_____

_____

_____

Apply Concepts

3 Draw an *X* over each appliance that changes electrical energy to mechanical energy. You may use an appliance more than once.

Circle each appliance that is designed to change electrical energy into heat energy.

Draw a square around each appliance that changes electrical energy to sound energy.

Draw a triangle around each appliance that changes electrical energy to light energy.

4 What is the device in the picture to the right called? What would happen if you put this device near a pile of iron nails?

_____

_____

_____

5

A. What are some resources used to produce electrical energy at energy generating stations?

_____

_____

_____

_____

B. Describe three ways that you can conserve electrical energy.

_____

_____

_____

_____

Take It Home! Discuss with your family ways that you could conserve electrical energy. You might talk about ways to use less energy or about things you can do by hand instead of using electrical appliances.

OHIO **4.PS.2** Energy can be transformed from one form to another or can be transferred from one location to another. **4.SIA.1** Observe and ask questions about the natural environment; **4.SIA.5** Communicate about observations, investigations and explanations; and

S.T.E.M.
Engineering & Technology

How It Works:
The Electric Grid

At home, you flip a switch and a light comes on. The electricity to power the light comes from generating stations. Generating stations are a part of a larger system know as the *electric grid*. Generators, high voltage steel towers, conductors, insulators, and your home appliances are all parts of this system.

At generating stations, generators transform kinetic energy into electrical energy.

From the generating stations, electrical energy travels over electrical lines on tall steel towers. These lines are made up of a conductor and an insulator.

Coal is a fossil fuel. There is plenty of it in the United States. Most of our electricity comes from burning coal.

Wind turbines are large generators. Turbines use energy from wind to generate electricity.

Troubleshooting

During prolonged hot weather, many people use air conditioning units to remain cool. How could this affect the electric grid and the environment?

_____

_____

Show How It Works

Water falling through a turbine can generate electricity. Most hydroelectric generating stations have a dam that blocks a river. A lake forms behind the dam and provides a constant source of falling water. The dam also floods areas that were once dry land. Draw a picture that shows what you think the area behind the dam looked like before the dam was built.

A hydroelectric dam uses energy from moving water to generate electricity.

Research the benefits and risks for each of the first three sources of electrical energy listed below. Fill out the chart. Then, identify the energy source described in the last entry.

Electrical energy source	Benefits	Risks
Wind turbines	do not pollute air, land, or water	
Coal-burning generating stations		Coal mines change the landscape; they can cause land, air, and water pollution.
Hydroelectric dams	use water, a renewable resource	
	do not pollute air, land, or water	These produce toxic wastes that must be stored for a very long time.

Build On It!

Rise to the engineering design challenge—complete **Build in Some Science: An Attractive Option** on the Inquiry Flipchart.

Unit 8 Review

Name _____

Vocabulary Review

Use the terms in the box to complete the sentences.

circuit
conductor
electric current
electric motor
generator
insulator
magnet
static electricity

1. A path along which electric charges flow is called

   a(n) _____.

2. An object that attracts iron and a few other metals is called

   a(n) _____.

3. A device that changes electrical energy into mechanical energy

   is a(n) _____.

4. A material through which electricity travels easily is

   called a(n) _____.

5. The buildup of electric charges on an object is

   called _____.

6. A material that resists the movement of electricity through

   it is called a(n) _____.

7. A device that produces an electric current by
   converting mechanical energy to electrical energy is

   a(n) _____.

8. The flow of electric charges along a path is called

   a(n) _____.

Science Concepts

Fill in the letter of the choice that best answers the question.

9. Carlita hangs two balloons from a desk. When they hang normally, they are close together but do not touch. Carlita rubs both balloons with a wool cloth. What happens when she lets the balloons hang near one another?

   (A) They push each other away.

   (B) They touch each other and pop.

   (C) They touch each other and stick together.

   (D) They are close together but do not touch.

10. Ari is combing his hair. After a while, he notices that the comb attracts the hairs on his head as shown below.

   Which explanation best describes why the hairs are attracted to the comb?

   (A) Combing the hairs caused them to lose their static charge.

   (B) Combing the hairs caused the comb to lose its static charge.

   (C) Combing the hairs gave them a charge that is opposite the charge on the comb.

   Combing the hairs gave them a charge that is the same as the charge the comb.

11. Identify the parts of an electromagnet.

   (A) battery, battery holder, nail, copper wire

   (B) battery, battery holder, bulb, copper wire

   (C) battery, battery holder, nail, bulb

   (D) battery, battery holder, switch, copper wire

12. When an electric current runs through a doorbell buzzer, a mechanism inside vibrates back and forth to make the buzzer work. When someone pushes the button on a doorbell, how does energy transform?

   (A) Electrical energy transforms into heat, then sound.

   (B) Electrical energy transforms into motion, then sound.

   (C) Motion energy transforms into electrical energy, then back to motion.

   (D) Sound energy transforms into motion, then back to sound.

13. Jayden uses various objects to complete a circuit. He compares how brightly a bulb glows using each object. His results are shown below.

Object	Glow
nail	very bright
crayon	dim
eraser	very dim
pencil lead	bright

   Which object is the best electrical conductor?

   (A) nail

   (B) eraser

   (C) crayon

   (D) pencil lead

14. While planning an investigation, Harini draws four ways she could connect a battery, a paper clip, a light bulb, and some wire. Which arrangement below would light the bulb?

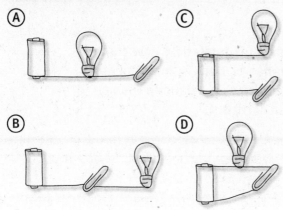

15. You rub a balloon on your hair on a dry day. Then, you bring a second balloon near the first one. How would you describe what happens to the balloons?

Ⓐ They repel each other.

Ⓑ They attract each other.

Ⓒ They neither attract nor repel each other.

Ⓓ Opposite charges make one balloon become larger and one smaller.

16. People use many sources of mechanical energy to generate electricity. Which frequently used source will eventually run out?

Ⓐ wind

Ⓑ coal

Ⓒ solar energy

Ⓓ running water

17. The picture below shows a large dam used to produce electricity. Water flows from the lake behind the dam to the river below it. Water passes through turbines connected to electric generators.

Which energy transformation takes place in the hydroelectric generating station?

Ⓐ heat energy into electrical energy

Ⓑ energy of motion into electrical energy

Ⓒ electrical energy into energy of motion

Ⓓ energy of motion and sound energy into electrical energy

18. When Tony left the room, he flipped the light switch. The light bulb stopped giving off light. What caused it to go out?

Ⓐ The tiny wires inside the bulb stopped moving, so it could not make light.

Ⓑ The electric current stopped, so no more electrical energy was changed into light.

Ⓒ The bulb became cooler, so the light bulb stopped changing heat energy into light.

Ⓓ The electric current stopped, so light could not be changed into electrical energy.

Apply Inquiry and Review the Big Idea

Write the answers to these questions.

19. Explain how a magnet and some wire can be used to generate electricity.

_____

_____

20. The amount of static electricity on a balloon can be estimated by how many pieces of confetti the balloon picks up at a distance of 1 cm. Yuma wants to find out if a dryer sheet produces less static electricity on a balloon than a piece of wool. Describe an investigation she can carry out.

_____

_____

_____

_____

_____

21. Eshe builds two circuits. After checking that all the bulbs work, she removes one bulb from each circuit, as shown below.

Circuit A

Circuit B

Explain why the bulb goes out in Circuit B but stays lighted in Circuit A.

_____

_____

_____

Interactive Glossary

As you learn about each term, add notes, drawings, or sentences in the extra space. This will help you remember what the terms mean. Here are some examples.

Fungi [FUHN•jeye] A kingdom of organisms that have a nucleus and get nutrients by decomposing other organisms

A mushroom is from the kingdom Fungi.

physical change [FIZ•ih•kuhl•CHAYNJ] Change in the size, shape, or state of matter with no new substance being formed

When I cut paper, the paper has a physical change.

Glossary Pronunciation Key

With every glossary term, there is also a phonetic respelling. A phonetic respelling writes the word the way it sounds, which can help you pronounce new or unfamiliar words. Use this key to help you understand the respellings.

Sound	As in	Phonetic Respelling	Sound	As in	Phonetic Respelling
a	bat	(BAT)	oh	over	(OH•ver)
ah	lock	(LAHK)	oo	pool	(POOL)
air	rare	(RAIR)	ow	out	(OWT)
ar	argue	(AR•gyoo)	oy	foil	(FOYL)
aw	law	(LAW)	s	cell	(SEL)
ay	face	(FAYS)		sit	(SIT)
ch	chapel	(CHAP•uhl)	sh	sheep	(SHEEP)
e	test	(TEST)	th	that	(THAT)
	metric	(MEH•trik)		thin	(THIN)
ee	eat	(EET)	u	pull	(PUL)
	feet	(FEET)	uh	medal	(MED•uhl)
	ski	(SKEE)		talent	(TAL•uhnt)
er	paper	(PAY•per)		pencil	(PEN•suhl)
	fern	(FERN)		onion	(UHN•yuhn)
eye	idea	(eye•DEE•uh)		playful	(PLAY•fuhl)
i	bit	(BIT)		dull	(DUHL)
ing	going	(GOH•ing)	y	yes	(YES)
k	card	(KARD)		ripe	(RYP)
	kite	(KYT)	z	bags	(BAGZ)
ngk	bank	(BANGK)	zh	treasure	(TREZH•er)

Interactive Glossary

A

adaptation [ad•uhp•TAY•shuhn] A trait or characteristic that helps an organism survive (p. 170)

advertisement [ad•ver•TYZ•muhnt] A public notice or announcement of information designed to communicate a message to a viewer or listener about a product or a service (p. 94)

atmosphere [AT•muhs•feer] The mixture of gases that surrounds Earth (p. 111)

B

behavioral adaptation [bih•HAYV•yu•ruhl ad•uhp•TAY•shuhn] Something an animal does that helps it survive (p. 175)

C

cast [KAST] A model of an organism, formed when sediment fills a mold and hardens (p. 215)

change of state [CHAYNJ uhv STAYT] A physical change that occurs when matter changes from one state to another, such as from a liquid to a gas

© Houghton Mifflin Harcourt Publishing Company

chemical change [KEM•ih•kuhl CHAYNJ]
Change in one or more substances, caused by a reaction, that forms a new and different substance (p. 271)

condensation [kahn•duhn•SAY•shuhn]
The process by which a gas changes into a liquid (p. 112)

chemical energy
[KEM•ih•kuhl EN•er•jee] Energy that can be released by a chemical change (p. 319)

conduction [kuhn•DUK•shuhn] The transfer, or movement, of heat between two objects that are touching

circuit [SER•kuht] A path along which electric charges can flow (p. 374)

conductor [kuhn•DUK•ter] A material that allows heat or electricity to move through it easily (pp. 334, 372)

computer model [kuhm•PYOO•ter MOD•l]
A computer program that models an event or an object (p. 55)

conservation of mass
[kahn•ser•VAY•shuhn uhv MAS] A law that states that matter cannot be made or destroyed; however, matter can change into a new form (p. 276)

Interactive Glossary

current electricity
[KER•uhnt ee•lek•TRIS•uh•tee] A kind of kinetic energy that flows as electric current (p. 358)

design [dih•zyn] To conceive something and to prepare the plans and drawings for it to be built (p. 72)

D

data [DEY•tuh] Individual facts, statistics, and items of information you observe (p. 41)

electric motor [ee•LEK•trik MOHT•er] A device that changes electrical energy into mechanical energy (p. 389)

E

density [DEN•suh•tee] The amount of matter present in a certain volume of a substance

electrical energy [ee•LEK•trih•kuhl EE•er•jee] A form of energy that comes from electric current (p. 319)

deposition [dep•uh•ZISH•uhn] The dropping or settling of eroded materials (p. 126)

electricity [ee•lek•TRIS•uh•tee] A form of energy (p. 354)

electromagnet [ee•lek•troh•MAG•nit] A temporary magnet caused by an electric current (p. 393)

environment [en•VY•ruhn•muhnt] All the living and nonliving things that surround and affect an organism (p. 168)

empirical evidence [im•PIR•uh•kuhl EV•uh•duhns] Data collected through direct observation or experience (p. 24)

erosion [uh•ROH•zhuhn] The process of moving weathered rock and sediment from one place to another (p. 126)

energy [EN•er•jee] The ability to do work and to cause changes in matter (p. 313)

evaporation [ee•vap•uh•RAY•shuhn] The process by which a liquid changes into a gas (p. 111)

engineering [en•juh•NIR•ing] The use of scientific and mathematical principles to develop something practical (p. 71)

evidence [EV•uh•duhns] Information collected during a scientific investigation (p. 10)

Interactive Glossary

extinction [ek•STINGKT•shuhn] A plant or animal species that is no longer living or existing (p. 194)

gas [GAS] The state of matter that does not have a definite volume or a definite shape (p. 256)

flood plain [FLUD PLAYN] The wide, flat area alongside a river (p. 142)

generator [JEN•er•ay•ter] A device that makes an electric current by converting mechanical energy to electrical energy (p. 395)

fossil [FAHS•uhl] The remains or traces of a plant or animal that lived long ago (p. 215)

groundwater [GROWND•waw•ter] Water located within the gaps and pores in rocks below Earth's surface (p. 114)

heat [HEET] The energy that moves between objects at different temperatures (p. 321)

hypothesis [hy•PAHTH•uh•sis] A possible explanation or answer to a question; a testable statement (p. 9)

index fossil [IN•deks FAHS•uhl] A fossil of a type of organism that lived in many places during a relatively short time span (p. 229)

inference [IN•fer•uhns] An untested conclusion based on observations (p. 19)

instinct [IN•stinkt] A behavior an animal knows how to do without having to learn it (p. 175)

insulator [IN•suh•layt•er] A material that does not allow heat or electricity to move through it easily (pp. 336, 372)

investigation [in•ves•tuh•GAY•shuhn] A procedure carried out to gather data about an object or an event (p. 7)

Interactive Glossary

K

kinetic energy [kih•NET•ik EN•er•jee]
The energy of motion (p. 314)

L

landform [LAND•fawrm] Any recognizable feature on Earth's surface shaped by natural causes (p. 140)

liquid [LIK•wid] The state of matter that has a definite volume but not a definite shape (p. 256)

M

magnet [MAG•nit] An object that attracts iron and a few other—but not all—metals (p. 390)

mass [MAS] The amount of matter in an object (p. 112)

mass extinction [MAS ek•STINGK•shuhn]
A period in which a large number of species become extinct (p. 236)

matter [MAT•er] Anything that takes up space and has mass (p. 252)

mechanical energy [muh•KAN•ih•kuhl EN•er•jee] The total potential and kinetic energy of an object (p. 314)

mold [MOHLD] An impression of an organism, formed when sediment hardens around the organism (p. 215)

microscope [MY•kruh•skohp] A tool for looking at objects that cannot be seen with the eye alone (p. 35)

O

observation [ahb•zuhr•VAY•shuhn] Information collected by using the five senses (p. 7)

mixture [MIKS•cher] A combination of two or more different substances that keep their identities (p. 289)

P

pan balance [PAN BAL•uhns] A tool that measures mass with units called grams (g) (p. 36)

model [MOD•l] A representation of something real that is too big, too small, too far away, or has too many parts to investigate directly (p. 53)

Interactive Glossary

parallel circuit [PAIR•uh•lel SER•kit]
An electric circuit that has more than one
path for the electric charges to follow (p. 377)

potential energy
[poh•TEN•shuhl EN•er•jee] Energy an object
has because of its position or its condition
(p. 314)

physical adaptation
[FIZ•ih•kuhl ad•uhp•TAY•shuhn]
An adaptation to a body part (p. 171)

precipitation
[pree•sip•uh•TAY•shuhn] Water that falls
from clouds to Earth's surface (p. 113)

physical change [FIZ•ih•kuhl CHAYNJ]
A change in which a new substance is
not formed (p. 270)

prototype [PROH•tuh•typ] An original or test
model on which something is based (p. 73)

physical property
[FIZ•ih•kuhl PRAHP•er•tee] A characteristic
of matter that you can observe or measure
directly

R

reaction [ree•AK•shuhn] The process
through which new substances are formed
during a chemical change (p. 271)

runoff [RUN•awf] Water that does not soak into the ground and instead flows across Earth's surface (p. 115)

series circuit [SIR•eez SER•kit] An electric circuit in which the electrical charges have only one path to follow (p. 377)

S

science [SY•uhns] The study of the natural world (p. 5)

solid [SAHL•id] The state of matter that has a definite volume and a definite shape (p. 257)

scientist [SY•uhn•tist] A person who asks questions about the natural world (p. 5)

solution [suh•LOO•shuhn] A mixture that has the same composition throughout because all the parts are mixed evenly (p. 290)

spring scale [SPRING SKAYL] A tool used to measure forces, such as weight, in units called newtons (N) (p. 36)

sediment [SED•uh•ment] Sand, bits of rock, fossils, and other matter carried and deposited by water, wind, or ice (p. 127)

Interactive Glossary

states of matter [STAYTS UHV MAT•er]
The physical forms (such as solid, liquid, and gas) that matter can exist in

temperature [TEM•per•uh•cher]
The measure of the energy of motion in the particles of matter, which we feel as how hot or cold something is (p. 254)

static electricity
[STAT•ik ee•lek•TRIS•uh•tee] The buildup of charges on an object (p. 356)

thermal energy [THUR•muhl EN•er•jee]
The total kinetic energy of the particles in a substance (p. 321)

succession [suhk•SESH•uhn] A gradual change in the kinds of organisms in an ecosystem (p. 186)

three-dimensional model
[THREE-di•MEN•shuh•nuhl MOD•l] A model that has the dimension of height as well as width and length (p. 55)

technology [tek•NOL•uh•jee] Any designed system, product, or process used to solve problems (p. 87)

tool [TOOL] Anything used to help people shape, build, or produce things to meet their needs (p. 86)

triple beam balance
[TRI-**puhl** BEEM BAL•**uhns**] An accurate tool to use for measuring mass (p. 36)

two-dimensional model [TOO-**di**•MEN•**shuh**•**nuhl** MOD•**l**] A model that has the dimensions of length and width only (p. 53)

V

volcano [**vahl**•KAY•**noh**] A place where hot gases, ash, and melted rock come out of the ground onto Earth's surface (p. 148)

volume [VAHL•**yoom**] The amount of space an object takes up (p. 252)

W

water cycle [WAWT•**er** SY•**kuhl**] The process in which water continuously moves from Earth's surface into the atmosphere and back again (p. 111)

weathering [WETH•**er**•**ing**] The breaking down of rocks on Earth's surface into smaller pieces (p. 125)

Index

compact fluorescent light (CFL), 92–93

compare, as science skill, 19

Compare and Contrast, 139, 183, 251, 371

Comparisons, 51

compression
of gases, 260–261, 273
temperature and, 272

compressor, 265

computer models, 55, 223

computer programs, robots and, 101

computers
disposal of, 94
electromagnets in, 393
energy for, 319, 379
energy transformations in, 388

concave mirror, 39

conclusions, drawing, 13, 42

condensation, 112
of gases, 112, 258–259, 275
temperature and, 274–275
in the water cycle, 110–111

condensation point, 259

conductor, electrical, 372, 372–373

conductor, thermal, 334, 334–335

conservation, of ecosystems, 193, 195

conservation of mass, 276, 276–277, 285

construction tools, 86–87, 88

contamination. *See* **pollution.**

continental drift, fossil evidence of, 230–231

contraction, of matter, 272–273

convex mirror, 39

cooking, chemical changes in, 270

copper, 291, 358

Cormack, Allan McLeod, 304

Cousteau, Jacques, 205

craters, 235

critical thinking skills, 24–25

critique, in critical thinking, 24

CT scan machine, 304

Culpepper, Martin, 49–50

Curie, Marie, 303–304

current. *See* **electric current.**

current electricity, 358, 358–359

D

dams
beaver, 188–189
for flood control, 151
hydroelectric, 394, 395, 400
sediment movement and, 127

data, 41
analyzing, 12–13, 24, 42–43
communicating, 12–13, 19, 42–43
descriptions as, 41
displaying, 22, 40–41
drawing conclusions from, 13, 42–43
empirical, 24–25
measurement tools in, 36–37
numbers as, 41
real-time, 56
recording, 22, 36–37, 41, 74
using, 42–43

database, 43

decision making, by robots, 101

deck, in skateboards, 75

degree Celsius (°C), 37

degree Fahrenheit (°F), 37

de Lorena, Guglielmo, 205

delta, river, 127, 140

density
of food, 255
of ice, 272–273
as physical property, 255
separating mixtures by, 292

deposition, 126
by glaciers, 130–131
landforms and, 126–127, 132–133, 140–141
of rocks, 126–127
from water, 126–127, 132–133
by wind, 128–129

desert environments, 128, 174–175

design, 72. *See also* **design process.**

designed system, 90–91

designed world, 90

design process, 72–77
communicating results in, 73, 77
problem definition, 73, 74
prototypes in, 73, 74–77
redesigning in, 73, 76–77
in river valleys, 150–151
summary of steps in, 72–73
testing and improving in, 73, 76

desk, 88

Details, 31, 167, 225, 269, 311, 353

Devonian Sea, 233

dew, 112, 259, 275

diagrams, 41, 53

Diebold, John, 49–50

dinosaurs
describing, 242
dung fossils, 241
extinction of, 194, 235, 241
walking movements in, 223

displaying data, 22, 40–41

dissolve, 291

glass, heat conduction and, 334, 337

glass eye, 71

gloves, 336, 372

glow stick, 322–323

goal, in system design, 91

gram (g), 36

Grand Canyon (Arizona), 132, 142, 226–227

graphs
bar, 41
circle, 41, 295

grasslands, 170–171

gravity
erosion by, 126, 128–129, 130
glaciers and, 143
landslides and, 144

grazing, ecosystem changes from, 189

Great Lakes, 130–131, 143, 190

Great Lakes Science Center (Cleveland, Ohio), 361

Green Belt Movement, 201

green energy, 331

groundwater, 114
in aquifers, 116–117
caves and, 142
in the water cycle, 110–111, 114, 116–117

hail, 113. *See also* precipitation.

hair
as insulator, 336
static electricity in, 357

hair dryer, 378, 389

hammer, 86

hand lens, 34, 35

Hawai'i, volcanoes in, 148–149

heat, 321
conductor of, 334–335

as energy transfer, 320–321
in homes, 338–339
insulator of, 336, 338–339
thermal energy and, 321
thermos and, 337

Hebgen Lake Earthquake of 1959, 149

hectare, 149

high voltage steel towers, 399

highways, environmental change from, 192

Hocking Hills (Ohio), 107–108

hologram, 39

homes
electrical wiring in, 378–379
electricity uses in, 388–389
energy in, 318–319
heat proofing in, 338–339

hot spot, 159, 160

hot weather, clothing for, 155–156

Hounsfield, Godfrey, 304

Howard, Ayanna, 101–102

human impacts
beneficial, 193
on ecosystem changes, 192–193, 195
on groundwater aquifers, 116

hurricane, satellite images of, 56

hydroelectric dam, 394, 395, 400

hypothesis (plural, *hypotheses*), 9
evidence for, 12
experimental testing of, 25

hypothesizing, 21

ice
in clouds, 112

density of, 272–273
fossils in, 214
in glaciers, 130–131
for refrigeration, 265

ice ages, 184, 228

icebox, 265

Iceland, volcanoes in, 148

ice sculpture, 320

icicles, 259

identification guide, 10–11

igniter, piezoelectric, 345

index fossil, 229

infer, as science skill, 18–19

inference, 18–19, 19

inland sea, 146

input, in system design, 91

Inquiry Skills
Analyze and Extend, 48, 62, 84, 100, 158, 182, 204, 244, 268, 286, 302, 330, 344, 368, 370
Draw Conclusions, 48, 62, 84, 99–100, 158, 182, 204, 244, 268, 286, 302, 330, 344, 368, 370
Make a Prediction, 267
Record Your Data, 47, 83, 99, 157, 181, 203, 243, 285, 301, 329, 369
Record Your Observations, 61, 267, 344, 367
Set a Purpose, 47, 61, 83, 99, 157, 181, 203, 243, 267, 285, 301, 329, 343, 367, 369
State Your Hypothesis, 203, 243, 343
Think About the Procedure, 47, 61, 83, 99, 157, 203, 243, 267, 285, 301, 329, 343, 367, 369

insects. *See also* animals.
in amber, 214

in still water, 173
weathering by, 125
logical reasoning, 24
loudness, 316

Maathai, Wangari, 201
magnetic field, 390–391
magnetic force
    at magnetic poles, 390–391
    in mixture separation, 293
magnetic pole, 390–391
magnetism, 390
magnets, 390
    electromagnets, 392–393
    in generators, 395
    poles in, 390–391
magnifying box, 35
Main Idea and Details, 31, 225,
    269, 311, 353
Main Ideas, 3, 85, 213
Make a Prediction, 267
maps
    as model, 53
    of the ocean floor, 49–50
    by surveyors, 71
    weather, 57
marine biologist, 21
Mars
    diameter of, 54
    robotic exploration of, 101
    surface of, 10
mass
    conservation of, 276–277, 285
    measurement of, 36
    as physical property, 252, 255
mass extinction, 234, 234–235,
    241
math skills, 22–23
matter, 252. *See also* **states of
    matter.**

changes of state in, 258–259,
    274–275
compression and expansion of,
    260–261, 272–273
mixtures, 288–289, 292–293
particles in, 256–257
physical and chemical changes
    in, 270–271
physical properties of, 252–257,
    390
rate of change in, 274, 278
solutions, 290–291
temperature and, 274
meanders, 145
measurement tools, 36–37
measuring, 22
mechanical energy, 314,
    314–315
mechanical engineer, 49
medicine, as technology
    product, 88
melting, 258, 274
melting point, 259
meltwater, 115
mental model, 52–53
mercury (metal), 92
Mercury (planet), 54
mesh screen, in mixture
    separation, 293
Mesosaurus, 230–231
Mesozoic Era, 228–229, 235
metals
    alloys, 294–295
    heat conduction and, 334–335
    insulation of, 336
meteor impacts, mass
    extinctions and, 235
meteorologist, 20, 56–57
metric units, 36
microscope, 35
minerals
    fossil replacement by, 215

piezoelectric, 345
mining, 192
mirrors, 337
Mississippi River, 145
mixture, 289
    properties of, 288–289
    separating, 292–293
model, scientific, 53
    computer, 55, 223
    in investigations, 10
    limitations of, 53
    mental, 52–53
    scale, 55
    of the solar system, 52–55
    three-dimensional, 55
    two-dimensional, 52–53, 57
    weather, 56–57
mold, fossil, 215
moraine, 131, 141
mosses, 186
mountains
    formation of, 140, 146
    plate tectonics and, 160
    valleys and, 142–143
    volcanic, 141, 148
mudslides, 185
museum, research in, 33, 43
mushroom rocks, 128
music, 316–317

Namibia (Africa), sand dunes
    in, 128–129
Native Americans, solar
    system model of, 52
native species, 190–191
natural gas, 319
natural history museum, 33
natural resources
    conservation of, 193, 195
    nonrenewable, 92, 319, 395